LaGrange Public Library
LaGrange, Illinois 60525
708-352-0576

LAW AND THE
LONG WAR

LAW AND THE LONG WAR

THE FUTURE OF JUSTICE IN THE AGE OF TERROR

Benjamin Wittes

THE PENGUIN PRESS | NEW YORK | 2008

THE PENGUIN PRESS
Published by the Penguin Group
Penguin Group (USA) Inc., 375 Hudson Street,
New York, New York 10014, U.S.A. • Penguin Group (Canada), 90 Eglinton Avenue
East, Suite 700, Toronto, Ontario, Canada M4P 2Y3 (a division of
Pearson Penguin Canada Inc.) • Penguin Books Ltd, 80 Strand, London WC2R 0RL,
England • Penguin Ireland, 25 St. Stephen's Green, Dublin 2, Ireland
(a division of Penguin Books Ltd) • Penguin Books Australia Ltd,
250 Camberwell Road, Camberwell, Victoria 3124, Australia (a division of Pearson
Australia Group Pty Ltd) • Penguin Books India Pvt Ltd, 11 Community Centre,
Panchsheel Park, New Delhi – 110 017, India • Penguin Group (NZ),
67 Apollo Drive, Rosedale, North Shore 0632, New Zealand (a division of Pearson
New Zealand Ltd) • Penguin Books (South Africa) (Pty) Ltd, 24 Sturdee Avenue,
Rosebank, Johannesburg 2196, South Africa

Penguin Books Ltd, Registered Offices:
80 Strand, London WC2R 0RL, England

First published in 2008 by The Penguin Press,
a member of Penguin Group (USA) Inc.

Copyright © Benjamin Wittes, 2008
All rights reserved

LIBRARY OF CONGRESS CATALOGING IN PUBLICATION DATA

Wittes, Benjamin.
Law and the long war : the future of justice in the age of terror / Benjamin Wittes.
p.   cm.
Includes bibliographical references and index.
ISBN: 978-1-59420-179-0
1. Terrorism—United States.   2. War on Terrorism, 2001-—Law and legislation—
United States.   3. Justice, Administration of—United States.   I. Title.
KF9430.W58   2008
345.73'02—dc22

2008012494

Printed in the United States of America
1   3   5   7   9   10   8   6   4   2

DESIGNED BY AMANDA DEWEY

For Gabriel

Contents

INTRODUCTION *1*

One: THE LAW OF SEPTEMBER 10 *19*

Two: THE ADMINISTRATION'S RESPONSE *44*

Three: THE REAL GUANTÁNAMO *72*

Four: THE NECESSITY AND IMPOSSIBILITY
OF JUDICIAL REVIEW *103*

Five: THE CASE FOR CONGRESS *131*

Six: THE TWIN PROBLEMS OF DETENTION AND TRIAL *151*

Seven: AN HONEST INTERROGATION LAW *183*

Eight: SURVEILLANCE LAW FOR A NEW CENTURY *219*

CONCLUSION *256*

ACKNOWLEDGMENTS *261*

NOTES *265*

INDEX *297*

LAW AND THE
LONG WAR

Introduction

THE TERRORIST MASTERMIND had slipped through their fingers before, and American forces were not about to let it happen again. At one point the previous year, they had actually arrested him but, not realizing who he was, had let him go. Unable to track him down now, they managed instead to locate and detain his wife, who was living in a remote mountainous region. For several days, they interrogated her at an air base, but she repeatedly insisted that he was dead. Finally, they tried a new tactic. They noisily put a plane on a nearby runway, its engines running. As the commanding officer later recalled: "We then informed [her] that the plane was there to take her three sons to [a repressive country nearby] unless she told us where her husband was and his aliases. If she did not do this then she would have two minutes to say goodbye to her sons. . . . We left her for ten minutes or so with paper and pencil to write down the information we required." Having threatened, in essence, to kill her sons—for nobody doubted what the secret police would do to them when they arrived at their destination—the interrogators got the information they wanted. And they got their man, disguised as a farm laborer, that evening.

What followed was a protracted habeas corpus action. Lawyers representing the high-value detainee decried the coercive interrogation of his wife, the threat to his children, and the savage beating he incurred on his arrest. (The medical officer accompanying the troops that detained him had shouted to the commanding officer to call his men off "unless you want to take back a corpse.") Human rights groups uniformly condemned the interrogation tactic as torture; major newspapers weighed in on their side. The military, meanwhile, insisted that the courts had no jurisdiction over any such overseas military action, which had in any event been lawful and had yielded essential intelligence and the capture of a very big fish. As of this writing, the lower courts have deemed themselves powerless to hear the case; the Supreme Court is considering the matter.

Should the courts hear the case, notwithstanding an act of Congress that explicitly precludes review? If so, how should they rule? Is such a tactic—garnering information from a mother by threatening to have her sons beheaded by a totalitarian regime—ever legitimate? And in a society committed both to law and to victory in a global struggle against terrorism, who should judge?

In the years since September 11, 2001, a gulf has opened up between the views of elites, mostly but far from exclusively liberals, and majority opinion on such questions of presidential power as detention, surveillance, interrogation, and trial of suspected terrorists. This gulf involves both the scope of these authorities—call them the powers of presidential preemption—and, perhaps more importantly, their source. This gulf was only accentuated by the Supreme Court's opinion in *Hamdan v. Rumsfeld*,[1] the resulting Military Commissions Act,[2] President Bush's disclosure of the CIA's secret prisons for high-value detainees in September 2006,[3] the National Security Agency's warrantless wiretapping program and the resulting legislative battles over electronic surveillance, and continuing Supreme Court litigation over detentions at Guantánamo Bay, Cuba. Public opinion has tended to regard these issues pragmatically—tolerating tough measures and contemplating with relative equanimity the deprivation of certain rights to terrorist suspects that are nonnegotiable in a civilian context. For prevailing opinion in the academy, the press, and the human rights world, however, the standards of international humanitarian law represent moral absolutes, the administration's flexible approach to them an affront to the rule of law, and the courts the principal line of defense against excessive executive power and its abuse. In functioning democracies, the argument goes, victims of uncivilized government conduct, no matter how odious these victims may be, must have access to the courts for redress—the threat of tyrannical government being ultimately greater than whatever threat even the worst criminals or terrorists may pose. In the end, the rules that limit governmental power have to be tough and the courts have to be available to make them meaningful.

But let me now confess that I have adjusted somewhat the facts of my opening anecdote, which is indeed the true story of the capture of an uncommonly evil and dangerous man: The plane was really a train; the country was Germany; the soldiers were British, not American; the year was 1946. And the high-value detainee was no Al Qaeda figure, not even a figure who posed a great prospective danger, but one of the great mass murderers of all time: Rudolf Hoess, the commandant of Auschwitz. The resulting habeas litigation, de rigueur today, was beyond anyone's wildest imagination then.[4] The stark reality is that absent an interrogation tactic that "shocks the conscience,"[5] Hoess—like his colleague Josef Mengele—might well have escaped justice, Nuremberg lost an important witness, and history denied his crucial accounts of the factory where more than a million people died.

If the tactic—and the absence of any judicial review of its use—does not suddenly seem more defensible, you have proven yourself both a principled opponent of abusive interrogation and truly committed to judicial oversight of legally dicey wartime practices. My purpose in this book is to shake somewhat the certainty of your nonconsequentialism and, in particular, your faith in judges as the essential check on such executive behavior. I share neither your certainty nor your faith and can only thank God that neither did the British soldiers who captured Rudolf Hoess. For those wholly comfortable with the operation morally or legally—those who would breezily defend it as a matter of unreviewable military discretion—my purpose is also to shake your certainty, albeit in a somewhat different manner. I wish to convince you that strong presidential action in the current conflict cannot rely exclusively—

or even chiefly—on the president's own constitutional powers. In the fight against global terrorism, the powers of presidential preemption will not remain vital without support from outside the executive branch.

This book is about that gulf between the centers of gravity of elite and mass opinion, the space in which the realities of America's genuine security needs meet the inadequacy of its laws and put stress upon the liberalism of its values. It is for those not content to give the president a free hand in a long war but also suspicious that courts can and should supervise detentions and interrogations and doubtful that such operations are, in any event, easily subjected to absolute moral rules. This is uncomfortable territory, for the slope is indeed as slippery as slopes get—and slippery, I should say, on a hill with two distinct bottoms. At one lies a government capable of torture with impunity, the very essence of tyranny. At the other lies a government incapacitated from expeditiously taking those steps necessary to protect the public from catastrophic attack. Those of us who occupy this space stand vulnerable at once to the charge of having forsaken American values and to the charge of having done so with insufficient vigor to enable the executive branch to win.

In reality, however, this is the intellectual and practical territory in which wars have been won with liberty preserved. If the United States is to win the current war on terror in the context of stable, democratic, constitutional government, I venture the guess that it is within this space—not with either a dogmatic commitment to executive power or an undying faith in the wisdom of judges—that it will do so.

NEARLY SIX DECADES after Hoess's capture, an American military panel at Guantánamo Bay, Cuba, considered the case of a man named Ghassan Abdallah Ghazi Al Shirbi. The panel was a Combatant Status Review Tribunal (CSRT), a peculiar creature set up by the military in Guantánamo not, like military commissions, to try detainees for crimes but to determine whether the government had properly classified each detainee as an enemy combatant. In its public summary of the evidence against Al Shirbi, the government made some serious allegations: He was associated with Al Qaeda. He had traveled from his native Saudi Arabia to Faisalabad, Pakistan, where he lived in a safe house with a senior Al Qaeda operative. He taught English to the other residents of the safe house and "received specialized training on remote control devices for use in explosives to detonate bombs against Afghani and United States forces." He was observed "chatting and laughing like pals with Usama bin Laden during a face-to-face meeting at [a] terrorist training camp." His nickname among the Guantánamo detainees is the "electronic builder" and "is known as 'Abu Zubaydah's right hand man' "—a reference to an Al Qaeda bigwig whom U.S. forces had captured.

At his hearing, Al Shirbi made no secret of who he was. "Honestly I did not come here to defend myself," he began. The tribunal, he said, "gathered here to look at what you have written and you will come up with a classification if this is an enemy combatant or not. If they come up with the classification enemy combatant, it is my honor to have this classification in this world until the end, until eternity, God be my witness." After a long rant against capitalism, Al Shirbi began chanting in Arabic: "May God help me fight the infidels. . . ."[6] Before one of the special military tribunals set up after September 11 to try enemy fighters for war crimes, the government charged Al Shirbi with conspiracy to murder and attack civilians and to commit terrorist acts.[7] He rejected legal representation and freely admitted the allegations against him. "I fought against the United States, I took arms. . . . I'm going to make it short and easy for you guys. I'm going to say what I did . . . without denying anything. I'm proud of what I did and there isn't any reason of fighting what I did," he told the military commission. "I came here to tell you that I did what I did and I'm willing to pay the price no matter how much you sentence me even if I spend hundreds of years in jail. In fact, it's going to be an honor—a medal of honor to me."[8] Despite such admissions, the government has been unable to convict Al Shirbi of any crime. His criminal case died when the Supreme Court tossed out the administration's original military commission system, and, as of this writing, a new case has not yet materialized. He remains at Guantánamo with no charges pending against him.

Faruq Ali Ahmed, a teenage Yemeni, also traveled to Afghanistan in 2001— and he also ended up facing a CSRT at Guantánamo Bay. Unlike Al Shirbi, Ali

Ahmed did not effectively admit to being an Al Qaeda operative, a Taliban fighter, or anything else. He had come to Afghanistan, he told the tribunal, "to teach the kids" the Koran. He conceded that he had turned over his passport to someone he thought might be Taliban, and he had stayed in a house run by people he "assumed" were Taliban. But he denied belonging to the group. He denied taking military training, and he denied traveling with a large group of mujahadeen fleeing the fighting at Tora Bora—some of whom, the government later alleged, he had met in high school. At least some of the government's other evidence against him seems to have come from a detainee who—after a very rough interrogation—implicated a lot of people. All of this troubled Ali Ahmed's personal representative, a nonlegal military officer assigned to assist him before the CSRT. The personal representative appended a brief memo to the tribunal's unanimous decision that Ali Ahmed was, in fact, detainable forever. "I do feel with some certainty," the personal representative wrote, that the detainee who gave evidence against Ali Ahmed "has lied about other detainees to receive preferable treatment and to cause them problems while in custody."

"Had the Tribunal taken this evidence out as unreliable, then the position we have taken is that a teacher of the Koran (to the Taliban's children) is an enemy combatant (partially because he slept under a Taliban roof)."[9] In later hearings, the military suggested that some of Ali Ahmed's high school acquaintances had become close to Osama Bin Laden and that his own name had appeared on a list of Al Qaeda operatives.[10] But all public documents relating to his case do not come close to answering the question of whether he is a dangerous operative or an innocent teacher.

How should the law consider cases of men like Al Shirbi and Ali Ahmed? According to the military, they are simply "enemy combatants," detainable at the administration's discretion until the war on terrorism is over—whatever that might mean and whenever it might come about. According to human rights groups, by contrast, they are both by dint of their incarcerations victims of human rights abuses. This country's legal obligation, to the extent it cannot prove criminal charges against them, is to set them free. As Amnesty

International put it, "the solution in principle is simple, and the government must turn its energies to this end. It should either charge the detainees with recognizable criminal offences and bring them to trial in the ordinary civilian courts, or it should release them with full protections against further abuses."[11]

The solution, even in principle, is actually not simple at all.

Al Shirbi is a man whom no society with an instinct for self-preservation would release blithely. Yet our legal system has at best an underdeveloped vocabulary for discussing men like him. We don't quite know how to put them on trial, but they are not quite like enemy soldiers, whom armies routinely detain without trials, and they are potentially more dangerous to the population at large than either soldiers or criminals. What's more, the legal system's vocabulary for distinguishing between people like Al Shirbi and those whose cases are murkier—and Ali Ahmed's case is one of many that is far murkier—is less developed still. Simply labeling them both "combatants" is inadequate, and seeing their detentions as raising comparable human rights questions absurd. Confronting these cases seriously requires more than interpreting existing law, the job of the courts, or carrying out existing law, the job of the president. It involves the crafting of new legal frameworks altogether; rethinking questions of why we lock people up, under what authority, and with what sort of review; and hybridizing intellectual and legal categories American and international law has traditionally kept distinct.

THIS IS THE STORY of the legal architecture of the war on terrorism—the rules that govern the American side of the fight and, perhaps more importantly, the rules that govern how those rules get made. It is, at one level, a story of failure: how this country has thus far failed to build a viable legal structure for its war; how it has failed as a political and legal culture to address seriously the questions of what to do with the modern Rudolf Hoesses (and the many more would-be Rudolf Hoesses) and how to distinguish them from the peasants, teachers, students, and other civilians among whom they hide; and how the legal battles it has fought with itself over the past several years have collectively avoided the hard project of designing new legal systems for a conflict unlike any that this country has ever faced.

In important respects, this is a critique of the Bush administration, whose consistent—sometimes mindless—aggressiveness and fixation on executive authority consistently blinded it to the need to solicit the backing of Congress and the courts for actions that were bound to be controversial. It is also a defense of the Bush administration, many of whose tactics in the fight were better grounded in precedent and more defensible than its legion of critics allowed. As such, it is also a critique of the administration's critics, who often failed to distinguish between human rights norms to which this country has actually committed itself and those to which human rights groups wished it had committed itself; they have thereby denied the administration the flexibility it legitimately required. It is a critique of the Supreme Court, which has used the legal disputes over the war on terrorism to carve itself a seat at the table in foreign and military policy matters over which it has, for good reasons, a historically limited role. Perhaps most of all, it is a critique of the Congress of the United States, which has sat on its hands and refused to assert its own proper role in designing a coherent legal structure for the war; to this day, America's national legislature continues to avoid addressing the questions only it can usefully answer.

At another level, the book is also a plea for a different approach in the future, an effort to begin putting the powers of presidential preemption on a solid legal foundation for the long term. Like the conflict itself, this approach is messy and inelegant, lacking all of the purity of either the administration's infatuation with presidential power or the civil libertarian love affair with judicial power. It also lacks completeness, for the ideas I advance are predicated explicitly on the notion that we have not yet built the legal and doctrinal architecture that will govern this area. I do not pretend to know in full those details, and I mistrust grand claims as to the ultimate design. I have provided here a sketch, an outline of a first draft of the statutory regimes that might undergird a sound long-term structure for a conflict that is not going away any time soon.

Animating this outline are two convictions born of the failures of the last six years: The first is that any proper legal architecture for this war will at once restrain the executive branch far more than the Bush administration has wanted to be restrained yet at the same time enable it far more than civil libertarians and human rights groups find congenial. It will empower judges to review executive behavior more robustly than the Bush administration finds comfortable, and far less robustly than human rights groups wish to see. It will also, almost invariably, contain significant holes of the type that permit aggressive, flexible executive action—which, as the Hoess example vividly illustrates, is not always pretty. International conflict stubbornly resists the concept of law as people generally understand it in more civilized settings. This point is an uncomfortable one. How satisfying it is, after all, to talk about war and military actions in the language of international conventions, statutes, war crimes, and customary international law. Yet if we face the matter entirely honestly, we cannot escape the fact that legal rules are inevitably less absolute, less truly legal, in this context than, for example, in the domestic civilian context. The Nuremberg trials, after all, involved *ex post facto* prosecutions of the sort most condemned by the American Constitution—yet we see them as a great victory for international justice. In the name of that higher justice, the world proclaimed rape a crime of genocide and torture after the fact in evaluating criminality in Rwanda and the former Yugoslavia.[12] Even some of the most committed human rights advocates will allow that with a ticking nuclear bomb in New York City and a suspect in custody, all bets are off as to interrogation tactics; they contend in this situation merely that the law should not countenance the step that any patriot or humanitarian would take to avert a catastrophe. Abraham Lincoln defied the chief justice of the United States over habeas corpus, and history views Lincoln as the country's greatest president and Chief Justice Roger Taney as one of the villains of his era. The subject matter of warfare has a way of making—and not only in extreme cases—legal principles look a bit flabby.

Discerning the reason requires no great imagination: The stakes are too high for anything else. A society can accept in the name of liberty the consequences of allowing even the worst criminal the rights we would all want were we facing trial. The worst that will happen is he escapes justice and goes on to commit additional crimes. While those crimes may be horrible, even the worst individual crimes represent manageable horrors from a societywide point of view. Terrorism, by contrast, involves horrors on an altogether different scale. And international conflict at its core is about avoiding harms—particularly catastrophic harms—prospectively, not retroactively accounting for them. No society can afford inviolable principles and inflexible rules concerning those steps on which its ultimate fate or interests depend. In a mature legal architecture for the war on terror, the principles themselves will somehow have to recognize this reality.

The second point is that the eventual design of a mature legal architecture for this war cannot come into being chiefly through dialogue between the executive and judicial branches of government—the president grasping and the courts slapping his hand. Neither unilateral rule making on the part of the president nor judicial review of whatever rules he makes up can mold a stable long-term architecture for a war that defies all of the usual norms of war. The only institution capable of delivering such a body of law is the Congress of the United States—the very branch of government that has been, in the years since September 11, 2001, least active and involved in the process of designing the rules.

In the years since the attacks, Congress has roused itself a few times, always in response to the president's call; the USA PATRIOT Act, the Detainee Treatment Act, and the Military Commissions Act present the most significant examples. But these are the exceptions. The broad mechanism for decision making about the legal structure of the war has consisted of executive actions followed by review in the courts of the validity of those actions, invariably contested under extant statutes and precedents. The absence of the national legislature from some of the most significant policy discussions of our time has brought about deleterious consequences at a number of levels. At a theoretical level, it has been unfortunate because Congress has its own independent duty to legislate in response to problems that arise in the course of the nation's life. After all, America's constitutional design presupposes that each branch of government will *assert* its powers, that those powers will clash, and that this clash will prevent the accumulation of power in any one branch. Yet in the war on terrorism, Congress has done very nearly the opposite of countering the executive's rather considerable ambitions. It has run from its own powers on questions on which its assertion of rightful authority would be helpful, and it has sloughed off the difficult choices onto the two branches of government less capable than itself of designing new systems for novel problems.

This abandonment of the field has also been unfortunate at a policy level, where it has inevitably lost nuance, flexibility, and imagination in envisioning the appropriate regime. Congress has left the courts to split the difference between polar arguments to which few Americans would actually sign on and others that badly frame the terms of what should be a much broader debate. To cite only one example, one can imagine a world of legitimate policy options to handle the detention of American citizens caught fighting for Al Qaeda. But instead of exploring those options, Congress has left the judiciary to seek the "right answer" by groping its way between a few Civil War–era precedents and a few World War II–era precedents—none of which obviously controls the current situation. Ultimately, the task of imagining the regime must become the legislative task it has so obviously been for so long.

THE NOTION THAT CONGRESS ought to play a substantial role in writing the law of the American response to terrorism would not surprise a middle-school civics class. Designing legal systems for complex and novel circumstances that preexisting law addresses inadequately is perhaps the quintessential legislative function. At its core, it is decidedly neither an executive nor a judicial one. Yet somehow, in the years since the attacks, America has become bogged down in a heartfelt, earnest, passionate debate over what the law already is, rather than over what it should be. It is a discussion of past precedent, instead of future needs, a legalistic debate about the issues at stake, rather than a policy debate about them, and it forsakes the political and legal burden of writing law with which to govern ourselves. This debate has obscured an important fact: We do not have a lot of law here. We have, rather, underdeveloped strands of law intended for other purposes, interacting in peculiar and

often perverse ways. Both sides in this debate like to pretend these strands answer the questions at hand—and answer them in accord with their own favored approaches. That both sides can claim as much with equal good faith
suggests that the law is more of a sphinx than either admits.

In the initial aftermath of the attacks, the Bush administration quite reasonably chose to see the confrontation with Al Qaeda as a legal war—that is,
as a military conflict under international and domestic law that triggered the
president's extensive constitutional war powers. Congress bought this premise, passing at President Bush's request a broad Authorization for the Use of
Military Force.[13] In so doing, it tapped into a preexisting and largely mori-
bund body of law the executive branch had last taken advantage of during the
aftermath of World War II. This body of law allowed the detention and trial
of enemy fighters with the barest minimum of judicial oversight. The administration used it to justify nonstatutory orders authorizing military commission trials, extensive detentions at Guantánamo Bay, Cuba, and elsewhere,
and even detentions of citizens domestically. In addition, the administration
tapped the president's war powers in its aggressive approach to interrogations
and to domestic surveillance. In all these areas, the shift to the war paradigm
allowed the administration to make its own rules, rather than to go to Congress to seek permission and legitimization for controversial steps that seemed
in tension with preexisting statutes and international norms.

In the short term, the war model seemed to involve a relatively precise
analogy, and the flexibility it gave the administration was undoubtedly useful.
After all, the initial action in the war on terror involved a major overseas military deployment, alliances with armed groups, and hostilities with other
armed groups. It involved the toppling of a government and the installation
of a new one. More generally, it involved the projection of American force all
over the world and followed a major attack on American soil—including on
the seat of the American military itself.

But the model was always imperfect. And the war on terror has, in any
event, now entered a different phase, one in which the spasmodic bursts of
overt military power that characterized the earlier phase and looked most like
traditional warfare have given way to something more elastic that takes place

in slower motion and requires more innovative, long-term legal approaches. Particularly with respect to detention rules, the laws of war just do not fit very well. While they sufficed in a pinch, they have come to resemble an old worn overcoat draped over a shivering child who walked outside underdressed. The tailoring for another wearer is obvious. The overcoat's age combined with the child's youth makes it seem almost like a costume. The flaws in the fit create gaps which the cold air rushes to fill. Nobody looking at this child would imagine his parents wanted him to wear that coat for the rest of the winter. Indeed, there would be costs for doing so.

The costs to America of persisting with the war model after the initial crisis passed have been hard to overstate. Yes, the war's legal structures have proven adequate to their main function; we have not suffered any more domestic attacks, and that is no small thing. Yet America has continued, as it were, to wear this coat, rather than getting one that actually fits, at great cost to its international image and to the confidence many of its own citizens have in its justice. Relying on the laws of war has required endless litigation—litigation that has made the courts into arbiters of counterterrorism policy. The unity of purpose that prevailed in America in the period immediately following the 2001 attacks has eroded, giving the conflict with Al Qaeda a partisan sheen that it ought not have. The question is whether a legal architecture for the war that reflected greater societal consensus in the form of the blessing of the nation's legislature, and thereby the consent of the public, would have delivered the same results at lower cost. I believe it would have, and that it still could.

Enhanced presidential powers during wartime are defensible conceptually in large measure because they are temporary; they last only as long as the crisis. Because of the indefinite nature of the long war on terror, allowing the president to exercise for its duration the traditional powers his office accrues during wartime involves permitting those powers to attach perhaps permanently. What's more, as the war on terror progressed, it became clear that a lot of its major operations were not, in fact, military in nature. Prosecutions of some important terrorist defendants have taken place in civilian courts, for example. And much of the international conflict has taken place not in battlefield combat in Iraq or Afghanistan but through the operation of foreign law enforcement in Europe and elsewhere. Indeed, for all its insistence on war as the appropriate model for the conflict with Al Qaeda, the Bush administration has not been consistent in practice at all. For all of these reasons, the longer the conflict has gone on, the less apt the pure war model has become, and the less comfortable the public—and particularly the courts—has become with the exertion of presidential powers not specifically authorized by the legislature, much less actions taken in active tension with laws the legislature has passed.

The result has been a series of confrontations between the executive branch and the judicial branch, which has sought to rein in unilateral executive action as the war has gone on. The first of these was a pair of Supreme Court cases in 2004—*Rasul v. Bush*[14] and *Hamdi v. Rumsfeld*[15]—in which the Court declared that it had jurisdiction over detainees at Guantánamo Bay and could therefore hear their habeas corpus petitions; the justices also, while acknowledging the war as a legal war, demanded that the military grant some form of due process to a citizen it was holding domestically as an enemy combatant. In response, the administration sought and received from Congress a law stripping the courts of jurisdiction over Guantánamo in an attempt to restore the status quo that existed before the decision.[16] The court, however, was not done. In 2006, it decided in *Hamdan v. Rumsfeld*[17] that this new law did not apply to cases pending on its date of passage—that is, to the hundreds of cases filed between the time the Court decided the first case and the time Congress acted to overturn it. In the same decision, the justices struck down President Bush's administrative plan for trials at Guantánamo by military commission, ruling that the plan deviated from military and international law and had not been specifically authorized by the legislature. *Hamdan* forced the administration once again to go to Congress—and once again it got more or less what it wanted. In the Military Commissions Act, Congress again sought to wipe out the court's habeas jurisdiction—including over pending cases—and it authorized the military commission trials. The country now finds itself in a third round of litigation, with the Supreme Court poised to rule on whether the statute's efforts to deny it jurisdiction over Guantánamo Bay violate the Constitution. If the justices determine again that they have the power to hear these cases, the courts will then turn to whether the processes Congress and the administration have set up pass muster.

The litigation to date has been at once momentous and, well, something less than momentous. This dichotomy reflects a peculiarity in the Supreme Court's work in the counterterrorism arena, which has set the table for a judicial posture in warfare far more aggressive than anything the Court has actually done so far. Taken on their own, the Court's specific pronouncements have been far less consequential than many commentators imagine. In neither *Rasul* nor *Hamdan* did the Court act on constitutional grounds, leaving Congress free in both instances to change the laws the Court interpreted—which the legislature promptly did. In neither case did the Court forbid the policy course the administration had chosen to take; for all the attention the cases garnered, they precluded neither military detentions at Guantánamo without charge nor trial by tribunals lacking the normal safeguards of both the civilian justice system and the general court martial. In both decisions, the administration suffered dramatic setbacks that amounted in practical terms merely to a requirement to seek congressional permission for what it wanted to do—congressional permission that proved, in both cases, relatively easy to obtain. Such is the oddity of these celebrated victories for the rule of law—for so all right-thinking people proclaimed them—that, should a similar situation arise again, they collectively would not prevent the administration from acting more or less as it did in detaining and interrogating, sometimes brutally, such a bevy of terrorist suspects as it rounded up in Afghanistan in 2001 and 2002.

What the Supreme Court has done is carve itself a seat at the table. It has intimated, without ever deciding, that a constitutional basis for its actions exists—in addition to the statutory bases on which it decided the cases—meaning that its authority over overseas detentions may be an inherent feature of judicial power, not a policy question on which the legislature and executive can work their will. Whether the votes exist on the Court to go this extra step we will find out soon enough. But the specter of a vastly different judicial posture in this area now haunts the executive branch—one in which the justices assert an inherent authority to review executive detention and interrogation practices, divine rights to apply with that jurisdiction based on due process and vaguely worded international humanitarian law principles not clearly implemented in U.S. law, and allow their own power to follow the military's anywhere in the world. Such a posture would constitute an earthquake in the relationships among all three branches of government, and the doctrinal seeds for it have all been planted. Whether they ultimately take root depends on factors extrinsic to the war on terror—particularly the future composition of a Supreme Court now closely divided on these questions. It also will pivot on the manner in which the political branches posture the legal foundations of the war in the future. Building a strong legislative architecture now may be the only way to avert a major expansion of judicial power over foreign policy and warfare.

It is also, I believe, the only hope for any kind of counterterrorism policy that a broad cross-section of both mass and elite opinion will support. Over the past few years, a large literature has grown up around the merits of the administration's and the judiciary's approaches to the conflict—most of it polemical, some scholarly, and only a little of it useful in guiding the future development of American law. Any number of commentators has denounced the administration's approach with varying degrees of sophistication. A smaller group has risen to its defense, attacking the Supreme Court for its intrusions into the executive's proper sphere. The literature debating whether the Bush administration presents a threat to American democracy or its best hope for effective confrontation with Al Qaeda is as large as it is unavailing.

Yet basic facts that should be at the core of any serious discussion of this subject are curiously missing from the debate. Most fundamentally, who are these detainees over whose fate we all so earnestly argue? The administration's sympathizers describe them confidently as terrorists or combatants; its critics no less confidently assure us that many are innocent laborers, students, and relief workers. Neither side cites much evidence for its view. Initially, the datalessness of the debate was unavoidable; there was no data to cite. The administration had released so little information about whom it was holding that some degree of speculation was inevitable. In the last few years, however, the available data has grown far richer as the administration has begun releasing large volumes of material. Yet the debate has not kept pace.[18] Designing legal rules is difficult indeed if one has not seriously studied the population to whom those rules would apply.

Even under the best of circumstances, writing rules to at once authorize and regulate the powers of presidential preemption is a daunting project. One of the reasons, I suspect, that we have preferred as a society to pretend that the answers to our current questions lie in age-old precedents, in the text of the Constitution, and in the will of "the Founders" is that the prospect of writing our own rules intimidates us so. But our denial will not do any longer. The Founders in so many ways never imagined the situation their progeny would face, and we delude ourselves to the extent that we mine their work for the answers to problems that defy even analogy to any they considered. To make law for our current conflict, contemporary America will need to apply its own values, its own instincts, and its own evaluations of risk. And it will need to undertake this project in the institution of its government which exists in order to write new rules for new circumstances.

In these pages, therefore, in addition to analyzing how America came to its current legal impasse, I have tried to suggest legislative strategies to address the range of issues currently in controversy: new rules for the detention of America's enemies, for their trials and their interrogations and transfers to foreign governments, and new law to replace or supplement surveillance laws rendered obsolete by the march of technology. The level of specificity in these ideas varies a great deal—from a set of broad instincts about surveillance law, an area where rampant government secrecy precludes more granular proposals, to fairly detailed suggestions about the reform of detention practices. The idea here is not a kind of comprehensive legislative package, a Counterterrorism Reform Act of 2009. It is, rather, a set of ideas that emerges from a common instinct: the belief that Congress has yet to put its mark on the law of terrorism and that the maturation of this essential body of law will founder badly until it does so. It is an attempt to force the reader—and to force myself, frankly—to begin thinking about the powers of presidential preemption in pervasively statutory terms, to imagine how America might break its current stalemate and position its law for a long war with a dangerous foe.

ONE

The Law of September 10

R ANDY MOSS IS, perhaps, an unlikely man to have toiled at removing the executive branch's fetters in what later became the war on
terrorism. For one thing, Moss did not serve in the Bush administration, but, rather, ran the Justice Department's Office of Legal Counsel
(OLC) during the waning years of its supposedly weak-kneed Democratic
predecessor. For another, he could hardly differ more in substance, style, or
public presentation from the infamous John Yoo. A quiet, careful lawyer,
Moss does not wear his politics on his sleeve, and in any event, he by no means
qualifies as a conservative. He has spent a great deal of time since his return to
private practice defending federal campaign finance laws. He is the picture of
liberal moderation—a fact that makes his cameo appearance in the report of
the 9/11 Commission all the more noteworthy.

In late 1998, President Clinton wanted to get Osama bin Laden, and the
CIA had concocted a plan to use tribal mercenaries in Afghanistan to kidnap
him, hold him for a spell, and then turn him over to the agency. As the 9/11
Commission recounts the incident, then-current legal authority "instructed
the CIA to capture Bin Ladin and to use lethal force only in self-defense. Work
now began on a new memorandum that would give the tribals more latitude.

The intention was to say that they could use lethal force if the attempted capture seemed impossible to complete successfully." The early drafts "emphasized that [they] authorized only a capture operation"; assassinations, after all, would violate a presidential executive order. But "the CIA's leaders urged strengthening the language to allow the tribals to be paid whether Bin Ladin was captured *or* killed." Then they pushed even further:

> They finally agreed . . . that an extraordinary step was necessary. The new memorandum would allow the killing of Bin Ladin if the CIA and the tribals judged that capture was not feasible (a judgment it already seemed clear they had reached). The Justice Department lawyer who worked on the draft [Moss] told us that what was envisioned was a group of tribals assaulting a location, leading to a shoot-out. Bin Ladin and others would be captured if possible, but probably would be killed. The administration's position was that under the law of armed conflict, killing a person who posed an imminent threat to the United States would be an act of self-defense, not an assassination.[1]

Details of the plan and of Moss's precise legal theory remain classified. The operation in question never took place, in part because Attorney General Janet Reno harbored anxieties about its proximity to an assassination, in part because the CIA deemed the likelihood of success low and the likelihood of substantial civilian casualties high. Still, even this bare outline of a still-born operation significantly complicates the caricature that both sides of the legal war on terror have sought to paint. Here, after all, was the Clinton administration thinking aggressively about the powers of presidential preemption with respect to Al Qaeda violence. Pivotally, it was not contemplating action in the narrow confines of criminal justice but under the law of armed conflict as well. The operation Moss reviewed appeared to contemplate something in between what we have since learned to call a "rendition"—a kidnapping orchestrated by the CIA—and a targeted killing. It was the Clinton administration, not the Bush administration, that put these themes in play—and long before September 11. When lawyers at the National Security Council later presented a document for Clinton's signature authorizing a shoot-down of Bin Laden's helicopters or planes, journalist Steve Coll recounted, "there was no pretense . . . that bin Laden would be captured for trial. Clinton signed it."[2]

THAT SEPTEMBER 11 triggered a seismic shift in America's legal approach to terrorism has become a kind of article of faith both for the administration and its critics. The significance of the shift differs according to the speaker. From the administration's perspective, it took America from an anemic law enforcement approach to terrorism to an approach premised on an actual state of war between this country and Al Qaeda—one that triggered the full panoply of presidential war powers. "For decades, the United States had dealt with terrorism primarily as a crime subject to the law enforcement and criminal justice systems," wrote John Yoo, one of the architects of the administration's approach. "In response to previous al Qaeda attacks, the United States dispatched FBI agents to investigate the 'crime scene' and tried to apprehend terrorist 'suspects.' . . . Efforts to capture or kill al Qaeda leader Osama bin Laden throughout the 1990s were shelved, out of concerns that the Justice Department did not have enough evidence to satisfy the legal standard for a criminal arrest." By contrast, Yoo wrote, "Here is how we at the Justice Department sat down to think about September 11. On that clear, sunny day, four coordinated attacks had taken place in rapid succession, aimed at critical buildings at the heart of our national financial system and our nation's capital." If, he concluded, "a nation-state had carried out the same attacks on the same targets, there would have been no question about whether a state of war would have existed. . . . Why should status as an international terrorist organization rather than a nation-state make a difference as to whether we are at war?"[3]

Such accounts play on certain favored conservative themes, portraying Democrats as soft on things about which leadership requires steadfastness. They mingle Cold War–era criticisms that liberals are "soft on communism" with the more domestic theme that they are "soft on crime"—although with the twist that they accuse liberals of wanting to treat America's enemies as

mere criminals, rather than as military opponents. In contrast, the administration's narrative portrays itself as having taken a tough approach, one
that for the first time took the threat seriously and saw it for what it was.
September 11 marked the turning point, after which America went on a war
footing.

The critics tell a different story. In their account, America went from a society committed to the rule of law, even in tough situations, to one unbounded
by it. Following the attacks, in this version, the administration tossed out
long-settled understandings of international law concerning the detention,
interrogation, and trial of terrorists; brushed aside the historic role of the
courts in overseeing government action; and otherwise ran roughshod over
civil liberties and human rights. The result, as Joseph Margulies—who represented Guantánamo detainees in the *Rasul* case—put it, "has created a human
rights debacle that will eventually take its place alongside other wartime mis-
adventures, including the internment of Japanese-Americans during World
War II, the prosecutions under the Espionage and Sedition Acts during World
War I, and the suspension of the writ of habeas corpus during the Civil War."[4]
After September 11, Margulies contended, the administration has claimed "all
the authority that could conceivably flow to the executive branch during a
time of armed conflict, but accept[ed] none of the restrictions. The result is
unchecked, almost imperial power. . . . All of this power is limited only by the
president's promise to exercise it wisely."[5] This version too plays on preexisting themes—specifically, the post-Watergate fear of unchecked presidential
power, particularly among liberals concerning conservative administrations.

Yet these two irreconcilable stories have one critical feature in common:
the notion that a tremendous shift occurred on September 11, one that represented a dramatic break with the past—not one merely of degree or of emphasis but one of kind. This point no doubt contains elements of truth; the
operative fabric of American law did change enormously in the wake of the
attacks. But as the example of Randy Moss illustrates, it changed somewhat
less enormously than the common wisdom on both sides imagines. America
has never taken a pure law enforcement approach to terrorism, and it does
not now take a pure wartime approach. Indeed, from the use of Guantánamo

Bay to evade judicial scrutiny, to indefinite detention, to extraordinary rendition, to military commissions, to the scope and meaning of the Geneva
Conventions, to the interrogation of military and CIA detainees, the law of
September 11 has much deeper roots in the law that preceded it—call it the
law of September 10—than either the administration or its foes like to pretend.

ON SEPTEMBER 10, 2001, the United States had no consistent legal approach
for thinking about terrorists. To be sure, the federal government had chiefly
deployed the criminal law in its confrontation with Al Qaeda. Federal prosecutors had convicted the first World Trade Center bombing conspirators.[6]
They had brought down as well the terrorist cell around Sheikh Omar Abdel
Rahman.[7] And they had garnered a conviction against a would-be Al Qaeda
attacker named Ahmed Ressam, whom authorities had caught carrying explosives across the Canadian border for an intended bombing at Los Angeles International Airport on New Year's Eve 1999.[8] A grand jury in New York had
even indicted Osama bin Laden himself.[9]

Yet the United States prior to September 11 by no means confined itself to
the use of law enforcement tools in confronting terrorism in general or Al
Qaeda in particular. Rather, policy makers, regarding counterterrorism as a
priority but not considering it a fundamental or overarching orientation for
American foreign policy and power, used the variety of powers at the government's disposal without belaboring the question of what paradigm they were
employing.

The military's role in counterterrorism operations, for example, long predated the 2001 attacks. Ronald Reagan ordered air strikes on Libya following
terrorist operations sponsored by that regime in 1986. Clinton, in the wake of
the African embassy bombings in 1998, famously launched cruise missile attacks on suspected Al Qaeda targets in Afghanistan and the Sudan. This latter
response required a specific legal understanding of the conflict with Al Qaeda
as something more than a law enforcement problem. We don't, after all, attack mere criminal suspects with Tomahawk missiles.

The 1998 operations bear particular attention. Clinton's choice of targets, specifically the decision to attack a Sudanese pharmaceutical plant suspected of producing chemical weapons components, garnered a great deal of criticism. Coming as the strikes did in the midst of the Monica Lewinsky scandal, Clinton's motives as well drew fire; many people dismissed the action as a "*Wag the Dog* scenario"—a reference to a movie in which a president mired in a sex scandal manufactures an overseas military confrontation to distract attention from his problems. But it is important to note as well what was *not* controversial about these strikes: the conceptual framework in which they took place. Within the administration, officials had begun thinking about Al Qaeda operatives as—in addition to criminals—legitimate military targets.

"There was little question at either the National Security Council or the CIA that under American law it was entirely permissible to kill Osama bin Laden and his top aides, at least after evidence showed they were responsible for the Africa attacks," wrote Coll. "The ban on assassinations . . . did not apply to military targets, the Office of Legal Counsel in Clinton's Justice Department had previously ruled in classified opinions." And terrorist camps "in Afghanistan were legitimate military targets under this definition, the White House lawyers agreed."[10] This idea of fighting terrorism on parallel tracks—a law enforcement track and a military and intelligence track—predated even the Clinton administration. From its creation during the Reagan administration, the CIA's Counterterrorism Center had an interdisciplinary quality. It imagined capturing terrorists when possible and bringing them to justice or neutralizing them by other means when doing so would preempt an attack.[11]

Indeed, the parallel use of criminal and military authorities in 1998 struck almost nobody as eccentric. Whatever else they may be, after all, terrorist acts clearly involve crimes of all sorts—from mass murder to frauds, identity thefts, and financial crimes. Attacks on American embassies or other official targets, however, are also presumptively acts of war, and Bin Laden had self-consciously and very publicly declared war on the United States. What's more, he located his bases of operations far beyond the normal reach of American law enforcement. Any serious effort to get him, therefore, would necessarily implicate presidential powers beyond those of civilian law enforcement.

September 11 certainly accelerated the change. After the attacks, the weight of the American response to Al Qaeda shifted decisively towards American military power—by then bolstered legally by Congress's Authorization for the Use of Military Force (AUMF)—and away somewhat from law enforcement powers. During the Clinton era, some operations against Bin Laden were halted or hampered because of legal concerns; the administration was still betwixt and between legal paradigms.[12] But it's important to understand the shift that has taken place, rather than as some dramatic break with the past on a particular day, as movement along a spectrum over time. September 11 catalyzed a change that had begun a long time earlier and that had already progressed remarkably far.

The overarching conception of the fight against Al Qaeda as, at least in part, a matter of warfare is by no means the only area in which the Bush administration's response to the attacks drew on the legal approaches of its predecessors. One can see the connective tissue far more broadly. After September 11, for example, the roundup and deportation of large numbers of Arab and Muslim aliens under immigration laws raised many hackles. But immigration authorities under both parties had long used the power of deportation to remove aliens suspected of terrorist ties from the country—sometimes using secret evidence of those affiliations to do so.[13] The Bush administration's innovation here lay only in using these powers sweepingly and secretively.[14] Similarly, after Hamas started its campaign to disrupt the Palestinian-Israeli peace process in the mid-1990s, a series of laws and executive orders sought to interrupt terrorist financing by prohibiting domestic "material support" for designated terrorists abroad. In the wake of September 11, the Bush administration made aggressive use of these powers; it did not, however, create them.

Even the most controversial and seemingly innovative of the administration's actions turn out, on closer inspection, to elaborate on, amplify, or revive preexisting currents of American law and practice. Consider, for example, the tactic of so-called extraordinary rendition, in which the CIA snatches a terror suspect abroad and turns him over to a foreign government for interrogation or detention. This program became infamous in the years that followed September 11 because of allegations that the administration was subcontracting torture to authoritarian-allied governments. According to the man who ran the program initially at CIA, however, it actually began back in 1995.

Michael Scheuer ran the agency's Osama bin Laden unit from its creation until 1999. In his account, given in congressional testimony in April 2007, "The rendition program was initiated because President Clinton and [National Security aides Anthony] Lake, [Sandy] Berger and [Richard] Clarke requested that the CIA begin to attack and dismantle al Qaeda. These men made it clear from the first that they did not want to bring those captured to the United States or to hold them in U.S. custody." Instead, "President Clinton and his national security team directed the CIA to take each captured al Qaeda leader to the country which had an outstanding legal process for him." Under Clinton, Scheuer testified, interrogation was never a priority, and there was a hard and fast rule that "we could only focus on al Qaeda leaders who were wanted somewhere for a legal process." Still, it was understood that rendered suspects would not be treated with kid gloves. The "CIA warned the president and his National Security Council that the U.S. State Department had and would identify the countries to which the captured fighters were being delivered as human rights abusers," Scheuer testified. "In response, President Clinton and his team asked if CIA could get each receiving country to guarantee that it would treat the person according to its own laws. This was no problem, and we did so." And while officials of both the Clinton and Bush administrations have emphasized that these diplomatic assurances were meaningful promises of humane treatment, Scheuer regarded them as something of a farce: "There [were] no qualms at all about sending people to Cairo and kind of joking up our sleeves about what would happen to those people in Cairo—in Egyptian prison," he said.[15]

Richard Clarke, the National Security Council's key counterterrorism official, dated the rendition program even earlier, as did another former NSC official, Daniel Benjamin.[16] Defining "extraordinary renditions" as "operations to apprehend terrorists abroad, usually without the knowledge of and almost always without public acknowledgment of the host government," Clarke cited a "terrorist snatch" during the Reagan administration. "By the mid-1990s these snatches were becoming routine . . . activity. Sometimes FBI arrest teams, sometimes CIA personnel, had been regularly dragging terrorists back to stand trial in the United States or flying them to incarceration in other countries." In Clark's account, it was the military establishment, not timidity on the part of the White House, that stood in the way of more aggressive use of renditions back then. "The fact is," he wrote, that "President Clinton approved every snatch that he was asked to review. Every snatch CIA, Justice, or Defense proposed during my tenure as [Counterterrorism Security Group] chairman, from 1992 to 2001, was approved."

The Clinton administration at the highest levels undertook these operations fully aware that they posed legally dicey problems. Clarke recalled:

The first time I proposed a snatch, in 1993, the White House Counsel, Lloyd Cutler, demanded a meeting with the president to explain how it violated international law. Clinton had seemed to be siding with Cutler until Al Gore belatedly joined the meeting, having just flown overnight from South Africa. Clinton recapped the arguments on both sides for Gore: Lloyd says this. Dick says that. Gore laughed and said, "That's a no-brainer. Of course it's a violation of international law, that's why it's a covert action. The guy is a terrorist. Go grab his ass."[17]

These operations were not pretty, and they were not all that different—except in frequency—from the ones the Bush administration undertook after the advent of the war on terrorism. In 1995, for example, American agents operating in Croatia helped abduct Talaat Fouad Qassem, an Egyptian terrorist who had been sentenced to death in absentia and was suspected of being involved in the assassination of former Egyptian President Anwar Sadat. After Croatian authorities nabbed Qassem in Zagreb and turned him over to U.S. agents, they interrogated him on a ship and then passed him on to the Egyptians. His fate is unknown, but Egyptian human rights monitors believe he was executed. In 1998, working in Albania, CIA operatives helped Albanian security officials wiretap a group of militants. After discovering that the militants were having substantial communications with Ayman al Zawahiri, Al

Qaeda's number two official, they convinced the Egyptians to issue a warrant for one of the militants. Over the succeeding months, Albanian officials—with the CIA's assistance—captured five of the suspects and killed a sixth. As *New Yorker* writer Jane Mayer recounted the incident, "These men were bound, blindfolded, and taken to an abandoned airbase, then flown by jet to Cairo for interrogation. [One of them] later alleged that he suffered electrical shocks to his genitals, was hung from his limbs, and was kept in a cell in filthy water up to his knees. Two other suspects, who had been sentenced to death in absentia, were hanged."[18] Then–CIA director George Tenet testified in 2002 that the agency "had rendered 70 terrorists to justice" before September 11.[19]

The rendition program, to be sure, changed under the Bush administration after September 11. For one thing, its use surely grew more frequent, giving rise to a greater likelihood of errors, some of which appear to have happened.[20] Another difference was that the CIA was keen after September 11 to interrogate the captives, whereas interrogation had not been a previous priority. The result, according to Scheuer, is that the agency ended up holding detainees itself, whereas it had previously limited its role to shipping them to allied governments.[21] But again, it is important to appreciate what didn't change. The core of the policy was already in place.

ON ITS FACE, the administration's policies concerning detention and interrogation of terrorist suspects appear to offer a decided contrast. These policies were not in place prior to September 11. They were new. They were different. And they shocked the world.

As was the case with rendition, however, they were at least a little bit less new and less different than the common wisdom imagines. Consider interrogation first. On the surface, the law of September 10 gave little quarter to harsh interrogation tactics. The Geneva Conventions forbid them in sweeping language.[22] And in a string of cases, the Supreme Court made clear not merely that abusive interrogations were out of bounds in law enforcement and that statements obtained improperly were inadmissible, but that authorities had an affirmative obligation to warn suspects of their rights to counsel and to keep silent.[23] In the international arena, the United States signed the U.N. Convention Against Torture, which bans not merely torture but also "other acts of cruel, inhuman or degrading treatment or punishment which do not amount to torture."[24] The convention specifies as well that "No exceptional circumstances whatsoever, whether a state of war or a threat of war, internal political instability or any other public emergency, may be invoked as a justification of torture."[25] Congress enacted legislation to implement America's obligations under the treaty.[26] And in 1996, it also passed the War Crimes Act, which generally made a crime out of any "grave breach" of the Geneva Conventions—including the requirements of Article 3, common to all of the conventions, to eschew "violence to life and person, in particular murder of all kinds, mutilation, cruel treatment and torture" and "outrages upon personal dignity, in particular, humiliating and degrading treatment."[27] In the years before September 11, nobody was arguing—as the Justice Department claimed in the infamous "Torture memo" of August 2002—that the legal definition of torture was limited to pain "equivalent in intensity to the pain accompanying serious physical injury, such as organ failure, impairment of bodily function, or even death" or that enforcing the statute in the context of fighting terrorists could "represent an unconstitutional infringement of the president's authority to conduct war."[28]

At the same time, as a young scholar named William Levi has shown, American interrogation policy has always existed at two levels: High-minded prohibitions of all coercive tactics have coexisted with policies that, in the granular terms of actual implementation, have allowed a great deal more flexibility than the top-line rhetoric would suggest. What's more, the CIA has always had more permissive guidelines than the military, which in any event did not always interpret the Geneva Conventions to forbid unpleasant interrogation behavior. In Levi's account, based on declassified interrogation manuals both from the Defense Department and from the agency, both military and intelligence interrogators—even after ratification of the Geneva Conventions—used techniques including drugs and physical pressure short of overt torture. The military considered slaps and techniques to induce disorientation as consistent with the conventions, and CIA manuals encouraged the use of sensory deprivation to lower the resistance of detainees to the approaches of their interrogators. Levi remarkably found that "almost without exception, the techniques approved at any one time post-9/11 for military interrogations of *unlawful combatants* . . . would have been understood to fall *within* the constraints of the Geneva Conventions for protected Prisoners of War at one point or another before 1969." Levi showed that over the course of the 1960s and early 1970s, the rules gradually tightened, particularly in the case of the military. But in the CIA's case, interrogation standards never entirely forbade tactics that would be categorically barred in the domestic criminal justice setting. What's more, as American policy moved towards greater restrictiveness, the CIA also started encouraging the use of allied foreign governments as proxies. American forces trained Latin American governments in the use of tactics forbidden to themselves, and the advent of the rendition program gave CIA personnel access to the fruits of interrogations they could never have lawfully carried out. America's interrogation rules, in other words, may have condemned torture and other cruel treatment, but they always seemed to have left stopgaps to deal with the Rudolf Hoesses of the world.[29]

Detention is a somewhat different story. The Bush administration probably took no step more controversial than holding captives neither as criminal suspects nor as prisoners of war but in indefinite detention as unlawful enemy combatants—and holding them in this status at Guantánamo Bay, Cuba, in the belief that the base there, in addition to ensuring security and isolation, would sit beyond the reach of the American court system. No decision the administration has made, except perhaps the decision to loosen interrogation standards, has drawn more opprobrium or more impassioned charges of lawlessness and outright tyranny. And, to be sure, it was a highly aggressive move—as carried out, foolishly so. That said, every component of it had a stronger basis in the law of September 10 than the administration's critics allow.

Start with the use of the base itself. The idea of holding aliens at Guantánamo by way of impairing their access to American courts was by no means new. Rather, it had recent and bipartisan pedigree, and some degree of judicial backing as well. In late 1991, following a coup in Haiti, large numbers of refugees took to rickety boats and tried to make the dangerous crossing to

Florida. The first Bush administration, keen to avoid a refugee influx during an election year, sent the Coast Guard out to interdict the incoming boats, and it shipped the thousands of refugees it picked up to Guantánamo. The base in the years before September 11 had much the same appeal it sported after the attacks. As Brandt Goldstein wrote in his history of one piece of Haitian refugee litigation,

> the base had the necessary infrastructure and an advantageous location. It was less than 125 miles from Haiti but well beyond U.S. borders, with severely limited access from the mainland. That gave the government effective control over the press and any other group that might seek contact with the refugees.
>
> But the most important factor behind the decision was a legal one: Justice Department officials believed that American law didn't apply to foreigners on an overseas military base. Assuming that Justice was right, [immigration officials] could process the asylum seekers on Guantánamo without following all the requirements of domestic immigration law. And the government would have a strong argument for getting [a] lawsuit thrown out of court.[30]

The administration's arguments in the lawsuits that developed over the Guantánamo Haitians have a familiar ring. Asked by one federal judge whether the American lease of Guantánamo, which gives this country "complete jurisdiction and control" there for as long as it wants but reserves ultimate sovereignty to Cuba, means that American law must apply, a government lawyer argued that "Guantánamo is a military base in a foreign country" and insisted that "it is not United States territory." Detainees there are "outside the United States and therefore they have no judicially cognizable rights in United States courts." Incredulous, the judge asked, "You're saying, if I hear you correctly that [the government], assuming that they are arbitrary and capricious and even *cruel,* that the courts would have no jurisdiction because the conduct did not occur on U.S. soil? That's what you're saying?" Responded government counsel, "That's correct, Your Honor."[31]

The first Bush administration wasn't interested in holding the Haitians long term. In fact, it wanted nothing more than to be rid of them and forcibly repatriated most within a matter of months, while bringing to the United States those whose asylum claims it could not ignore. To discourage the flow of refugees, it ultimately adopted a policy of immediate return: Those it picked up on the high seas went directly back to Haiti with no asylum hearings at all. But one group at Guantánamo caused a particular problem: those whom the Coast Guard brought to the base before the direct-return policy, who had credible asylum claims yet who tested positive for HIV. At the time, American law barred entrance to those carrying HIV, and while the administration had latitude to waive that restriction, bringing HIV-positive Haitians to the United States during an election year was not in the cards. So the administration placed these people and their families in a makeshift camp for indefinite detention. These Haitians were not, it bears emphasis, enemies of the United States: They were political refugees with a devastating illness.

As a candidate, Bill Clinton attacked Bush's Haiti policy. As president, he adopted it. He did not rescind the direct-return policy, and despite having announced that he would lift the HIV immigration ban, he did not close the camp at Guantánamo, which remained open until a federal district court in Brooklyn forced him to shut it down.[32] What's more, his Justice Department made sure that all court rulings applying American law on Guantánamo were stricken from the books. The Supreme Court itself vacated one ruling by the Second Circuit Court of Appeals in New York. And after the administration brought all of the HIV-positive Haitians to the United States following their victory in the Brooklyn court, the administration settled that case without an appeal by paying a large sum of money to the plaintiffs for court costs in exchange for their agreement to vacate their win in the district court.[33] As an anonymous presidential adviser told Goldstein, the administration wanted to preserve "maximum flexibility" on Guantánamo, "confident that they would do the right thing but not wanting to be forced by the law to have to do so."[34]

This decision turned out to be lucky for the administration, for shortly thereafter Clinton faced two new refugee crises, one from Haiti and one from Cuba. And once again, Guantánamo became the facility of choice for the detention of people accused of no wrongdoing whom this country was unwilling either to admit or to forcibly repatriate. The matter ultimately came before the Eleventh Circuit Court of Appeals, which disagreed with the two other courts that had considered the question. The court held, as it had in an earlier case, that "we again reject the argument that our leased military bases abroad which continue under the sovereignty of foreign nations, hostile or friendly, are 'functionally equivalent' to being land borders or ports of entry of the United States or otherwise within the United States." The court explicitly rejected the notion "that 'control and *jurisdiction*' is equivalent to sovereignty" and therefore triggers the applicability of American law.[35]

In other words, by the time September 11 took place, two administrations of opposite parties had used Guantánamo for the indefinite detention of aliens who meant America no harm but merely wanted to seek its shelter from repressive regimes. The administrations had done so precisely to avoid the scrutiny of American courts, and they had argued directly to those courts that Guantánamo should be considered beyond their purview. While some judicial decisions had sought to impose American law, including American constitutional norms, on the base, those decisions had not survived. The only case law that remained on the books solidly supported the government's right to use Guantánamo in this fashion. Whatever one thinks of the morality of using a base abroad to warehouse foreign nationals suspected of association with Al Qaeda or the Taliban, it was hardly a stretch on the part of the second Bush administration in the wake of September 11 to use the base for a purpose so similar to those of its predecessors.

THE CONCEPT of indefinite detention also bears examination, for the American legal tradition does not, in fact, condemn it quite as strongly as does our civil libertarian rhetoric. The Haitian and Cuban detainees at Guantánamo in the 1990s are not the only groups of people this country has locked up for long periods without formally charging with any crime. I don't mean just those detentions America has, as a society, come to deeply regret—like the internment of Japanese Americans during World War II. I mean, rather, detentions the

U.S. legal system accepts and to which the public does not give much thought. It is part of our civic mythology that our system does not lock up people except when it can prove their guilt of a crime. The mythology is true in a few senses. In contrast to authoritarian societies, democracies avoid detaining people arbitrarily or punishing them to discourage political dissent. In general, the touchstone of legitimacy of any incarceration is suspicion of wrongdoing of some kind. But this is a rule with many exceptions.

Of most obvious relevance to the current struggle is the notion that the military detains the enemy during wartime. Prisoner-of-war detentions may not last long in practice; then again, they may. They are indefinite in the sense that they end only upon the termination of a military struggle that may go on at great length—and whose termination is fundamentally a political judgment, not a legal one. At the outset of World War II, the newly captured POW had no idea whether his detention would last six months, six years, or sixty years. While long-term military stalemates had not occurred in recent European history, the educated prisoner of war knew that such historical episodes as the Thirty Years War or, more ominously still for him, the Hundred Years War implied that—at least in theory—his detention could eat up most or all of the rest of his life.

To cite an example closer to home, it is a fairly routine matter—though not an easy one—to lock up the mentally ill based on the expectation that they will pose a danger to the community. All states authorize the detention of the mentally ill under some circumstances. And while the Supreme Court has placed considerable limitations on this practice, it has also repeatedly upheld its constitutionality.[36] Generally speaking, states are entitled to commit to detention those people whom they can prove by clear and convincing evidence—not necessarily proof beyond a reasonable doubt—suffer from a mental illness and, as a consequence, pose a danger to themselves or others.[37] The Court has even upheld laws that authorize the civil commitment of violent sexual offenders after they have completed their prison terms—effectively locking away people who have already served their time yet who seem likely to offend again if let loose in society.[38] The analogy to severe mental illness for detentions in the war on terror may sound a bit strained, yet it is actually quite telling. In both instances, the government holds people based not on crimes they have committed but on violent acts that a condition in their lives—mental illness in one case, enemy combatant status in the other—may lead them to take in the future. In both cases, the detention goes on as long as reviewing authorities consider the detainee dangerous. In both cases, as well, that condition might persist permanently.

There are two major differences between enemy combatant detention and civil commitment of the mentally ill—and these differences cut in opposite directions. The first is that as a society, we attach no negative moral judgment to mental illness. A paranoid schizophrenic who, left free, may kill people properly warrants pity, not anger or hatred; he suffers, after all, from a disease he did not bring upon himself. The government detains him solely to protect society against the symptoms of that disease—much the way it also has the power to quarantine individuals with particularly dangerous communicable diseases. By contrast, most Westerners attach enormous negative moral judgment to membership in Al Qaeda or the Taliban. It's hard to see conceptually why locking up members of such groups, against whom Congress has authorized military force, based on their dangerousness should be forbidden when the detention of disease sufferers based on the circumstances of their victimhood is so accepted.

The second difference is that the legal process associated with a civil commitment is significantly more established, and more elaborate, than the still-developing and quite skeletal processes that govern enemy combatant detentions. Civil commitments are less controversial today than they were when they were easier, when they—and, indeed, the concept of mental illness itself—were criticized as a mechanism for punishing social deviance.[39] Enemy combatant detentions have likewise suffered from the suspicions that inherently accrue to legal processes lacking in transparency and rigor. But this distinction, it is important to note, is not a conceptual distinction, but a practical one. It would, after all, be possible to construct a more rigorous enemy combatant detention regime, even one in which the rights of the detainee were as robust as the rights of the schizophrenic in the civil commitment proceeding. Many of the objections to enemy combatant detentions, however, have been objections in principle, not merely objections to the manner in which they take place.

Long-term detentions domestically have also occurred in the context of immigration law with surprising frequency. The government routinely detains aliens who are awaiting deportation. It also locks up aliens who arrive on this country's shores yet are both inadmissible under the law and, for one reason or another, impossible to return to their home countries. Traditionally, the courts have regarded this sort of detention as just the tough luck of the alien in question, no matter how long it has gone on. Courts have even tolerated the government's use of secret evidence in identifying people as excludable for national security reasons—and thereby consigning them to indefinite lockup while awaiting return to countries that won't take them. "Courts have long recognized the power to expel or exclude aliens as a fundamental sovereign attribute exercised by the Government's political departments largely immune from judicial control," the Supreme Court wrote in 1953 about one such case. "That exclusion by the United States plus other nations' inhospitality results in present hardship cannot be ignored," the Court majority bloodlessly stated. But ignore the hardship it did: "we do not think that respondent's continued exclusion" and resulting detention on Ellis Island "deprives him of any statutory or constitutional right."[40]

Long-term detention of inadmissible aliens has continued until quite recently. The most prominent modern example—though far from the only one—is the detention of large numbers of Cubans who came to the United States as part of the Mariel boat lift in 1980. During that episode, 125,000 Cubans set out for American shores; the vast majority of these people were permitted to settle in the United States, despite having arrived illegally. Because of past criminal records in Cuba or serious mental health problems, however, many hundreds were detained. When Cuba refused to take them back, they ended up in a kind of long-term limbo, although the government later "paroled" them into the United States—that is, released them into the country without formally admitting them. When these and other Mariel parolees committed crimes and therefore rendered themselves inadmissible, the government detained them anew. For many years, the courts tolerated this situation. As of 2004, there were 750 Mariel Cubans in immigration detention. Approximately 300 people who could not return to other countries were detained as well.[41]

The Supreme Court began reining in indefinite detention in the immigration context a few short months before September 11. In the 2001 case of a stateless career criminal who was slated for deportation but whose government refused to take him back and who therefore got stuck in a kind of detention limbo, the Court interpreted the immigration laws so as to avoid authorizing such detentions to go on forever when the government had no prospect of actually effectuating its deportation order. Reading the law otherwise, the Court reasoned, would raise serious due process concerns.[42] In 2005, the Court extended this ruling to people like the Mariel Cubans, who had never been formally admitted to the United States at all.[43] The result is that immigration detentions of this sort are a lot more difficult than they used to be.

But while the Court signaled anxiety about such detentions, it did not bar them altogether. While a majority of the justices strongly suggested that such indefinite detentions might violate due process, they ruled on the basis of statutory law only—meaning that Congress could simply alter the law to authorize them if it chose. Given President Bush's new appointments to the Court, a revised statute might well pass muster.[44] What's more, even the Court's reading of the current statute does not clearly rule out *all* indefinite detentions. Justice Stephen Breyer seemed to carve out an exception for suspected terrorists and to suggest that the government might be able to justify holding them, as distinct from common criminals or mere visa violators.[45] Congress, as part of the USA PATRIOT Act, followed up with a new statutory provision designed to do just that.[46] To top it off, Breyer also made clear that the government was entitled to set and enforce conditions associated with the release of these aliens and that it could lock up anew, at least temporarily, those who did not fulfill those conditions.[47]

To put it simply, while the law of September 10 did not smile on indefinite, noncriminal detentions, the legal system tolerated it in a number of contexts far less pressing than the neutralization of sworn enemies of the country against whom Congress had authorized military force.

THE FINAL COMPONENT of the Bush administration's Guantánamo strategy was the decision to hold Al Qaeda and Taliban operatives neither as prisoners of war nor as criminal suspects but as unlawful enemy combatants. This decision represented a sharp break with past American practice in the modern era. It did not, however, constitute much of a break with American law, which had always preserved the option of holding enemies in a noncriminal status beneath that of prisoner of war.

Traditionally, the laws of war have distinguished between the prisoner of war—the privileged belligerent—and the unlawful combatant. The privileged belligerent, the soldier who fights honorably and in accord with the laws of war, is entitled, when captured, to a highly civilized detention, including the crucial benefit of immunity from criminal prosecution for any offense save war crimes. In other words, he is regarded as an honorable arm of his state, whose detention is a regrettable necessity but with whom the detaining state has no individual bone to pick. By contrast, the laws of war traditionally granted the unlawful combatant, the fighter who does not fight according to the laws of war or who hides among civilians, no such solicitude. The detaining state is entitled to prosecute unlawful combatants, and often shot them.[48] As the Supreme Court aptly summarized the difference in 1942:

> Lawful combatants are subject to capture and detention as prisoners of war by opposing military forces. Unlawful combatants are likewise subject to capture and detention, but in addition they are subject to trial and punishment by military tribunals for acts which render their belligerency unlawful. The spy who secretly and without uniform passes the military lines of a belligerent in time of war, seeking to gather military information and

communicate it to the enemy, or an enemy combatant who without uniform comes secretly through the lines for the purpose of waging war by
destruction of life or property, are familiar examples of belligerents who
are generally deemed not to be entitled to the status of prisoners of war,
but to be offenders against the law of war subject to trial and punishment
by military tribunals. . . .[49]

Since the signing of the Geneva Conventions in 1949, a significant gap has
opened between American views of this difference and those of many other
countries. The Third Geneva Convention specifies in great detail the protections and benefits owed the prisoner of war; it says nary a word about what
states may do to unlawful combatants in international conflicts, save a requirement that they hold a "competent tribunal" before denying anyone POW treatment in circumstances of doubt as to his proper status. International law has
tended to rub the category almost out of existence. Starting in the late 1970s,
many nations ratified an addendum, colloquially known as Protocol I, to the
convention that treats many members of guerrilla groups as prisoners of wars.[50]
Prevailing international sentiment has also treated the prosecution of those not
granted prisoner-of-war status as all but obligatory. In other words, under this
view, any detainee must be a prisoner of war protected by the Third Convention, be put on trial for war crimes, or be treated as a civilian protected by the
Fourth Convention, which deals with civilian protections in circumstances of
conflict or military occupation. As Canadian law professor Marco Sassòli put it,
critiquing the Bush administration's position, "The U.S. administration claims
that the persons it holds in Guantánamo are neither combatants nor civilians,
but 'unlawful combatants.' . . . However, according to the text, context, and
aim of the Third and Fourth Conventions, no one can fall between the two
conventions and thus be protected by neither of the two."[51]

American practice since World War II has tracked these developments. For
example, the American military held no detainees as unlawful enemy combatants during the Vietnam War; despite the fact that many Viet Cong did not
meet the criteria for prisoners of war, the military either afforded them POW
treatment anyway as a matter of discretion or turned them over to the South

Vietnamese for prosecution.[52] And the U.S. Army's regulations for detentions have largely conformed to the sort of gapless coverage that Sassòli describes. Under the current version of these regulations, a detainee is categorized as a prisoner of war, an "innocent civilian who should be immediately returned to his home or released," or as a "civilian internee who for reasons of operational security, or probable cause incident to criminal investigation, should be detained." The regulations do not seem to contemplate anyone's detention as a combatant who is entitled neither to treatment as a POW nor to further criminal proceedings. "Persons who have been determined by a competent tribunal not to be entitled to prisoner of war status may not be executed, imprisoned, or otherwise penalized without further proceedings to determine what acts they have committed and what penalty should be imposed," the regulations state.[53]

American law, however, has also preserved a less generous approach. The United States did not ratify Protocol I, specifically because it might confer privileges on unlawful combatants. In his message to Congress announcing that he would not submit the treaty to the Senate for approval, Ronald Reagan described it as "fundamentally and irreconcilably flawed. It contains provisions that would undermine humanitarian law and endanger civilians in war. . . . [One] provision would grant combatant status to irregular forces even if they do not satisfy the traditional requirements to distinguish themselves from the civilian population and otherwise comply with the laws of war. This would endanger civilians among whom terrorists and other irregulars attempt to conceal themselves. These problems are so fundamental in character that they cannot be remedied through reservations. . . ."[54] In other words, the United States had specifically guarded its right to maintain a distinct category of unprivileged belligerent for whom prosecution is an option but not a requirement.

The real innovation of the Bush administration lay not in reviving a category of detainees whose existence the military had allowed to lapse in practice while maintaining in principle. It lay, rather, in dispensing with the requirement of the Third Geneva Convention, to allow "competent tribunals" to make these judgments individually for each detainee.[55] Instead, Bush declared as a blanket matter that no Taliban or Al Qaeda detainees could qualify as prisoners of war.[56] Though a close call legally, this decision was, without question, a thumb in the eye to international expectations. It was also a profoundly stupid decision tactically. It sent a message of contempt to the world for the Geneva Conventions, a body of international law the United States had always championed, simply to avoid holding tribunals that would have inconvenienced the United States far less than has failing to hold them. These tribunals are not trials. They are historically minimal affairs. The detainees do not get lawyers. They have no appeal. There is no obligation to give detainees extensive due process protections or access to evidence. They are just a kind of screening device, a chance for the detainee to tell his story in a quasi-formal setting—a chance to work out misunderstandings. Holding tribunals for detainees in this conflict should have been an easy call.

This is especially true because doing so would likely have had no substantive implications at all. Al Qaeda, after all, not only is not a signatory to the conventions but professes an avowed intention to target civilians and fight outside the constraints of the laws of war. It is unthinkable that any Al Qaeda operative could qualify as a POW. Taliban soldiers present a tougher case; the Taliban, after all, was the army of the closest thing that existed to a government of Afghanistan, a country that had ratified the conventions. Still, the Taliban was not by and large an internationally recognized government, and to qualify for POW status for its troops, a nongovernmental militia must meet four criteria: a responsible command structure, a "fixed distinctive sign recognizable at a distance," "carrying arms openly," and complying with the laws of war.[57] Taliban fighters do none of these things. So had the military held these tribunals, they would not have qualified for privileged treatment either. Holding these "Article 5 tribunals," however, would probably have identified a few noncombatants earlier and assuaged world anxieties about American intentions with respect to international norms.

Indeed, the hard question these detentions posed—and still pose—is not which detainee is entitled to POW status. It is how to distinguish *any* combatants from *noncombatants*—those unlucky civilians who found themselves in the wrong place at the wrong time and got rounded up with the fighters. Assuming that wheat could be reliably separated from the chaff, detaining Taliban or Al Qaeda fighters as unlawful combatants had solid grounding in the law of September 10 and should not have been controversial.

This idea of revitalizing legal doctrines and propositions that had lapsed in practice yet persisted in law is perhaps even more visible in the administration's decision to try detainees accused of war crimes by military commission, rather than either by general court martial or in civilian courts. The military commission, a kind of ad hoc tribunal that historically meted out punishments during wartime, was for all real-world purposes a dead institution.[58] Used sporadically throughout American history, commissions had not shown up since the World War II era. As a formal legal matter, however, they seemed to remain available. When the Supreme Court okayed their use in 1942 for German saboteurs, including an American citizen, it cited several statutory authorities—direct parallels for each of which remained on the books in 2001.[59] While developments in American and international law after World War II arguably created rights that trial by commission would violate, the Supreme Court had never declared inappropriate the use of military commissions or forsworn the dramatic deviations from federal trial norms they involve and that the Court had once okayed. There was, in short, little reason to imagine that a commission trial at Guantánamo that lacked all of the procedural protections of a civilian trial or a general court martial would be legally impossible.

THERE IS, IN FACT, only one major arena in which the administration's course after the attacks lacked some substantial grounding in the law of September 10: its decision to conduct electronic surveillance domestically outside of the authority of the Foreign Intelligence Surveillance Act (FISA)—the law that since 1978 has authorized and regulated domestic wiretapping in national security cases. Federal law, after all, specifies explicitly that FISA represents the "exclusive means" by which the executive branch can conduct national security wiretapping of Americans.[60] And while a current of legal thought since the the passage of FISA's passage has asserted that the president has inherent power to conduct such surveillance—and that he can therefore override the law if need be—no administration since the passage of FISA had relied on that theory to circumvent its requirements. Most commentators, rather, believed that FISA both codified and limited the president's power and took seriously the notion that acting outside it was a crime.

This field, however, is the exception. In general, looking back on the law the day before the attacks, it is remarkable how many components of a muscular legal architecture for a war on terror had been preserved in American law or had already taken root in American behavior. Laid out like the pieces of a jigsaw puzzle dumped onto a table, they were there for an administration and a Congress that wanted to assemble a structure to govern a new orientation for American policy—a conflict that was neither pure war nor pure law enforcement. The great mistake of the Bush administration was that it never tried to enlist Congress's aid in putting the puzzle together but tried instead to go it alone and use and aggrandize each piece separately.

Two

The Administration's Response

THE BUSH ADMINISTRATION deserves neither the credit it claims nor the blame it accrues for its decision in the immediate aftermath of September 11 to treat the conflict with Al Qaeda as, legally speaking, a war. While it is often a mistake to assume that history's course proceeded inevitably, in this case it is not a mistake. The war model developed neither because of the administration's laudably creative tough-mindedness nor because of its lawlessness, but because, in the short term, no remotely viable alternative existed. Al Qaeda had attacked the United States, including a successful assault on the seat of its military and an unsuccessful one on either the Capitol or the White House. Given that the group had ensconced itself in a safe haven in Afghanistan—far beyond the reach of U.S. courts or civilian law enforcement—and had allied itself with the de facto government of that state, the only means of striking its leadership was military. This fact alone necessitated to some degree a war-based approach.

At the outset of the conflict, the model presented relatively little controversy. Congress passed the Authorization for Use of Military Force a scant week after the attacks with only a single vote against the measure in either legislative house.[1] The resolution gave the president the legal authority "to use all necessary and appropriate force against those nations, organizations, or persons he determines planned, authorized, committed, or aided the terrorist attacks that occurred on September 11, 2001, or harbored such organizations or persons, in order to prevent any future acts of international terrorism against the United States. . . ."[2] While individual commentators argued vainly for a law enforcement approach, the argument gained little traction, and for good reason. Treating a conflict of this scale as a matter of criminal law would preclude the kind of speed, flexibility, and agility that such a dynamic confrontation would obviously require. It would offer no tangible support for the muscular use of the American military needed to bring down the Taliban government. And it would necessitate years of litigation to neutralize each detained suspect—many of whom may not have committed crimes at all or may have committed crimes that the government would be unable to prove. Being an enemy of the United States, after all, is not a crime, nor necessarily is fighting American forces.

By contrast, treating the conflict as a legal war offered maximal operational flexibility. The model provided a recognized framework for American forces to bomb Taliban positions, a framework under which they could also legitimately kill Al Qaeda and Taliban operatives in battle. It also allowed the military to detain such people and interrogate them long term. And trial remained an option—either in civilian courts or in military commissions. At a rhetorical level, the war model also projected seriousness about the problem, announcing a commitment to the fight that went beyond the struggle against organized crime, drugs, or other mere law enforcement priorities. In the short term, war was the only way to invoke the full range of presidential powers that George W. Bush wished to bring to bear on Al Qaeda—and that any other president would likewise have wanted to invoke.

Yet even early on, war was an imperfect idea—intellectually and legally—for the range of problems that Al Qaeda posed. To some degree, the administration's rhetoric acknowledged this from the beginning. Within days of the attacks, Bush had labeled this conflict "a new kind of war" and Al Qaeda "a different type of enemy"—implying that it might not resemble more traditional wars all that much.[3] Expanding on this notion in late September, then–Defense Secretary Donald Rumsfeld wrote:

> This war will not necessarily be one in which we pore over military targets and mass forces to seize those targets. Instead, military force will likely be one of many tools we use to stop individuals, groups and countries that engage in terrorism.
>
> Our response may include firing cruise missiles into military targets somewhere in the world; we are just as likely to engage in electronic combat to track and stop investments moving through offshore banking centers. The uniforms of this conflict will be bankers' pinstripes and programmers' grunge just as assuredly as desert camouflage.
>
> This is not a war against an individual, a group, a religion or a country. Rather, our opponent is a global network of terrorist organizations and their state sponsors, committed to denying free people the opportunity to live as they choose. While we may engage militarily against foreign governments that sponsor terrorism, we may also seek to make allies of the people those governments suppress.
>
> Even the vocabulary of this war will be different. When we "invade the enemy's territory," we may well be invading his cyberspace. There may not be as many beachheads stormed as opportunities denied. Forget about "exit strategies"; we're looking at a sustained engagement that carries no deadlines. . . .
>
> The public may see some dramatic military engagements that produce no apparent victory, or may be unaware of other actions that lead to major victories. "Battles" will be fought by customs officers stopping suspicious persons at our borders and diplomats securing cooperation against money laundering.[4]

Rumsfeld's account of the incipient war, when one stops and analyzes it, is extraordinary. It begins with the frank recognition that military force represents only one of a range of powers America's effort to take on the enemy "may in-

clude." Military action gets no honored place alongside computer program-
ming and banking, or the work of Customs officers and diplomats. Rumsfeld
talks about forming alliances with people while fighting their governments—
not something countries generally do when at war. And he talks about an engagement of indefinite duration composed of battles that the public may not
see. Rumsfeld calls all of this "a new kind of war," but he describes something
that goes beyond war altogether. He describes, rather, an overarching policy
orientation for all of the levers of American power, one that would use the
president's war authorities but by no means be limited to them.

This has proven an apt description of the war on terrorism in practice. The
conflict has involved military force at times. It has also involved civilian law
enforcement, not merely by the U.S. government but by allied governments as
well. It has involved covert actions. It has proceeded under immigration authorities and banking regulations, through training and liaison with foreign
police and intelligence organizations, and through biomedical research and
countless other expressions of federal power. In the short run, the administration was able to harness this entire array of operational and policy powers
under the rubric of the president's war-making authorities, and the stretch
seemed natural enough to suffice in the pinch. Presidents, after all, have long
rallied the country in support of war efforts, deploying the full range of their
powers to mobilize nonmilitary components of society, particularly industry,
in support of military objectives.

In the longer term, however, the harness has strained. The reason is that in
contrast to past conflicts, it's not clear that this one *is* primarily military at all.
Put another way, it's not clear that Bush has mobilized other authorities in
support of his military powers, rather than the other way around or some
more balanced, mutually supporting arrangement. The capture of certain
high-value detainees—September 11 plotters Khalid Sheikh Mohammed and
Ramzi Bin al-Shibh, for example—came not as a result of the deployment of
American military force in Afghanistan but because of sustained intelligence
cooperation with Pakinstani authorities. Many of the biggest victories in the
conflict have taken the form of foiled terrorist plots, in which the lead actors
have been European law enforcement authorities acting in cooperation with

American officials. The military's role has certainly been substantial, in terms of putting the enemy on defense and changing the geopolitical landscape in Afghanistan. But the war on terrorism would have been an utter failure had that been the only thing the United States had done to confront Al Qaeda.

In their more candid moments, administration officials, including President Bush himself, acknowledge freely that this conflict is something more than pure warfare. The United States, Bush said at a press conference in 2007, is employing "a variety of methodologies to deal with [terrorists]: one is intelligence, one is law enforcement, and one is military. We got to use all assets at [our] disposal to find them and bring them to justice before they hurt our people again."[5] The rhetoric once more reveals a great deal. Bush is not talking about harnessing nonmilitary powers to achieve a military objective. Taken at face value, rather, his words describe using military (and other) means to pursue a nonmilitary objective: bringing terrorists to justice.

Indeed, by continuing after the immediate crisis to rely on the concept of war as the principal source of its power, the administration put a great deal of weight on the core legal assumptions that underlie warfare and the powers it grants to the president in the American legal tradition. Just as the word "war" doesn't quite describe the war on terror intellectually or in practical terms, it doesn't quite work legally either—at least not if the goal is a legal architecture that grants the president the powers he needs yet also generates the sort of accountability for the use of those powers that might sustain them with long-term public confidence.

For a vivid example, let us return to the problem of detentions. Here a great gulf exists between the baseline assumptions of the laws of war and the laws governing the criminal justice system; so it matters a great deal which model the government adopts in terms of how it handles those it arrests. In the criminal arena, the law serves a punitive purpose, and it therefore requires the government to prove beyond a reasonable doubt all material facts it alleges against an individual to support his incarceration. Detention of a combatant in wartime, by contrast, imputes no wrongdoing to the detainee, yet the laws of war also require far less by way of establishing his amenability to detention in the first instance than does the criminal law. In fact, the laws of war generally presume that there exists little or no doubt that a captured enemy fighter is, indeed, a captured enemy fighter. This premise, in the context of the war on terrorism, is simply false. Detentions in the current conflict are rife with factual ambiguity and uncertainty—precisely because of the irregularity of the battles and the contempt Al Qaeda harbors for rules of warfare that evolved to protect civilians from the rawest consequences of geopolitics.

Nor does the assumption that no negative moral evaluation of the detainees attends their detentions hold in this conflict. To the contrary, detention at Guantánamo Bay involves a frightful assertion of individual moral culpability; labels like the "worst of the worst" and "bad people" have issued from the highest levels of American government.[6] And how could it be otherwise? We don't, after all, consider individual Al Qaeda fighters to be worthy adversaries—honorable arms of a state or organization with which we have a dispute unbridgeable except by force. We consider them, rather, as clever and highly dangerous murderers, dangerous not merely in their status as agents of their organization but dangerous *as individuals.* The laws of war offer no useful vocabulary for such people.

Indeed, the laws of war presuppose detentions to be a temporary incapacitation of the fighters until the warring parties make peace and arrange their repatriation. No such presumption makes any sense here either. This conflict, rather, seems like a permanent state of affairs and, if it someday does end, it will end only because all members of Al Qaeda are caught or killed. Releasing detainees then would only reignite the conflict.

This problem of there being no endpoint for hostilities is a profound one for any conception of this conflict as traditional warfare. In one sense, the end of hostilities is always conjectural; a warring party never knows the date on which it will prevail or concede defeat. So the emergency powers that the president accrues as a function of war inevitably have a temporally open-ended dimension. He has them for as long as it takes to win.

But the war on terrorism adds a layer of conceptual open-endedness to the temporal one we already tolerate. We have no idea even what the end of hostilities might look like. It surely requires more than that American troops fully pacify Iraq and Afghanistan, since Al Qaeda operates worldwide. It presumably requires more than the capture of Osama bin Laden, Ayman al Zawahiri, and their chief lieutenants, since Al Qaeda is a diffuse network of cells that receives inspiration and a certain level of support from its command hierarchy but could operate to some degree even if its hierarchy were decapitated. Even if one were confident that all such cells had been dismantled, this is not the imperial Japanese army, which regenerated through conscription and the sovereign powers of a government to raise an army. Al Qaeda regenerates because of a deep strain of illiberalism that has taken root in certain segments of Muslim society worldwide. This is what Bush means, I suppose, when he terms the conflict "an ideological struggle" as a way of unifying the various "methodologies" the government has at its disposal for dealing with terrorists.[7] But that very formulation renders the end of hostilities hard to envisage. Taken seriously, the war model imagines holding Al Qaeda operatives without charge and without proof of the individual facts that justify their detentions until such time as violent Islamist extremism is sufficiently discredited as to be incapable of attracting new recruits to the cause. John Yoo, one of the architects of the administration's legal response, can assure his readers that "there is no reason to believe [the conflict with Al Qaeda] will go on for a generation. . . . Our current conflict is with al Qaeda, and we can declare hostilities over when it can no longer attack the United States in a meaningful way."[8] But the point rings hollow. Victory in the war on terrorism is so remote, conceptually as well as temporally, that in practical terms the use of wartime detention authorities amounts to an executive power to detain permanently and quasi-punitively anyone in the world suspected of belligerency on behalf of the enemy or providing material support of that belligerency.

The problem of the end of hostilities is not limited to detentions. The administration at various times has relied on the inherent powers of the president as commander in chief to justify several of its most aggressive interrogation and surveillance tactics as well. The infamous "Torture Memo" went so far as to claim that any statute that impaired the president's ability to fight the war could be tossed aside. And the administration relied on the president's inherent powers to create a new trial mechanism without consulting the legislature. Such claims of executive authority would challenge contemporary civil libertarian sensibilities even if made on a temporary basis. It's far harder to justify them when their temporary nature is less than clear. Broad presidential war powers are only defensible insofar as they represent a temporary aggrandizement of executive power to handle a crisis. To rely on their applicability in this conflict over the long term is really to describe a permanent state of emergency with a corresponding growth of executive power and a diminution of checks upon it.

This suited key figures in the Bush administration just fine. They harbored open ambitions—quite separate from and long predating the war on terrorism—to restore executive prerogatives that, in their judgment, had eroded in the post-Watergate era. Yoo, for example, had written scholarly work arguing for broad presidential war and treaty powers.[9] More importantly, the ambition to expand presidential powers had deep roots in Vice President Cheney's career and that of his longtime counsel, David Addington. "[L]ong before 9/11," wrote Jack Goldsmith, who sparred with the vice president's office repeatedly in his brief tenure as head of the Justice Department's OLC after Yoo's departure, Addington "and his boss had set out to reverse what they saw as Congress's illegitimate decades-long intrusions on 'unitary' executive power."[10] Indeed, prior to the attacks, the administration had begun aggressively asserting unilateral executive powers and had demonstrated a willingness, even an eagerness, to spend political capital on enhancing presidential authorities. The White House, to cite one telling harbinger of things to come, had courted controversy by refusing to give the Government Accountability Office access to information about with whom the vice president's energy policy task force had met.[11]

In the years that followed the attacks, this idea of revitalizing and reinforcing presidential power merged in the minds of the administration and its critics alike with the idea that the president required more robust authorities to confront Al Qaeda. Inherent presidential power became synonymous with muscular action, while cooperation with the other two branches of government became synonymous with constraints on the executive and limitations on its flexibility. The administration disdained Congress and sought legislative authorization for its actions only when forced by the courts. It saw going to Congress as an implicit acknowledgment that it lacked the inherent power to do what it needed, as an acknowledgment that it had to ask permission. Doing so, the administration repeatedly concluded, both abandoned the principle that it could act on its own and risked getting conditions attached to authorities it could assert unconditionally if it left Congress out of the picture. Cheney and Addington, wrote Goldsmith,

> viewed power as the absence of constraint. These men believed that the president would be best equipped to identify and defeat the uncertain, shifting, and lethal new enemy by eliminating all hurdles to the exercise of his power. They had no sense of trading constraint for power. It seemed never to occur to them that it might be possible to increase the president's strength and effectiveness by accepting small limits on his prerogatives in order to secure more significant support from Congress, the courts, or allies. They believed cooperation and compromise signaled weakness and emboldened the enemies of America and the executive branch. When it came to terrorism, they viewed every encounter outside the innermost core of most trusted advisors as a zero-sum game that if they didn't win they would necessarily lose.[12]

When the possibility of going to Congress would arise, Addington would ask two questions. "Do we have the legal power to do it ourselves?" and "Might Congress limit our options in ways that jeopardize American lives?"[13]

The critics, ironically, saw the relationship between inherent executive power and broad presidential counterterrorism authorities in somewhat the same way—and opposed both with almost equal vigor. With a few notable exceptions, they consistently confused objections to claims of inherent presidential power with claims that the administration was going too far in the substance of what it sought to do.

The administration's plan to try terrorists in military commissions, rather than in civilian courts, offers a window into this conflation. Little question existed that the military could, in principle, try terrorist suspects in front of military tribunals that lacked the procedural niceties of either civilian courts or the general courts martial before which American service members face trial. The military had held such commissions in the past, and no intervening law had banned them. Just as clearly, however, the revival of such an institution would stand on firmer ground were it fixed in statute. Yet the administration did not go this route, insisting that it had all the authority it needed between the general congressional authorization to use force, the extant statutes that archaically made reference to military commissions, and the inherent powers of the president.[14] Going to Congress would merely permit the legislature to impose limitations.

For their part, human rights and civil liberties groups did not confine their objections to the question of where the administration got the authority to conduct such trials. Rather, they merged this idea with a broader set of objections to any trials that did not fully comport with modern norms. The American Civil Liberties Union, for example, argued that commissions were illegitimate because only aliens, not U.S. citizens, were subject to trial before them—and they were therefore discriminatory.[15] Human rights groups argued against them on grounds that they might admit evidence obtained under torture.[16] Because of the administration's reliance on the inherent powers of the presidency in wartime, the substantive objections to its policy merged with objections to an unrelated idea on which a robust response to Al Qaeda need not have depended.

This merger was not in any sense inevitable. The questions of the scope of presidential antiterrorism powers and the source of those powers, in fact, ought to be distinct from one another. It is possible, after all, to believe that the executive branch requires broad authorities to fight Al Qaeda and other terrorists who mean America harm yet to believe at the same time that those powers do not flow ineluctably from the nature of the presidency itself. That is, it is possible to believe that Congress ought to give the president a fairly free hand, but that how free a hand is a matter for the legislature to decide, not one on which the Framers of the Constitution pronounced two centuries ago. Conversely, one could conclude also that the presidency possesses certain inherent powers in this area with which Congress may not tamper, but that these are narrow and bounded by constitutional restrictions on presidential actions.

The irony was that relying on the war paradigm, untailored to the oddities of this conflict, precluded the administration's attainment of important policy goals even as it created flexibility in other areas. Relying on the laws of war made it relatively easy to detain suspects, for example, but difficult to garner public confidence in the detentions. It facilitated in the short term aggressive surveillance and interrogation tactics. But the further into the conflict America waded and the less military the day-to-day operation of the conflict came to appear, the harder it became to sustain public support for such activities. If what the administration required, in other words, was a regime that permitted it maximum flexibility in the long run, the war model was less promising than its tantalizing executive-centeredness made it seem to officials caught up in the moment and predisposed ideologically to favor it.

RATHER THAN A PROJECT in adapting the laws of war for a novel conflict or in imagining how far it could leverage them to justify the substantive powers that it required, the administration needed a different, rather deeper, enterprise. It needed a law-building project for something that had gone beyond war altogether—an effort to assemble the disparate puzzle pieces that the law of September 10 had scattered about the table into some kind of coherent law of terrorism, a body of law that could sustain the powers of presidential preemption before the courts and the public. This project would have begun with a single simple question: Given that America finds itself locked in a long-term struggle with violent Islamist extremism, what authorities does its government need to wage the fight and prevail in it and from where might those authorities come?

Given the breadth and ambition of such an undertaking, no administration would have contemplated it immediately after the attacks. At that point, the proper course was the one the administration took—deploying every available component of the law of September 10 on an à la carte basis and not dwelling overmuch on its source—and the administration did it quite effectively. War offered the power to deploy the military, so America went into a state of war. The criminal justice system offered tools, so the FBI launched the biggest criminal investigation in history. The immigration system offered the ability to detain and deport large numbers of people who had some connection to the investigation and who were living unlawfully in the United States. So the administration used the immigration law to justify a dragnet, in which it snared hundreds of people. It also sought and received expansions of its surveillance powers in the USA PATRIOT Act. Some of these steps garnered no controversy, some of them significant objections. None of them, however, was an oddity of the Bush administration. They, or something very much like them, represented what any presidential administration would have done when airplanes started unexpectedly hitting buildings. The administration's failure, rather, began somewhat later—the exact moment is hard to pinpoint—when it confused the ad hoc approach the crisis had necessitated with a viable permanent legal architecture for the struggle.

Recognizing that what it needed was a new legal regime—or even a new set of legal regimes—would have required a wholly different approach. The institution that builds new legal structures in our democracy, after all, is Congress, not the White House. While Republicans controlled Congress for much of the relevant time period, going to Congress would have involved holding negotiations, making concessions, and potentially accepting a measure of legislative restraint on the military's and the CIA's operational flexibility. Yet Congress is ultimately capable of delivering more durable, comprehensive—and more imaginative—law than the executive branch can make up on its own. While the executive branch can, if it chooses, go it alone, when it does, it is oddly confined by past precedents. The president can, for example, choose to view the conflict as war or he can bring criminal cases. But when he invokes a body of law, that body of law then constrains him. He cannot, on his own, easily declare the conflict what it so obviously is—a hybrid problem that requires its own rules. If the executive branch holds detainees under the rules of warfare, for example, it confines itself to conduct that it can defend, in some sense, as consistent with the laws of war. If it brings a criminal case, it invokes huge bodies of criminal case law that limit its ability to obtain and use evidence. It can't simply declare that the war on terrorism represents a sui generis situation, requiring authorities drawn from a variety of legal sources and—in some instances—made up out of whole cloth. Congress, to a great degree, can do this. So while going to Congress risks sacrificing certain short-term flexibility, it permits far greater flexibility in the conceptualization of the regime.

Going to Congress would also have generated political and legal legitimacy for decisions that were becoming increasingly controversial. Because a congressional enactment represents the collective judgment of the people's elected representatives, it carries weight—both to the public and to the courts—that executive rule making will often lack. It is no small thing for an administration to be able to say, in response to public controversy over a broad wiretapping program, that Congress carefully considered the authority and voted to grant it to the intelligence community. It is no small thing, when detentions become controversial, to be able to declare that Congress debated how to handle suspected Al Qaeda operatives and specifically decided not to subject them to the normal criminal process but to treat them in accordance with a prescribed set of rules. Creating a law of terrorism would have required patient work with a branch of government composed of a multiplicity of mercurial actors, but doing that hard work would have paid big dividends. And the administration's failure to do it has cost it many times the price it would have had to pay.

The administration's failure to do this work was all the more mystifying in light of its impressive record of getting what it wanted from Congress when it did bother to ask. The administration generally had its way with the legislature irrespective of which party controlled the body. With the Senate under tenuous Democratic control in 2001, for example, Congress passed the Patriot Act, which included all of the major enhancements to law enforcement and intelligence authorities after the attacks. In 2006, the administration got the law reauthorized. In the wake of the Supreme Court's 2004 *Rasul* decision, with Congress solidly in Republican control, the administration got the high court's decision reversed legislatively. The Supreme Court had asserted jurisdiction over detentions at Guantánamo, and lawsuits proliferated in response. Congress, at the administration's request, passed the Detainee Treatment Act

(DTA) to get the cases thrown out of court. After the Supreme Court balked in *Hamdan*, Congress did so again in the Military Commissions Act (MCA), acting once more at the behest of the administration; for good measure it wrote into law a plan for military commission trials strikingly similar to the ones the administration had sought to impose as a regulatory matter. In both the DTA and the MCA, the White House had to engage in a certain degree of negotiation and accept a small measure of restraint. But in both instances, it ended up in the main with the legislature's ratifying its position, not undermining it.

Even after the Democrats seized control of Congress in the 2006 midterm elections, the administration's ability to get what it needed from the legislature did not wane overmuch. The following year, the intelligence community declared that it needed emergency updates to the FISA to allow for warrantless wiretapping in situations in which it reasonably believed the target of the intercepted communication to be abroad—even if the other party were an American citizen in the United States. Democrats in Congress made noise about refusing or scaling back the proposal, but then they buckled and gave the administration what it wanted, at least on a temporary basis.[17] As of this writing, Congress was poised to make a version of this authority permanent, though still haggling over the details.

This relative success with the legislature should not surprise anyone. The presidency is a unitary actor who actually has to conduct the operations at the heart of the conflict. The administration can present a single position; the president can declare his policy needs and fight for them. Congress, by contrast, is by its nature fractured into blocs and individuals. It depends on the executive branch for information about executive needs. And it is always vulnerable, when it refuses the president his requests, to allegations that it tied his hands against a dangerous adversary. Republicans in Congress were both ideologically and politically inclined to give the administration what it wanted; Democrats, even to the extent they would want to impose onerous restraints, lived in fear of being painted as obstructionists or soft on Al Qaeda. Given these constraints—structural and political—on muscular legislative behavior, it would have been amazing had the legislature energetically asserted itself in opposition to, as opposed to in cooperation with, the president. In the American system, Congress never takes the lead in a crisis—that is what the presidency is for. Had the administration gone to Congress and asked for its help in writing a long-term architecture for the conflict, it would surely have found a partner for the project.

This judgment is not mere 20/20 hindsight. It was knowable early. From outside the administration came high-profile warnings that plans for military commissions without specific congressional sanction would founder in the courts.[18] And sober voices inside the administration too knew that the cause of a robust response to Al Qaeda would be better served with legislative buy-in than with all the political accountability for controversial choices concentrated in the president.

Former OLC chief Goldsmith recounts a White House meeting in February 2004 to discuss the Supreme Court's decision to hear the first round of enemy combatant litigation. The solicitor general's office warned that the action was "bad news" and that the government might well lose. Goldsmith suggested going to Congress for additional support, an idea the solicitor general's office, the National Security Council legal adviser, and the Pentagon's general counsel all backed. "Why are you trying to give away the president's power?" vice-presidential counsel Addington responded. The idea died.[19]

As time went on, these voices became increasingly public. In the spring of 2006, for example, I participated in a panel discussion at American University law school on institutionalizing the war on terrorism in legislation. "I find the failure to involve Congress substantively and pervasively in a range of [key] decisions to be . . . inexcusable this far out," I argued. My harsh indictment of the administration went on at some length. The panel's moderator sought to give a pair of former administration officials the chance to respond. First, he turned to Goldsmith, who had served a stint at the Pentagon before taking over at the OLC. "I agree with almost everything Ben said," he responded. The moderator then turned to Bradford Berenson, who had worked in the White House Counsel's office in the days immediately after the attacks. He too publicly agreed: "Had I been White House counsel or attorney general during the past several years, it probably would have been my overriding priority to try to convince the president and the administration to do just what he proposes."[20] The incident surprised me at the time only for taking place in public. Privately, officials—and not just ex-officials—had long made little secret of their frustrations with the administration's thick-headed resistance to congressional involvement. Many knew they would stand on far more solid ground if they relied not merely on the president's own powers but on the legislature's as well. They knew also that Congress would not deny the president the authority he truly needed and that only chest-thumping executive-power machismo stood in the way of potentially productive engagement with the legislature.

The administration also had the example of its predecessor, which took an altogether different approach to developing a legal framework for controversial national-security authorities. The Bush administration scorned the Clinton administration's supposedly weak-kneed lawyers, who—as the previous chapter illustrated—do not deserve this caricature. Their approach, generally speaking, involved an attractive combination of tough-mindedness on the scope of law enforcement and intelligence powers with nondoctrinaire flexibility concerning their source and a willingness to accept modest restraints in exchange for clear legislative authorization for power.

Back in 1994, when the FBI caught CIA mole Aldrich Ames, it precipitated a mini-crisis in the law of national security surveillance. When Congress passed the FISA in 1978, it wrote the law to cover only electronic surveillance, not physical searches of the houses or offices of suspected foreign agents. The result was that the government would go to the so-called FISA court for warrants for wiretaps, but not when it wanted to conduct a national security search. Reluctant to use criminal search authorities in national security cases, because of the possibility of leaks, the government had continued to conduct physical searches in these instances without any warrant at all. Successive administrations had long claimed the inherent authority to do this—and the judicial authorities on the question were muddled. Generally, because the government conducted such surveillance for intelligence purposes, the targets never learned of them, so opportunities for the courts to rule on their validity did not often arise. Ames's case, however, was different. When the FBI had needed to search Ames's office, then–Attorney General Janet Reno had uncomfortably approved the search on her own authority. The government's criminal case against Ames depended pervasively on the fruits of that search, and he had a first-rate lawyer itching to attack it.

The Justice Department was nervous. If a court invalidated the Ames search, it would not only destroy the case against him, it would cast doubt on the ability of the government to use noncriminal searches in future cases as well. Partly with its eye on avoiding a legal showdown, the government allowed Ames a plea deal, one that granted his wife leniency she likely would not have received had the government not feared the litigation. Then the Justice Department went to Congress.

The amendment to the FISA it sought and obtained that year brought physical searches under the statute. "Our seeking legislation in no way should suggest that we do not believe we have inherent authority," Jamie Gorelick, Reno's deputy attorney general, said at the time. "We do . . . but as a policy matter, we thought it was better to have Congress and the judiciary involved." Ames's attorneys, she said, "had raised those issues and threatened to litigate. . . . And anytime you don't have a Supreme Court case on point, there's a risk. We thought we would prevail, but . . . this, I think, cements it."[21]

Gorelick's comments offer a striking contrast with the Bush administration's approach, fixated as it is not merely on making sure the executive has the powers that fighting Al Qaeda requires but on emphasizing that those powers are nonnegotiable and cannot be limited or regulated by anyone. Why, Gorelick's approach asks, rely on a nebulous, general constitutional authority that is not clearly articulated and whose vitality many lawyers, and some judges, doubt when you can supplement that authority with a clear statutory authorization? Indeed, although Gorelick believed that the Justice Department had the inherent constitutional authority to conduct physical searches, she also believed that accepting a measure of restraint by inviting the involvement of the other two branches would make the executive branch stronger, not weaker. Its authority would go from being controversial and untested to stable, regular, and accepted by both legislators and judges.

She was right. At the time of the 1994 amendment, the ACLU hotly opposed it.[22] The *Washington Post* clucked in an editorial that "moving the authorizing power [for physical searches] from the attorney general to the intelligence court won't provide the protection the Constitution guarantees" and insisted that a "more complete reform is needed."[23] Yet the controversy over "black bag jobs," as secret warrantless physical searches are derisively known, has died. Few, if any, observers today would prefer to go back to the days when the executive branch conducted physical searches without going to the Court. Rather, the fear among civil libertarians in general is not that the FISA court's jurisdiction is growing but that the Bush administration is bent on contracting it—placing more types of surveillance beyond its purview, as physical searches once were. Gorelick's comments back in 1994 in defense of her proposal on physical searches from attacks from the ACLU could today be an ACLU press release about FISA as a whole: "If you take . . . an ability by the executive on its own to authorize a search [versus] a process where it has to petition a court with rigorous factual evidence and that whole framework is under the guidance of Congress, I can't see how the second process isn't preferable to the first."[24]

Looking to Congress—and legislatively authorized judicial review—as potential boosters of a strong executive response to terrorism was not, of course, the path the Bush administration chose. And it's not hard to understand the seductive power of the arguments surrounding inherent presidential powers, particularly given the context and the character of the enemy. If the Constitution really grants the president the authority to take the steps needed to fight the bad guys, why ask duplicative permission from a mere legislative body? Congress, as Addington so regularly pointed out, might refuse. It might put limits on the activity. Why not just do what needs doing, making up whatever rules one considers optimal and changing them as circumstances themselves change? Why accept unnecessary restraint? The unilateral executive approach not only maximizes operational flexibility and minimizes the need for messy, protracted negotiations with a coordinate branch of government, it also establishes and reinforces the pattern of not asking—a pattern that might become important in the event of some exigent need for strong action that might discomfit Congress.

But the freedom is chimerical. Modern America is long past the stage as a

society where it will tolerate executive power unmediated by some other institution of government. One can still make a theoretical argument for an executive-
only approach to problems like global terrorism. In practice, however, the
argument is an unreal dream. When the president bypasses Congress—and
Congress so willingly lets him do so—the result will not, in fact, be unre-
strained executive latitude. It will be litigation, and another institution will
step in to fill the void: the courts. When the executive branch untethers itself
from statutory law, the courts will examine its actions with a more powerful
microscope. If they lack clear law to apply, they will tend to create it with
whatever surrogates might be available. The day has long passed when the executive branch can count on the courts to declare that the absence of a Congress saying "no" is the equivalent of the legislature's saying "yes."

The administration can bemoan this fact, and conservative commentators
can pen jeremiad tomes about usurping federal judges,[25] but they argue against
a big tide—the entire trend of modern American constitutional history. It's
not just the lessons of Watergate but a much longer trend toward bureaucra-
tization and oversight of executive action. The executive branch has expanded,
and so too have the checks on the executive branch. In modern America,
when the president seeks to deflate one of these checks, another inflates more
or less proportionately to take its place. More often than not, that new check
is a federal judge. Claims of executive power can often serve in the long run to
trigger aggrandizements of judicial power. What Gorelick knew and the Bush
administration denied to its great cost is that this trend can either strengthen
or weaken the executive—the president can harness these checks as legitimizing agents of strong executive action or he can position himself in conflict
with them and paralyze himself with litigation and controversy.

This point should have been obvious to anyone who has watched the
courts over time. Conservatives, who have critiqued the growth of judicial
power in American life for decades, should have been particularly sensitive to
it. Indeed, even John Yoo, one of the more ideological theoreticians of the executive power approach to the conflict, anticipated to some degree that the
courts would respond to muscular presidential actions with assertions of
power of their own. Writing in December 2001 about federal court jurisdic-

tion over Guantánamo Bay with another Justice Department lawyer, Patrick Philbin, he warned that while "the great weight of legal authority" is arrayed against such jurisdiction, "we cannot say with absolute certainty that [a habeas corpus] petition would be dismissed for lack of jurisdiction. . . . While we believe that the correct answer is that federal courts lack jurisdiction over habeas petitions filed by alien detainees held outside the sovereign territory of the United States, there remains some litigation risk that a district court might reach the opposite result."[26] Yet this awareness of "litigation risk" does not seem to have ever translated in Yoo's case into a more tactically sophisticated approach to getting the authorities the president might need. Addington, for his part, seems to have simply deluded himself as to the prospects of success before the Court. Goldsmith recalled that he "would often predict that the Supreme Court would not countermand the Commander in Chief in wartime." He described Addington as "surprisingly naïve about the factors that influenced Supreme Court decisionmaking" and "oblivious to how changes in context and culture" since the Civil War and World War II "might influence the Court's decision to approve presidential action."[27]

The more sophisticated voices within the Bush administration always knew their crew was playing with fire. When the Supreme Court first moved to consider whether it had jurisdiction over Guantánamo Bay, for example, I asked Goldsmith—a close friend who was then, unbeknownst to me, arguing internally for a congressional approach—what he thought the justices would do with the case. The relevant legal precedents seemed solidly on the government's side, I said, and I had a hard time imagining the Court would simply cast them aside. "When was the last time the Supreme Court granted" review, Goldsmith quipped acidly, "in order to decide that it *didn't* have jurisdiction over something?"[28] I thought about Goldsmith's question, and I knew he was right. The administration would lose, and when it lost in court, it would damage its own power. Goldsmith was contemptuous of the choice—and others were as well—but the administration as an institution for some reason considered going through that exercise preferable to doing business with a Republican Congress. After all, it preserved the illusion that the executive branch was acting on its own, was refusing to negotiate about the scope of its powers, was preserving maximum operational flexibility. Within months, the Supreme Court handed down *Rasul* and declared, as Goldsmith had shrewdly predicted, that it did have jurisdiction after all. The precedents didn't matter in the end. The Court simply wasn't willing to give the president a free hand, unconstrained by any oversight mechanism. And in the absence of any other oversight mechanism, it assumed the burden itself.

Even before *Rasul* was decided in June 2004, the problems of the administration's course were naked. Every major decision it had made had provoked controversy, most of it legal, much of it in the courts. In sharp contrast to what happened when Gorelick went to Congress over physical searches less than a decade earlier, the controversies were widening, not shrinking as time went on—and no wonder. The gaps in the war model posed genuine puzzles of great moral and legal complexity. To simply sweep them under the carpet by claiming that in "a different kind of war" the president has all the powers of a normal war yet few of its restraints, that the whole world is his battlefield, and that this state of affairs goes on in perpetuity is really akin to claiming a kind of worldwide martial law. It only stood to reason that the public—and the courts—would eventually grow uneasy.

Any doubt about this should have disappeared, at the very latest, by June 2004, when the Supreme Court issued its opinions in *Rasul* and in *Hamdi v. Rumsfeld,* a case involving a U.S. citizen held domestically as an enemy combatant. The holding in *Hamdi,* a decision involving a Saudi Taliban member who held American citizenship by virtue of having been born in Louisiana, was complicated; in it, the justices insisted that a citizen detainee receive a hearing in federal court to address the allegations against him. They also, however, affirmed the authority of the executive branch to detain until the end of the hostilities an American citizen fighting for the other side—the core of the administration's argument. *Hamdi* was a mixed bag for the administration. *Rasul* was not a mixed bag. The Court wholly repudiated the administration's contention—fully in line with those of its predecessors—that it could detain people at Guantánamo Bay to avoid the scrutiny of the federal courts. To do this, the justices had to cast aside long-standing doctrine on which they had spoken emphatically in the past. Back in 1950, the Court confronted the case of German prisoners of war convicted of war crimes by an American military commission. The Germans sought habeas review. But Justice Robert H. Jackson, writing for the Court, dismissed the case, saying: "We are cited to no instance where a Court, in this or any other country where the writ is known, has issued it on behalf of an alien enemy who, at no relevant time and in no stage of his captivity, has been within its territorial jurisdiction. Nothing in the text of the Constitution extends such a right, nor does anything in our statutes."[29]

That was 1950. By 2004, however, the Court was singing a different tune. The Abu Ghraib scandal broke even as the solicitor general's office was assuring the justices that the executive branch did not engage even in "mild torture."[30] Not only did the justices determine that they did have jurisdiction over detentions at Guantánamo, they did so in a way that carefully left open the question of whether their jurisdiction extended far beyond a base peculiarly leased to the "exclusive jurisdiction and control" of the United States. The *Rasul* decision should have been a giant flashing red light, a warning that the Court was not going to tolerate indefinite detention without a rigorous oversight scheme. It was not going to tolerate an executive-centered approach in which generalized congressional authorization to use force against Al Qaeda merged with inherent presidential powers to produce a range of broad detention, interrogation, and trial authorities with few checks, minimal procedural rights for the detained, and no known endpoint. In *Rasul,* the administration received a vivid illustration of the Court's willingness to alter doctrine to ensure accountability in the war on terrorism, and an equally vivid illustration of the point the administration should have intuited much earlier: that its assertions of executive authority would ultimately result in expanded judicial power.

The administration should have realized then, at the very latest, that it needed a comprehensive legal regime to support its actions, one that would have the blessing of Congress and to which a court could defer as the collective judgment of the American political system about a novel set of problems. Instead, it plowed on, bent more on reversing the Court's decision than on creating systems that might induce its confidence. This decision guaranteed that American detention policy would be thrashed out in a dialogue between the executive branch and the judiciary, rather than in a dialogue between the executive and the one branch most capable of creating an appropriately imaginative regime.

The administration responded to *Rasul* by setting up a two-layered review process for detentions at Guantánamo. Initially, it subjected each of the 558 detainees who remained at the base to review by panels it dubbed Combatant Status Review Tribunals (CSRT). These panels were set up to judge not the detainees' guilt or innocence of crimes but their status under the laws of war. That is, the CSRTs looked at whether or not the detainees had been properly categorized as "enemy combatants" subject to detention. The CSRTs heard classified government evidence as well as detainees' responses to unclassified summaries of that evidence. They found that 520 of the detainees had been properly classified. By contrast, the panels found 38 detainees to be "no longer enemy combatants"—a bizarre euphemism for erroneously detained.[31]

The administration gave those detainees whom the CSRTs deemed justifiably held an additional layer of review: annual examinations by parolelike boards called administrative review boards (ARB). The ARBs do not reexamine the question of the individual detainee's status. They look, rather, at whether the particular detainee remains too dangerous to relinquish from American custody. They recommend "release [of] the enemy combatant without limitations to his home State or a third State as appropriate," "transfer [of] the enemy combatant to his home State (or a third State as appropriate) with conditions agreed upon between that State and the United States," or continued detention by the United States.[32] The first round of ARBs, held in 2005, determined that 14 detainees could be released and 119 transferred. The second round, held in 2006, ordered no detainees released and 55 additional ones transferred.[33]

How one views this system depends, to a great degree, on the standard one measures it against. By the standards of the laws of war, the CSRTs are pretty generous. The Geneva Conventions, concerned less with separating combatants from noncombatants than with making sure that POWs do not get wrongly denied the privileges owed them, require only that a "competent tribunal" make status determinations.[34] Historically, these tribunals have been cursory affairs, panels assembled in the theater of combat as a rough check on detention judgments. They have not had elaborate procedural protections. And against them, the CSRTs measure up well. Detainees get to see a summary of the allegations against them; they get the assistance of a military officer to prepare their rebuttals; they can call witnesses if those witnesses are readily available; and they have an opportunity to tell their sides of the story. And the CSRTs resulted in the release of nearly 7 percent of detainees who came before them—a rate significantly higher than the rate of acquittal in federal court.[35] Still, against the standards of the criminal justice system, the process is pretty anemic. Detainees have no assistance of counsel before the tribunals; they have no way to address the details of the allegations, which are generally classified; the panels have no specialized legal training; and the burden of proof is on the detainee to prove the government's allegations wrong, not the other way around. What's more, neither the CSRTs nor the ARBs produce any kind of public record that a member of the press or public skeptical about a particular detention might examine to explain its reasonableness.

Most fundamentally, this beginning of system—and it was, in some respects, a better beginning than its fiercer critics allow—lacked any congressional buy-in. The administration once again had declined to ask Congress to enact its policy in statute but instead had implemented it in regulations. As a consequence, the rules reflected nobody's judgment but the military's own, and they could be changed at any moment they became inconvenient. Because the tribunals themselves were conducted out of the public eye, nobody outside the administration had any particular basis for confidence in them. Even to the extent that the nonclassified CSRT hearings justified the administration's detention decisions—and they did in a significant number of cases— holding them in secret under the executive's own authority ensured that they would lack both the visibility and the imprimatur of the legislature required to maximize public and judicial credibility.

The administration did go to Congress for one thing: to get the lawsuits that proliferated in the months after *Rasul* thrown out of court. By passing the Detainee Treatment Act (DTA) late in 2005, Congress sought to undo what the Court had done a year and a half earlier. It created a narrow appeal mechanism for CSRT determinations and trial verdicts by military commissions— of which there had been none of the latter at that time and still, to this day, have been none. Final judgments by the CSRTs and commissions, the act said, would be appealed to the D.C. Circuit Court of Appeals in Washington. Other than this process, however, "no court, justice, or judge shall have jurisdiction to hear or consider" any "application for a writ of habeas corpus filed by or on behalf of an alien detained by the Department of Defense at Guantánamo Bay, Cuba." Moreover, the statute barred "any other action against the United States or its agents relating to any aspect of the detention by the Department of Defense of an alien at Guantánamo Bay, Cuba." The CSRTs thus became a peculiar quasi-judicial institution for which its appeal alone was authorized by statute. The administration could make up the rules and alter them as it saw fit—but whatever the rules looked like, the D.C. Circuit could hear an appeal.

As part of the DTA, Congress also passed the so-called McCain Amendment, intended to prevent abusive interrogations by both the military and the CIA in its detention facilities, which were then still nominally secret. The law declared that "no individual in the custody or under the physical control of the United States Government, regardless of nationality or physical location, shall be subject to cruel, inhuman, or degrading treatment or punishment." It defined such treatment as that conduct "prohibited by the Fifth, Eighth, and Fourteenth Amendments to the Constitution of the United States." The administration quickly interpreted the treatment provisions of the DTA so narrowly as to read them almost out of existence.[36]

The jurisdiction-stripping language of the DTA seemed straightforward enough, but the Supreme Court had already made plain that it regarded an executive-only approach to these detentions as unpalatable. So it was no surprise when the Court a few months later in *Hamdan* did not deem itself barred from considering a detainee's attack on the administration's plan for military commissions. It turns out, the justices ruled, that the words "no court, justice, or judge shall have jurisdiction to hear or consider" any "application for a writ of habeas corpus" don't mean quite what they seem to say. The Court interpreted the law to apply only to new cases, filed after the DTA's passage. The majority claimed that the new law did not touch the hundreds of cases filed after *Rasul* and pending at the time Congress enacted the law.[37] The Court went on to strike down the military commissions, which, like the CSRTs, existed only in administrative orders, not statutory law. The justices ruled that the absence of congressional authorization rendered unacceptable the commissions' deviations from normal trial procedures. The absence of congressional sanction was now taking a big bite.

This time, the administration did go to Congress to authorize its policy choice; if it wanted to run military commissions, it now had no alternative. So in the fall of 2006, it prevailed on the legislature to enact the Military Commissions Act (MCA) which, unlike previous congressional enactments, created a statutory scheme for the policy the administration wished to pursue—in this case, trials without all the niceties of either the civilian justice system or the traditional military courts. But if this effort was more comprehensive than prior ones, it wasn't comprehensive enough. While the statute laid out trial procedures in some depth, it left the underlying questions of who can be detained, under what procedures, and with what sort of review altogether unaddressed. Because the military had slated so few detainees for trial, the relatively detailed procedures for commissions described in the MCA would have been to some degree a hypothetical advance even had they reflected a broad legislative consensus, rather than a partisan bill hastily cobbled together and pushed through on the eve of the midterm elections. The underlying structure for detentions, despite the new law, remains skeletal and peculiarly nonstatutory. Prior to passage of the MCA, the system involved a statutory appeals process layered on top of a nonstatutory trial and detention scheme. In the MCA, Congress wrote the trial scheme into law, but it once again neglected the foundation on which the whole enterprise rests: the detentions themselves.

The MCA also, for good measure, once again tried to undo the administration's compound defeat on the question of federal court habeas jurisdiction over Guantánamo. "No court, justice, or judge shall have jurisdiction to

hear or consider an application for a writ of habeas corpus filed by or on behalf of an alien detained by the United States who has been determined by the
United States to have been properly detained as an enemy combatant or is
awaiting such determination," the law reads. To make itself perfectly clear,
Congress added that this bar "shall apply to all cases, without exception, pending on or after the date of the enactment of this Act which relate to any aspect
of the detention, transfer, treatment, trial, or conditions of detention of an
alien detained by the United States since September 11, 2001."[38] By doing this,
it tried to ensure that the courts would have no power to dwell on its omis-
sions—that is, that the paucity of statutory foundation for the entire detention enterprise would stay out of court. But in asking for and receiving such a
fragmentary regime, the administration very likely underestimated once more
the judiciary's tenacity in demanding accountability as the price of its own
deference.

Indeed, this latter provision predictably led to another round of litigation.
As of this writing, nobody knows for sure whether the Supreme Court will
strike down this law and insist that, as a matter of constitutional law, it must
have a seat at the table over Guantánamo. But after three separate rounds of
this back-and-forth, the pattern that has developed is an unsubtle one that
doesn't look much like what a middle school civics class would recognize as
American democratic government. According to the civics class's version of
democracy, the president—faced with a novel problem—would go to the legislature and say, "Here is the problem and here is what I need to address it,"
and the legislature would respond, "Here is what you can have." The pattern
America has developed under the Bush administration looks entirely different: The president adopts a policy on his own. He refuses to seek congressional blessing for the core of his policy—and Congress does not insist that he do
so. He seeks congressional authority only when the courts explicitly demand
congressional permission and with the perverse purpose of shielding his policy from judicial review. The courts then pass retroactively on the propriety of
his efforts, always stopping short of forcing the release of detainees or telling
the administration it cannot do what it wants but never blessing the detentions or the policy. Nobody ever envisions the optimal system from scratch.

This pattern has repeated itself, as if on autopilot, for more than six years, during which time policy in the war on terrorism has grown more, never less, contentious. Over that time, something else has happened too: In the minds of many people in the press and the academy, and in both domestic and international public opinion, the detainees at Guantánamo Bay somehow morphed from terrorists into victims.

THREE

The Real Guantánamo

THE WEIRDNESS of the American naval base at Guantánamo Bay, Cuba, beggars easy description. Large iguanas roam the forty-five-square-mile tract of land as though they own the place. At roughly two thirds the size of Washington D.C., Guantánamo sits on either side of the bay that gave the base its name. Heavily armed Coast Guard speedboats zoom back and forth across the water, passing off-duty personnel lolling about on pontoon boats that motor pacifically in the lagoons off the main channel. Guantánamo is not far off America's shores, barely past Miami—a quick three-hour hop by Gulfstream jet from Andrews Air Force Base near Washington. And despite its being on the land mass of one of this country's most implacable enemies, you don't need a passport to get there. At the same time, it's a world away. The detention facilities there constitute a kind of prison within a prison, a lockup located in an oasis of America wedged between a sea of Cuban communism and the sea itself. And while you may have little sense of leaving the United States when you travel to Guantánamo, in a strange recognition of the facility's foreign status, you do need your passport to get back home.

The very oddities that make Guantánamo such a peculiar place to visit render it operationally—though not optically—ideal as a detention site. At once secure and nearby, Guantánamo operations are not subject to the discontent or objections of the host government. And at least until the outset of the war on terrorism, successive administrations had assumed as well that the area lay outside the purview of the American courts. At Guantánamo, they reasoned, the government can do as it likes—as long as it can take the political heat. And so, amid the lizards and the blazing heat, the military built a set of detention camps, which have indelibly etched into the public mind images of shackled, hooded prisoners in cages.

The images, however they might dominate public perceptions, bear little relation to Guantánamo's contemporary reality, which is coolly professional. The detention facilities at the base vary a great deal. As of April 2007, when I visited Guantánamo, only Camp 1 still had cells with mesh walls—and the military was then phasing detainees out of there as it completed its new facilities. Camp 4, which houses relatively compliant detainees, looks a lot like a basic prisoner-of-war camp. Dormitorylike barracks open onto a courtyard, of which detainees have the run. Detainees have access to English classes. It's not a resort, by any means, but inmates in many prisons in the United States would surely see it as an improvement were they shipped there. Camps 5 and 6, by contrast, are pretty grim. Built for the less cooperative and more dangerous detainees, they are the equivalent of a modern "supermax" prison. The facilities are clean, and detainees are fed well and have more exercise time than comparable high-security prisoners in the United States. Still, the military keeps them locked down most of the day in individual cells. It candidly admits that how much cooperation a detainee offers in interrogations helps determine in which camp he lives.

Running Guantánamo is a nightmare. Guards face intense stress. Between July 2005 and August 2006, detainees conducted 432 "bodily fluid attacks." Detainees in Camp 4—the facility for the most compliant detainees— conducted a violent uprising. Suicide attempts and hunger strikes have occurred relatively frequently—often requiring involuntary feeding to keep detainees alive. Maintaining the fewer than four hundred detainees present at that time required almost eleven hundred guards. The tension at Guantánamo is so palpable that one has no trouble imagining how, but for stringent military discipline, a site like this could degrade into anarchic brutality—as Abu Ghraib degraded in the face of command failures.[1]

Detention itself, even under worse conditions and of many more people, does not normally spark the controversy that has attended Guantánamo. America keeps more than two million people under lock and key these days domestically, many of them in prisons that make Guantánamo seem tame. The detainee population in Iraq dwarfs that of Guantánamo by almost two orders of magnitude, and these detainees get *less* legal process—yet they prompt little outcry. Guantánamo differs because detentions there seem to reflect arbitrary government power so close to home yet self-consciously kept offshore in a fashion too clever by half. Detentions there seem somehow punitive, yet the Pentagon has never publicly justified them on an individual basis. Its evidence that the detainees are who it claims mostly remains secret. And many Americans—and a growing international consensus—have come to doubt the very premise that the laws of war permit indefinite detentions of such people without criminal charges supported by proof in court beyond a reasonable doubt using admissible evidence.

Many Americans have come to doubt something else too: the premise that the people detained at Guantánamo warrant incarceration at all. This doubt flows in part from the frankly irresponsible rhetoric the administration used about its captives at the outset of the conflict. Presidential spokesman Ari Fleischer famously called them the "worst of the worst"[2] and Rumsfeld declared them "among the most dangerous, best trained vicious killers on the face of the earth."[3] This kind of talk quite reasonably spawned a cottage industry of doubt and evaluation. A law professor—and habeas lawyer—from Seton Hall University named Mark Denbeaux issued a report in February 2006, which evaluated 517 CSRT summaries of government evidence against detainees. Denbeaux and his coauthor found that 55 percent "of detainees are not determined to have committed any hostile acts against the United States or its coalition allies," that only 8 percent of detainees "were characterized as al Qaeda fighters," and that most detainees were not captured by American forces but by either the Northern Alliance or the Pakistani army.[4] Around the same time, *National Journal* published its own evaluation of the still-sketchy data released from the CSRT process. Far from the "worst of the worst," the magazine concluded, "Many [detainees] are not accused of hostilities against the United States or its allies. Most, when captured, were innocent of any terrorist activity, were Taliban foot soldiers at worst, and were often far less than that. And some, perhaps many, are guilty only of being foreigners in Afghanistan or Pakistan at the wrong time."[5] Within a few weeks of the publication of these reports, the *New York Times,* based on CSRT hearing transcripts, had editorialized that "far too many [detainees] seemed to be innocents or lowly foot soldiers simply caught up in the whirlwind after 9/11."[6] A few months later, "far too many" had turned in the eyes of the *Times* editorialists into "hundreds of innocent men . . . jailed at Guantánamo Bay without charges or rudimentary rights."[7] Four short years of the administration's Guantánamo policy had turned the "worst of the worst" into the oppressed of the earth.

This perverse turnabout simply would not have taken place had a strong and open legal architecture guided detention decisions at Guantánamo. Any person at any time can look up the basis for the incarceration of any of the two million people serving time in prisons in the United States. The government charges them in public and subjects its evidence freely to attack at trial. You don't have to go so far as to envision the criminal law as the basis for war-on-terrorism detentions to see how this open application of agreed-upon rules serves to justify criminal convictions over the years and to lessen doubt about the legitimacy of long-term imprisonments. Individual criminal cases provoke debate, sometimes passionate debate, and Americans disagree about numerous policy questions surrounding the criminal justice system at large. But the openness of that system, the fact that it carries out a set of rules we've agreed upon in advance, and the resulting ability of the public to examine each case on its own for compliance with those rules cumulatively ensure that doubts about any given conviction do not erode confidence in the mass of others. By contrast, the review systems the military belatedly set up at Guantánamo lacked all of the elements that would have rendered their judgments credible and durable. The government released no information about the detainees—not even their names—until litigation forced it to make disclosures. The rules it finally did apply, also under pressure from the courts, reflected no sort of consensus as to how to balance fairness and due process against the military's concerns about security and protecting intelligence sources and methods. And the public consequently could not consider these cases on their individual merits, only as a group.

When the public lacks information about a process to which it has not consented and in which people's long-term liberty is at stake, the government cannot reasonably expect its confidence. Our traditions of public trials and transparency in government action are simply too strong and well entrenched for Americans to tolerate a detention procedure based on trust in executive competence and goodwill to resolve complex disputes over facts and evidence. When the military compounds this basic flaw by releasing information in dribs and drabs and making it painstakingly difficult to figure out what happened to each detainee, when, and why, it breeds suspicion. And the lack of any solid information about the detainees ironically allows each observer to see in them more or less what he or she comes looking for. Those suspicious of the CSRT process had little trouble finding unfairness and arbitrary justice.[8] Journalists came looking for innocent detainees—as is their job—and they found detainees with compelling stories.[9] Some writers seemed to find oppressed innocence everywhere they looked.[10] On the other hand, a team at West Point, looking at the same data the Seton Hall report examined, determined that 73 percent of allegations against detainees described a "demonstrated threat" and 95 percent of allegations described at least a "potential threat."[11]

Over the years, the public data has grown richer. Because the CSRTs and ARBs did not provide a forum in which the government's evidence faced systematic testing, the data still cannot offer a comprehensive portrait of the detainee population at Guantánamo. But the many thousands of declassified pages of analytical memos, allegations, and transcripts related to detainee hearings nonetheless paint a more complicated and interesting portrait of the detainee population that is reflected in most public debate.

On one side, the public record now offers, at a minimum, a sketch of the government's CSRT evidence against each detainee—usually just a few sentences of allegations, sometimes significantly more. The government often supplemented these allegations in the annual ARB reviews, the parolelike hearings that followed CSRT judgments. Because the government never carried the burden of supporting its allegations rigorously, its evidence, to whatever extent it has evidence, remains classified, unavailable for the detainee to attack or the public to assess. These records, therefore, do not represent the facts the government could prove but offer a window into what it believes, rightly or wrongly, that its intelligence shows about each detainee.

On the other side, the public record also now generally includes the detainee's side of the story. These data too have limitations. The detainees lacked access to counsel to help them rebut government allegations. Their opportunity to call witnesses was seriously impaired; in fact, in the CSRT process, no detainee managed to call a witness other than those also detained at Guantánamo.[12] They generally lacked the ability to prove their stories true. Nonetheless, in both the CSRT process and during each round of ARB hearings, the military gave each detainee the opportunity to respond to the allegations against him. In the CSRTs, the majority of detainees took that opportunity. The number appearing at their hearings dwindled during the ARBs, but the cumulative impact of these opportunities is that of 572 detainees whose CSRT records the public can access, more than 70 percent made some statement that has been subsequently declassified.

The result is that in most cases, while the public still has nothing quite like the process of testing evidence in an adversarial court proceeding, it does now have some picture of both sides of the story. We can describe in some detail whom the government contends it captured and how those captives describe themselves. We can compare the government's collective portrait with the collective self-portrait of the detainees and examine the areas of congruence and incompatibility of these pictures. We can, in short, figure out how much really stands in dispute concerning this much fought over group of men. And the comparison illuminates a good deal, because it turns out that a lot of information about the detainees is *not* in dispute. Notwithstanding its over-blown rhetoric, the government does not deny it has erred in certain cases, and many detainees do not deny their belligerency.

Indeed, examining in detail the detainee population brings into stark relief the utter inadequacy of the administration's law-of-war approach to these long-term detentions and the urgent need for a more open and adversarial re-gime that reflects the will of more than one elected official. The system the military used probably approved the detentions of some innocent men—and the military's tardiness in building any system certainly delayed the release of innocents. But the greatest victim of the administration's failure to forge with Congress a process that separated rigorously and publicly those rightly de-tained from those wrongly detained was surely the government itself. For in an elaborate game of "heads I win, tails you lose," the government managed to lose in the public arena no matter what the evidence showed. Where CSRTs and ARBs sent detainees home, the government received no credit for this as a substantial check on its power. Where they brought out genuine factual dis-putes attending particular detentions, they lacked both the procedural rules and the perceived independence to resolve them credibly—the result being that they never served usefully to validate detentions in the public arena. Even, ironically, in the many cases in which no material factual dispute existed be-tween the detainees and the government, the secrecy of the process ensured that the public could not know. This was a needless self-inflicted wound, not only in the public relations arena but also insofar as it invited judicial skepti-cism and scrutiny. In many cases, a reasonable process would have had the ef-fect not of freeing scary people but of better selling to the world and to the American courts and public the need to keep them locked up and the propri-ety of doing so.

THE DETAINEES at Guantánamo came from literally all over the world. More than forty countries saw at least one of their nationals detained there. The lion's share, however, came from only three countries—Afghanistan, Saudi Arabia, and Yemen—which together contributed almost 65 percent of the total population. No other country contributed more than twenty-five detainees. The population at Guantánamo has been in a precipitous decline since even before the CSRT process began. Nearly 800 detainees have passed through Guantánamo at one point or another, yet only 558 detainees were there when the original CSRT process was launched. And of those subjected to ARB review, the military had cleared for release or transfer all but 273 by the time it completed the second round of ARBs in 2007. Actually effectuating these transfers presents enormous logistical headaches—and there has been a years-long lag in some cases between the decision to send detainees home and their actually leaving Guantánamo. But in principle, at least, the military now contends it needs to hold only a rump group of detainees, plus the handful of high-value detainees and the overlapping group it has designated for trial before military commissions. The residual population has continued shrinking over the course of the third round of ARBs, about which the military has not yet made extensive data public. During 2007, the Pentagon repatriated the overwhelming majority of the Saudi nationals—even some it had reason to regard as dangerous—under a program in which the Saudi government has sought to mitigate the risk they pose.[13] In this chapter, I deal almost entirely with data from the CSRTs and the first two rounds of ARBs.

The government's portrait of each detainee starts with a brief summary of evidence given to the detainee as part of the CSRT process. This document, in most cases, contains two categories of allegation. The first is a broad suggestion of some level of association with a group engaged in military hostilities against the United States—overwhelmingly either the Taliban or Al Qaeda or both. The military accused each detainee of being a member, a fighter, or an associate—or sometimes two of these in combination—of these groups. While it isn't quite clear how the military drew lines between these categories, in many instances, it produced a relatively simple top-line allegation. The government, for example, alleged that the detainee population that went through the CSRT process included the following:

- 68 members of Al Qaeda
- 9 Al Qaeda fighters

- 101 people associated with Al Qaeda
- 64 members of the Taliban
- 23 fighters for the Taliban
- 43 people associated with the Taliban[14]

But for many other detainees, the government had a harder time articulating even this highest altitude charge. In some instances, for example, it had understandable difficulty distinguishing between groups that were tightly intertwined—and therefore had trouble identifying a principal affiliation for individual detainees. The result is that it described 11 detainees as members of *both* Al Qaeda and the Taliban, 109 as affiliates of both groups, and 28 as affiliates of one and fighters for or members of the other.

In other cases, the military struggled to identify the level of attachment a detainee had demonstrated. It labeled four detainees, for example, as either affiliates or members of Al Qaeda and an additional one as either an affiliate or member of the Taliban. In an additional forty-six cases, reflecting an even greater level of ambiguity, it alleged that detainees were tied not to both groups but to *one group or the other,* or, stranger yet, *one group "and/or" the other.* The government accused thirty-nine detainees of being attached to unspecified groups hostile to coalition forces, and in twenty-four cases made no top-line allegations at all.

These troubles with basic classification reflect in some instances the amorphous structure of Al Qaeda and the Taliban. They undoubtedly also sometimes reflect weakness in the government evidence linking detainees to the groups and a certain sloppiness in the military's categorization of and standards for the detainees. Ultimately, the government labeled more than twice as many detainees as associated with the groups than it branded as "members" of them—and it branded almost four times as many detainees "members" as it did "fighters."[15]

Compounding these evidentiary difficulties was the fact that the vast majority of detainees were not captured by American forces. The Pakistani army caught a plurality crossing into their country after the American air attacks in Afghanistan began. The Northern Alliance also caught many detainees. Because a large number of Taliban fighters fled the battlefield in civilian clothing, the circumstances of their belligerency grew murkier than it would have been had they been caught on the battlefield itself. And it grew murkier still because American forces often learned the evidence surrounding their conduct secondhand from forces that lack the professionalism of American military personnel. The fact that U.S. forces offered bounties for Al Qaeda members, though it undoubtedly netted a bunch of genuine operatives, also made this problem worse.[16]

It is a grave mistake, however, to see all this ambiguity as evidence of a general triviality in the government's allegations against the detainees—as the authors of the Seton Hall reports describe it. The military also included a list of more specific allegations against each detainee, and these allegations are, generally speaking, not trivial at all—though many of them are vague, weakly sourced, entirely unsourced, or even stated as possibilities or likelihoods, rather than as certainties. Many detainees, if you take the government's portraits seriously, are committed jihadists. And while their individual stories differ considerably, there are important common threads that make them look like something other than innocent relief workers, laborers, and Koranic instructors—common threads the military could not regard as anything other than extremely dangerous. According to the government's summaries of CSRT and ARB evidence in the nonhigh-value cases, for example:

- At least 179 traveled to Afghanistan for jihad
- At least 234 stayed in Al Qaeda, Taliban, or other guest or safehouses.
- At least 317 detainees took military or terrorist training in Afghanistan
- At least 151 actually fought for the Taliban, many of them on the front lines against the Northern Alliance
- At least 160 were at Tora Bora
- At least 157 detainees' names or aliases were found on computers, hard drives, or physical lists of Al Qaeda operatives, material seized in raids on Al Qaeda safe houses and facilities
- At least 136 detainees were captured under circumstances—military surrenders, live combat actions, traveling in a large pack of Mujahideen,

or in the company of senior Al Qaeda figures, for example—that strongly suggest belligerency

• 34 detainees served on Osama bin Laden's security detail

The government processes also brought out a significant number of mistakes. The thirty-eight detainees found by the CSRTs to be erroneously categorized included a number of Uighurs—ethnic Turkic Central Asians from China who had traveled to Afghanistan to train for insurgent activity against Beijing but who clearly had no beef against the United States. Reflecting the oddity of these cases, however, commissions found other Uighurs, whose cases were materially similar, to be enemy combatants.[17] The commissions also seem to have believed certain non-Afghan detainees who claimed to have been in Afghanistan for innocent reasons. These stories, some of which seem a bit implausible in black and white, include a Turk who had stayed with a suspected Al Qaeda operative for two months,[18] a Saudi man whom the Taliban had imprisoned for five years,[19] a Yemeni man who claimed to be at the Afghanistan-Pakistan border doing drug deals,[20] an Uzbek who suggested that "special forces" had sent him from Tajikistan to Afghanistan by helicopter in an effort to get him out of the country,[21] and a Frenchman who lied about his nationality and identity on capture and contended he had traveled from Iran to Afghanistan two months after September 11 "just to visit," carrying ten thousand dollars in cash given him accidentally by a stranger.[22]

The saddest of these cases involve detainees, mostly but not exclusively Afghans, who got rounded up, sometimes in simple error and sometimes in confusion about which groups were really fighting America and its allies. There were some cases of simple mistaken identity. The government identified Shed Abdur Rahman, for example, as a high-ranking Taliban "military judge" who "tortured, maimed, and murdered" other Afghans in Taliban jails. The detainee—who was born in Pakistan—contended that he had "never even hit my own child at home and . . . never hurt anyone." Far from being a military judge, he said, "the only time I have ever been in Afghanistan was for two days to attend a funeral." The CSRT ultimately accepted his claim that he actually worked on a chicken farm.[23] The military claimed that Mohammed

Nasim "commanded a squad of Mujahidin fighters for a Kabul commander" and that his name "was referenced in intercepted radio transmissions regarding Northern Alliance troop movement." The detainee, by contrast, said he had "never been a commander. I never saw Kabul. I was always in my area, in my place, in my home farming. I was a farmer." His CSRT believed him, too.[24]

Other cases involved not mistaken identities per se but murky circumstances or the difficulty of distinguishing military from civilian functions in a regime run by a militia. For example, Janut Gul, whose CSRT record also calls him Hammdidullah, avoided conscription into the Taliban by becoming a civilian employee for the national airlines, of which he eventually became a top officer. The CSRTs struggled in many cases with claims by detainees that they performed only civilian functions. While in many instances, tribunals did not buy the distinction, Hammdidullah's tribunal did.[25] Likewise, in the case of Nasibullah Darwaish, whom the government described as a security commander for a Taliban-linked governor of an Afghan province, the detainee acknowledged that he served in that role under the current government of Hamid Karzai, but insisted that the governor he served was "not Taliban and he was nowhere near Taliban" and that "when I accepted the job as district chief of police that made me a lifetime enemy with Taliban."[26] The shifting alliances of Afghan politics left a goodly number of Afghan detainees claiming not that they were not combatants, but that they were not *enemy* combatants. Between the CSRTs and ARBs, the majority of these people have been cleared for removal from Guantánamo.

In general, however, the CSRTs did not free detainees but validated the government's allegations and the detention decisions based upon them. Because the government's top-line allegations are so confused, I have tried to simplify them, grouping the military's core allegations into a few loose categories. These categories are admittedly somewhat impressionistic, and there is a great deal of overlap among them. As such, reasonable minds can argue about which detainees belong in which box—and even how distinct the boxes really are. Moreover, the categories reflect nothing about the strength or quality of evidence against individual detainees, only about the nature of the claims the government has made about them. They are designed to provide a somewhat easier and more vivid picture of the detainee population as seen through the government's summaries of evidence. Taking all government allegations in both the CSRT and ARB processes as true, the population can be described as including:

- 25 members of Al Qaeda's leadership cadre. This category, which comprises 4 percent of the population, ranges from Khalid Sheik Mohammed to the movement's top money men and recruiters, the aides de camp of its chieftains, and the operational heads of and key participants in major Al Qaeda terrorist operations. It also includes some leaders of terrorist groups, like the Indonesian Jemmah Islamiyah, which allied themselves with Al Qaeda but retained some measure of independent identity.

- 182 lower-level Al Qaeda operatives, people who played a variety of roles in moving personnel and money, planning attacks, and carrying them out. This category, which makes up 32 percent of the population, includes Al Qaeda fighters with particularly close ties to the movement leaders—Bin Laden bodyguards and those who have sworn an oath of loyalty to him. It also includes fighters whose training bears some particular indicia of terrorism, as opposed to military combat. And it includes people who worked in Afghanistan and Pakistan for charities that operated as fronts for Al Qaeda, as well as operatives of terrorist groups like the Libyan Islamic Fighting Group, which are affiliated with Al Qaeda but remain to some degree distinct.

- 17 members of the Taliban's leadership cadre, ranging from ministers in the ultra-Islamist government and those who actively provided them high-level aid from outside the government to field commanders who led substantial numbers of soldiers. This group, 3 percent of the population, includes some people who could also reasonably be deemed Al Qaeda operatives, given the intertwined nature of the organizations. It also includes the leadership of native Afghan militias allied with the Taliban against coalition forces.

- 240 foreign fighters of varying levels of commitment and ferocity, from fervent international jihadists to the Gulf Arab youth who migrated to Afghanistan out of a relatively common desire for military "training" or a romantic religious attachment to the "pure" Islam of the Taliban. The government generally classifies these people, who make up a 42 percent plurality of the detainee population, as either Taliban or Al Qaeda, the groups that recruited them, trained them, and for whom they fought—or, in many cases, did not ultimately end up fighting. And there is undoubtedly a great deal of overlap among this group and the others. For present purposes, however, a foreign fighter is a non-Afghan who came to the region to fight or train but whom the government does not allege either to have had extensive access to high-level Al Qaeda operatives or to have planned or trained for terrorism—as opposed to military operations—specifically.

- 93 Taliban fighters and operatives. This group, which makes up 16 percent of the population, includes people who resemble conventional soldiers, as well as people who seem far closer to terrorists but are generally native Afghans whose principal affiliation is with their militia, not with Al Qaeda. It also includes fighters for the Taliban-allied militias, and other native Afghan groups fighting coalition forces in Afghanistan.

- 15 people who fell into none of these categories.

The government, as previously noted, did not disturb CSRT findings that thirty-eight detainees were "no longer enemy combatants," and the military cleared an additional fourteen for outright release in the first round of ARB review. Approximately thirty others had been cleared for release or transfer under procedures that predated the CSRTs but were still present when the military convened the tribunals.[27] These groups—those either cleared or sufficiently unthreatening to be quickly releasable anyway—comprised about 14 percent of the population that went through the CSRTs.

In other words, the government's portrait of the detainee population comprises a motley mixture of highly dangerous characters, buffoons who with

varying degrees of plausibility imagined themselves warriors, and a few unlucky people in the wrong place at the wrong time. Particularly after the addition of the high-value detainees in September 2006, the group certainly
included some of the "worst of the worst." But it principally comprised a different group: low- and mid-level Al Qaeda and Taliban operatives and the
foreign fighters they recruited to man the barricades in Afghanistan. This
group, the cannon fodder of international jihad, can pose a real menace both
to American soldiers in the field and to American (and non-American) civilians. But unlike the true worst of the worst, who have almost always committed crimes one could try to prosecute, the members of this group may have
done little more than train to fight against forces that later became American
allies. Unless one is prepared to stretch the law of conspiracy so far as to crimi-
nalize association with certain groups, some of these people are almost certainly innocent of criminal activity.

THE PICTURE looks different when considered from the point of view of the
detainees. Most detainees, after all, do not describe themselves as terrorists.
They tend, rather, to minimize their involvement. People whom the government labels Al Qaeda operatives call themselves relief workers; people whom
the government calls moneymen call themselves businessmen; people whom
the government calls jihadist fighters call themselves instructors in the Koran,
and some call themselves farmers.

Yet the picture looks a good deal less different than one might think from
a public debate that has tended to treat the detainees as a bloc. A substantial
percentage of detainees do not seriously contest their status. The Venn dia-
grams of the government's portrait of the detainees and their collective self-
portrait, rather, have a significant zone of overlap.

Start with the fact that of the 534 detainees found to be enemy combatants
by the CSRTs, 59 openly admit either membership or significant association
with Al Qaeda, the Taliban, or some other armed group the government considers militarily hostile to the United States. An additional 13 acknowledge
being Taliban but claim to have been pressed into service. In these cases, the

military can justify its detention judgments with reference to the detainees' statements alone. A further group of 64 detainees deny affiliation with Al Qaeda or the Taliban yet admit facts that, under the broad authority the laws of war give armed parties to detain the enemy, offer the government ample legal justification for its decisions. An additional group of 62 detainees admits to some lesser measure of affiliation—like staying in Taliban or Al Qaeda guesthouses or spending time at one of their training camps. In these cases, the detainees' statements alone only partially justify the detentions, but it's not hard to imagine how the classified evidence might push the government over the hump. Together, these groups amount to more than one third of the population the CSRTs deemed enemy combatants. While by no means a majority, this is a sizable block of detainees who concede at least something substantial in support of their detentions. The remaining detainees divide almost evenly between those who deny all the material allegations against them and those who make no statements at all. Each of these groups bears a more detailed examination.

Those who admit operating on behalf of the enemy are not necessarily the worst of the detainees—though some of them certainly are. "I helped out Bin Laden," an Afghan named Mohammed Hashim told his CSRT panel. "We were told by the Arabs, who had all the money, that they were planning an attack on the United States with 20 pilots." For five years, he said, "I have been a member of the Taliban," on behalf of whom "I took part in a lot of battles." Of the government's summary of evidence, he said, "All of it is true. There are no lies in there."[28] Walid Bin 'Attash quibbled with details but acknowledged proudly that he had taken part in the attack on the U.S.S. *Cole* and the East African embassy bombings:

> **Tribunal:** What exactly was his role as the—both the USS *Cole* and the—ah—embassy thing?
>
> **Detainee:** Many roles, I participated in the buying or purchasing of the explosives. I put together the plan for the operation a year and a half prior to the operation. Buying the boat and recruiting the members that did the operation. Buying the explosives . . .

[**Tribunal**] **President:** Where were you, physically, at the time of the *Cole* attacks?

Detainee: [I] was with Sheik Usama bin Laden in Kandahar.

President: And at the time of the embassy attacks?

Detainee: I was in Karachi meeting the operator, the guy that basically did the operation a few hours before the operation took place. . . . I was the link between Usama bin Laden and his deputy Sheikh Abu Hafs Al Masri and the cell chief in Nairobi.[29]

Khalid Sheikh Mohammed admitted to a long list of terrorist acts—perhaps more than he actually conducted—and declared: "I will not regret when I say I'm [an] enemy combatant."[30] Abdul Rahman Al Zahri, whom the government also accused of advance knowledge of the September 11 attacks, announced at his ARB hearing: "I do pose a threat to the United States and its allies. I admit to you it is my honor to be an enemy of the United States. I'm a Muslim jihadist . . ." Al Zahri denied membership in Al Qaeda but proudly declared that he trained at Al Qaeda camps and met with Bin Laden many times. "I'm not one of his men and not one of his individuals. I am one of his sons. I will kill myself for him and will also give my family and all of my money to him. I praise Mullah Omar. Relating to my relationship with [the] Taliban, it is a Muslim country. My duty toward them is like any duty of a Muslim person to defend the Taliban and its stay. . . . With the help of God, we will stand Mujahedin and terrorists against Americans."[31]

Most of the admissions are more pedestrian than these. Indeed, while the percentage of people the government describes as Al Qaeda operatives, Al Qaeda leadership, and senior Taliban is significantly higher among this group than among the Guantánamo population at large, it is not dramatically so. For most of the detainees who admit their roles, the frankness of their statements may reflect less the intensity or fervor of their commitment to jihad—which may well not exceed the commitment of many of those who deny everything—than simple honesty or the sense that the government's evidence is strong enough to render any denial fruitless. Many detainees acknowledged openly that they traveled to Afghanistan to train for and participate in the fight against the Northern Alliance.[32] Some dispute fighting American forces specifically or contend they never formally joined the Taliban or Al Qaeda as members. But they admit an affiliation with the other side in the fight. A typical example of this group is Adnan Muhammed Ali Al Saigh, whose CSRT hearing contains the following exchanges:

> **Tribunal President:** What do you have to say about that, are you or are you not with the Taliban?
>
> **Detainee:** I am.
>
> [The next allegation is then read to the tribunal]: *3a1. Detainee stated he answered an Islamic fatwah in Saudi Arabia to fight for the Taliban forces in Afghanistan.*
>
> **Detainee:** That is a religious activity, are you fighting my cause?
>
> . . .
>
> *3b. The Detainee participated in military operations against the coalition.*
>
> **Detainee:** I never participated.
>
> **Personal Representative:** When I spoke with the Detainee, he said he fought with the Taliban against the (forces led by General) Massoud but not against the American allies.
>
> **Detainee:** That's true.
>
> . . .
>
> **Tribunal Member:** Did you answer a fatwah from a religious leader in Saudi Arabia to go to Afghanistan?
>
> **Detainee:** Yes. . . . I went there to fight with the rest of the people.[33]

In many cases, detainees admit their affiliations in the course of seeking to minimize their roles. For example, Salim Hamdan, the detainee whose challenge to military commissions went all the way to the Supreme Court, did not deny that he served as Osama bin Laden's driver. But he said he was "forced" to do so.[34] Several admitted members of the Taliban argued that their work for the militia was purely civilian in nature. These include Abdul Haq Wasiq, the Taliban's deputy minister of intelligence, who describes being forcibly pressed into service and then promoted when his boss became ill. "[H]e told me to take his position until he got better. He got sick and didn't get better, so I continued doing the job. I confessed this and I will confess again. My job was against thieves and bribes; I was fighting against those kinds of people."[35] More plausibly, Mullah Norullah Noori acknowledged to his CSRT that he joined the Taliban and sometimes called himself a "soldier" but described his role as something closer to that of a civilian security guard. "I assured under the oath that against the United States or its allies, I never thought about fighting against them and I'm not thinking in the future to ever fight against them," he said.[36] At the margins, some of these cases may present a question under the laws of war, which do not treat civilian government workers as enemy fighters. In the case of the Taliban, which is a militia, that line is exceptionally difficult to draw. The type of hearing that might probe it meaningfully would require something far more calibrated and adversarial than the CSRTs.

A more sympathetic group is the thirteen detainees, nearly all Afghans, who claim—some quite plausibly—to have been forced against their will into low-level Taliban service. Abdul Rauf Aliza, for example, claimed that the Taliban threatened to take away his land unless he served them, so he carried food from a bakery to Taliban members.[37] Dawd Gul describes having been a brick maker whom the Taliban kidnapped and gave a gun. Since he could not shoot, he became an assistant to a Taliban cook.[38] Mohammed Sharif describes being taken forcibly by the Taliban from his village, something the Taliban did frequently to young men there. He would work twenty days or so every three months as a security guard, a cleaner, and a food and firewood carrier.[39] Under the rules of warfare, such people are ripe for capture and detention, just as they are—tragically—legitimate targets on the battlefield. As a matter of policy, however, assuming one believes their stories, locking them up for long periods of time makes little sense. The CSRT process treated them as enemy combatants. The ARB process, however, seemed relatively sensitive to the fact that impressed Taliban pose little danger to American forces. ARB hearings or other review mechanisms seem to have cleared all but two members of this group for either release or transfer.

A somewhat more complicated group of detainees—sixty-four in all— actively, sometimes passionately, denies affiliation with the Taliban or Al Qaeda yet nonetheless admits facts that strongly support their categorizations as enemy combatants. These detainees range a great deal in terms of the threat they likely pose. Fahed Nasser Mohamed, a Saudi detainee, denied in strong terms during his CSRT hearing that he had any relationship with the Taliban or Al Qaeda or that he had ever been to a terrorist training camp. He admitted, however, that he had gone to Afghanistan because "I met a man who told me about the idea of jihad" and "gave me the idea about fighting." While he claimed that his "opinion changed" after he got there and saw Afghans worshipping at graves, a practice he found religiously offensive, he nonetheless went to "a house" in Kabul "that was a cooking facility for the front line" and trained there on an AK47. He was captured as part of a surrender to Northern Alliance forces, escaped, and turned himself in again the following day.[40] Mohammed Ali Abdullah Bwazir of Yemen also refused to concede any affiliation with the enemy but did acknowledge traveling to Pakistan on a passport with a changed name, staying at a Taliban house in Quetta, and traveling to the front lines for humanitarian purposes in connnection with an Al Qaeda-linked charity. "Sometimes we visited the Taliban trenches" to preach, he told his ARB. "Yes, I've seen the Taliban and all I have for them is respect and love. They are not my enemies."[41] At the more dangerous end of the spectrum is Hafez Qari Mohamed Saad Iqbal Madni of Pakistan. He disclaimed to his CSRT any relationship with Al Qaeda, but acknowledged hanging out with major terrorist figures in Indonesia and boasting to them of his high-level Al Qaeda contacts. "To show that I was such a big person, I talked about Osama bin Laden and they asked me, did I see Osama bin Laden and I told them yes, when I was coming from Pakistan, I heard one of his announcements, in which he announced that the Muslims should not travel on non-Muslim airlines." His contacts, in turn, told him of their operational plans, including an effort the previous year to "blow up the American embassy in Jakarta." They also took him to a meeting where they were planning terrorist acts against hotels: "An American ambassador had a program in one of the hotels."[42] At the less dangerous end, a Pakistani named Zia Ul Shah acknowledged that he worked for the Taliban as a truck driver but only because they were the available employer; he always refused to enter combat areas, he claimed, and quit after September 11. Yet he also acknowledged driving a large group of Taliban fighters to surrender to Northern Alliance forces.[43]

Legally speaking, these sorts of admissions make detention decisions pretty easy. The laws of war permit the government to lock up the enemy, and these groups—even those claiming Taliban impressments—all acknowledge a level of affiliation with the enemy sufficient that the military would reasonably regard them as either fighting for the other side or directly and materially supporting the other side's fight. What's more, any regime the government might employ in place of or in addition to the laws of war—and I argue for a civilianized administrative detention regime in Chapter 7—would likewise permit noncriminal detention of many members of these groups. While in some instances, particularly the Taliban impressment cases, the policy and humanitarian arguments against long-term detention outweigh the security and intelligence benefits of holding people, these are prudential, not legal, considerations. Under one set of rules or another, American law does and should consider such people detainable for as long or as short a time as necessary to protect the country from them. There is, after all, no real dispute about the key fact at issue in any detention judgment: whether they have aligned themselves with the enemy. In the midst of an armed conflict, only a society whose Constitution truly is a suicide pact would require their freedom as a matter of law.

The legal question starts to get more difficult with the next group down the totem pole of admissions: those who deny membership but admit some nontrivial and yet nondispositive measure of affiliation. Some fourteen detainees, for example, admit to having stayed in Taliban or Al Qaeda housing but to nothing else. An additional fifteen admit to having spent time—often very short periods—in a training camp but not to any other activity indicative of membership. Thirty-three more admit to some other type of associational activity. Some claim to be refugees from the fighting in Afghanistan who traveled or camped with armed men fleeing the war zone. A Palestinian named Mahrar Rafat Al Quwari, for example, says he went to Afghanistan because he could live there without identification but fled to Tora Bora when the bombing started and Afghans began turning on Arabs. He worked briefly distributing food around the caves at Tora Bora but says he was never a part of the jihad.[44]

In many of these cases, it is easy to imagine that the government's classified evidence, were it available, would persuade one of a detainee's being properly categorized—there being a relatively narrow gap between a detainee's admissions and facts adequate to establish enemy combatant status. Yet unlike the cases of clearer admissions, there are at least some material issues of fact in dispute. Not everyone who spent time taking military-style training in Afghanistan was necessarily a Taliban fighter, after all. It's certainly possible that some recruits showed up, tested the waters, and realized that jihad was not for them. Likewise, some people who stayed in guest houses could have been prospective recruits, not actual ones, or even just guests. And some genuine refugees probably did get mixed in with the fighters in flight. In this group of cases, the government can draw partial support for its detention judgments from the statements of the detainees, but the statements don't get the military all the way home.

We come, then, to the many cases in which the detainees admit nothing. There are a few common themes among these 184 detainees, 160 of whom the CSRTs classified as enemy combatants. Twenty-three claim to have been doing charitable work, another 19 to have been teaching or studying the Koran. The rest are a mishmash of tales, plausible and tall. One man says he traveled to Afghanistan to escort his sister to her husband there.[45] Several say they went there to find better jobs.[46] Others traveled to Afghanistan or Pakistan for medical care.[47] Some went for family reasons,[48] out of attraction to the pure Islamic lifestyle of the Taliban's Afghanistan,[49] even for sightseeing purposes.[50] Compared to the detainee population at large, the deniers as a group seem to comprise a considerably smaller concentration of people whom the government portrays as foreign jihadist fighters and a significantly higher concentration of those it regards as Taliban operatives or leadership. Two of the high-value detainees transferred to Guantánamo in 2006 from the CIA's secret detention program—including Hambali, the operational chief of Al Qaeda's

Indonesian affiliate, Jemaah Islamiyah—deny the gravamen of government's allegations against them.[51] So do the preponderance of those the government set free as "no longer enemy combatants."

Many of the denying detainees are undoubtedly lying. In some cases, their stories are patently absurd; in others the circumstances under which American or allied forces captured the detainee belie his denial. An example of a simply incredible story is that of Bessam Muhammed Saleh Al Dubaikey, who claimed he traveled to Pakistan in the wake of September 11 to buy rare artifacts such as old coins. He ended up, however, buying a pair of mummies, which he sold on the Internet for a large sum of cash. He later hooked up with a man at a mosque, who turned out to be a leader in an Al Qaeda–linked charity, and the two traveled together looking for a group to which to donate the proceeds of the mummy sale—until they got arrested with ninety thousand dollars.[52] A Tajik man named Omar Hamzayavich Abdulayev was captured with three handwritten notebooks full of information about weapons systems, counterintelligence methods, chemistry, and poisons, and a small book listing the members of a jihadist group and the serial numbers of their weapons. Abdulayev claimed Pakistani intelligence officers forced him to copy down all this information, telling him he would go free if he did and beating him when he refused.[53] In many other cases, the stories have no obvious absurdities; they just ring false, and it's therefore easy to imagine the classified record resolving the preponderance of these cases on the government's side. In many instances, a more robust, more independent review mechanism would likely have made the same decisions as did the CSRTs but would have done so with far greater prestige.

This is not to say that all detainees are where they belong. In some instances, detainees' denials seemed alarmingly credible—particularly when coupled with especially thin government allegations. U.S. District Judge Joyce Hens Green, in one judicial opinion, expressed particular concern about the case of Murat Kurnaz, a Turk who lived as a permanent resident in Germany and whom the government accused of being a friend of a would-be suicide bomber and a part of a missionary organization called Jammat al Tabliq that Al Qaeda has infiltrated.[54] Kurnaz told his CSRT: "Now I hear Jamaat al Tabliq supports terrorism. I never knew that. . . . My reason for going to Pakistan wasn't to kill anyone or learn about weapons, it was to study Islam. In Germany, Islam was only taught on weekends; therefore, it would take a few years to learn what would only take a month in Pakistan." Kurnaz acknowledged a relationship with Selcuk Bilgin, the man suspected of participating in a suicide attack, but described the relationship as purely religious and nonviolent.[55] Bolstering the credibility of Kurnaz's statement is the fact that the government's classified evidence, which became public in 2005, seems terribly weak. In an excellent *Washington Post* article, reporter Carol D. Leonnig quoted accidentally declassified documents from American military intelligence, which had concluded that it had "no definite link/evidence of detainee having an association with Al Qaida or making any specific threat against the U.S." and was "not aware of evidence that Kurnaz was or is a member of Al Qaeda." Another document in Kurnaz's file, the *Post* reported, made clear that the "Germans confirmed this detainee has no connection to an al-Qaida cell in Germany." Even the suggestion that Bilgin was dirty turned out to be thin. German authorities never made a case against him. The German prosecutor who investigated him told the *Post* that there was no evidence of his being a suicide bomber and that authorities there had to drop the case. "We don't have proof the two wanted to go to Afghanistan or had any terrorist plans," he told Leonnig.[56] Kurnaz, after being found an enemy combatant by his CSRT and subject to continued detention in the first round of ARB hearings, was transferred to Germany and released following the second round of ARB hearings.[57]

Kurnaz's is not the only case in which a detainee's denial seems nonfrivolous. The government alleged that Abdul Razzak, an Afghan detainee, served as an "Al Qaida facilitator and smuggler," conducted an "escort mission" for Bin Laden, fought against the United States, "was a commander of a Taliban terrorist cell in Afghanistan," and "was involved in assassination attempts against Afghani government officials.[58] The detainee denied the allegations; while he acknowledged he had been forced to serve the Taliban as a driver early in the militia's rule, he claimed he had broken major opponents of the Taliban out of prison, opponents who later became significant figures in the government of Hamid Karzai. After that incident, he said, he fled the country and was abroad until after the Karzai government came to power.[59] Abdul Razzak never made headway with these claims in the military's review systems, and other detainees described serving under a Taliban commander named Abdul Razzak.[60] The detainee died of cancer at Guantánamo in late 2007. After his death, however, the *New York Times* published a report indicating that the man the paper called Abdul Razzaq Hekmati might have been telling the truth. Senior Afghan officials, including those whom the detainee had busted out of prison, described his case as a gross error and described him as a war hero against the Russians and a courageous opponent of the Taliban.[61] Given the shifting allegiances of Afghan factions, the murkey evidence, and the limitations of the CSRTs as a fact-finding mechanism, it would be surprising if more such cases did not exist.

In the majority of the denial cases, in fact, the detainee's statements are at least plausible, and the CSRTs were left resolving genuinely contested issues of fact, mostly in the government's favor. Particularly when dealing with detainees captured far from anything resembling a traditional battlefield setting, the tribunals had little credibility in carrying out this task. Perhaps the most troubling example of their failure here involved a group of six Algerian natives living in Bosnia. Bosnian authorities arrested them as an alleged Al Qaeda terrorist cell. And while the allegations against them were severe—one was supposedly a high-ranking operative in phone contact with Abu Zubaydah, and the group was suspected of plotting to bomb the American embassy in Sarajevo—the Bosnian courts ordered them freed for lack of evidence. Instead, authorities turned them over to the United States, which shipped them to Guantánamo, where the military held them based on intelligence data they could not attack. This evidence persuaded their CSRT panels, notwithstanding the detainees' strenuous denials. But the outsider has little basis to evaluate the integrity of what appears to be a series of civilian arrests outside of any combat setting.[62] In some instances, the CSRTs clearly struggled with the plausibility of detainee denials, and relatively weak evidence provoked dissents in the three-member CSRT panels' determination that a detainee met the criteria for detention. One such case involved Hassan Adel Hussein, a

Sudanese man accused of working for a pair of organizations the government later lamely claimed "may" be connected to Al Qaeda.[63] The detainee acknowledged in his ARB hearing that in his work in refugee camps, he saw Khalid Sheikh Mohammed from a distance and at one point worked for an organization run by Mohammed's brother, but he denied any connection to Al Qaeda.[64] The CSRT voted 2–1 to consider him an enemy combatant, though he was cleared for transfer by the first round of ARB hearings.[65] In some cases, CSRTs initially believed detainee denials and determined those detainees not to be enemy combatants, only to have the Pentagon order a do-over. New tribunals hearing new classified evidence then came to different conclusions.[66] Some of the cases, in short, are hard. Sometimes the CSRTs own processes and outcomes reflect the difficulty. In some cases, like Kurnaz's and Abdul Razzak's, the panels seem to have missed the difficulty. While I suspect that a more rigorous process would, in many cases, have ended up validating the government's detention choices, this is only an instinct—one based on seeing so many detainees telling such similar stories and the fact that it would have been an extraordinary coincidence indeed for the military's roundup of the enemy to have netted such a concentration of relief workers, students, teachers, job seekers and tourists as the detainees claim to be. I concede, however, that the facts do not compel this instinct. It is certainly possible that a significant fraction of these detainees are telling the truth, and it is positively likely that among those who are lying are a significant number about whom the government's classified evidence would fail to impress a reasonable fact finder under a more adversarial process.

The final large group of detainees is the 161 who have given no statement at all. For these detainees, we have only one side of the story: the government's. It is therefore difficult in general to draw conclusions about them. In some instances, as with the denials, the circumstances of a detainee's capture offer strong indication that his detention would pass muster. Some were captured with large groups of other fighters.[67] Others were part of significant Taliban surrenders.[68] Still others were captured in raids on safe houses in Pakistan, sometimes after firefights and sometimes in the company of senior Al Qaeda figures.[69] In a few other instances, like that of September 11 conspirator Ramzi

Binalshibh, one can safely assume based on the public record—including Binalshibh's own public statements—that the government would have no trouble establishing his amenability to detention, whatever process and standards it might use. All of these cases, however, represent the exceptions. In general, the cases without detainee statements represent a significant wild card. It is not clear how many of them would deny the allegations against them and how many are proudly enemies who simply chose not to dignify the CSRT and ARB processes with their participation. Nor do we know whether the government's evidence would satisfy a reasonable fact finder.

One final group of detainees warrants brief comment, for its members fit into none of the categories above: the Uighurs. In key respects, the Uighurs presented more of a policy problem than one of due process or fact-finding. In almost all of the twenty-two Uighur cases, the basic facts were not disputed: The Uighurs came to Afghanistan to train in order to fight for autonomy from the Chinese. By the standards to which the military subjected other foreign nationals who took training under the auspices of the Taliban, they clearly warranted the enemy combatant label. At the same time, they just as clearly had no interest in fighting against the United States and did not have much interest in international jihad either. Rather, they concerned themselves with their own regional conflict with a highly oppressive government. The CSRTs struggled with the Uighurs, some of whom they labeled as enemy combatants and some of whom they cleared; facing detainees who so tested the premises of the review mechanism, different tribunals reacted to them differently. That said, there was not much dispute over what should happen to them: Nobody really believed they should remain detained. The military itself had long been attempting to get rid of them and had cleared several for release or transfer even before the CSRTs took place. Effectuating this decision has presented a major logistical problem, because the Uighurs did not want to go back to China out of a reasonable fear of persecution and other countries proved unwilling to take them.[70] But from early on, in contrast to the other detainees, a basic consensus existed both as to who they were and as to what to do with them. By the time the first round of ARBs were completed, in fact, all but one of the Uighurs—the lone individual the government seems to have regarded as a part of enemy forces—had been cleared to leave.

All told, the public record supports the following breakdown of the government's enemy combatant determinations. In 27 percent of cases, the detainee's own statement validates his designation. In 3 percent of cases, notwithstanding a denial or no statement by the detainee, the alleged circumstances of his capture are so suggestive of belligerence that it seems overwhelmingly likely that the government has pegged him properly. In 1 percent of cases, detainees who deny or offer no statement concerning the allegations against them have faced criminal charges before military commissions, either the pre-MCA commissions or the more recent statutory tribunals—and should thus be considered reasonably detained pending trial. In 31 percent of cases, therefore, the public record one way or another supports the government's position with relative clarity. In an additional 11 percent of cases, the detainee's statement partially supports the designation, though not adequately to say comfortably that he is properly detained.

In 28 percent of cases, by contrast, the detainee gave a statement in which he denied affiliation with hostile forces and a contested issue of fact remains about his status. In 27 percent of cases, the detainee gave no statement and there exists no other basis to validate the government's claims.

This picture changes remarkably little when one examines the subset of Guantánamo detainees whom the government regarded as still requiring detention after the second round of ARBs. The percentage of detainees staying mum has risen a bit. The percentage of those whose detention the public record justifies in whole or in part has inched up. The percentage of those denying all allegations, conversely, has declined marginally.

What does change considerably in the subset of the population not cleared for release following the second ARB review is the severity of the government's allegations against the detainees. The percentage of the population the government describes as Al Qaeda's leadership doubles from 4 percent in the population subjected to CSRTs to 8 percent in the group that survived the second ARB process. The percentage the government casts as Al Qaeda operatives grows from 32 percent to 45 percent of the total, while the concentration of foreign fighters shrinks from 42 percent to 34 percent. The concentration of Taliban operatives drops in half, from 16 percent to 8 percent, while the concentration of Taliban leadership rises a small amount. In other words, more than half the population at Guantánamo the government insisted upon holding past the second ARB round falls into the three most serious categories of detainees: Al Qaeda and Taliban leadership and Al Qaeda operatives.

The change here would probably appear more dramatic were ongoing detention judgments purely a function of the given detainee's individual circumstances, but they're not. A big factor in whom the military releases is which foreign governments are willing and able to take responsibility for managing the risks they pose. The result is that all British detainees, even some whose files are pretty scary, have gone home, and Saudi detainees—once the second largest group at the base—are now scarce. But Yemenis, even some who seem to pose a less obvious threat than some of the Saudis and British who have gone home, continue to languish.[71]

That said, the administration has clearly taken big steps to concentrate the hard core at Guantánamo and send the bit players home. Officials were certainly stretching the truth when they declared the detainees at the base the "worst of the worst" in 2002. While the phrase still smacks of hyperbole, as a description of the population the government believes itself to be holding it approximates the truth today far more closely than it did when the White House actually said it.

IN SHORT, as a mechanism for adjudicating which detainees the government needed to hold on to and for how long, the review mechanisms the government set up almost certainly outperformed their dismal public reputation—probably by a country mile. The CSRT and ARB panels offered detainees a process considerably more generous than that required by the laws of war. Their members worked diligently and freed or transferred a lot of people. They also identified a large group of detainees about whose incarcerations no serious question of propriety should have existed. And they isolated that group of people about whom questions of fact remained. None of this comports with their public reputations as a meaningless layer of kangaroo court justice.

Yet if the goal was a review mechanism that would justify over the long term detention decisions to a public used to criminal justice norms and suspicious of arbitrary detentions of people not wearing enemy uniforms, these review processes failed utterly. They failed because detainees had too few procedural rights to challenge government allegations and offer their own evidence.[72] They failed because the government's evidentiary burden was so low that a finding that a given detainee was an enemy combatant meant literally no more than that he had failed to prove he was not one.[73] They failed because the decision-making panels had no independence from the military's chain of command and therefore could not credibly resolve contested factual matters in the government's favor without seeming merely to rubber stamp preexisting conclusions.[74] Perhaps most importantly, they failed because they operated in secret, so that both striking detainee admissions and the actions the panels took to free people remained almost entirely beneath the public radar.

A mature legal architecture would have done better: It would have given detainees sufficient procedural protections and set the government's evidentiary burden high enough that a finding in the government's favor would have meant something substantial. It would have employed a decision maker with sufficient independence that such a finding would have carried prestige and institutional heft. And it would have produced a public document explaining each decision so that the public need not argue about the many cases in which there existed no real dispute between the parties and might have understood the precise parameters of the contested questions at issue where a genuine dispute did exist. Such a process would surely have complicated the government's task. Charles Stimson, who oversaw detainee matters at the Pentagon for a spell, estimates that a more rigorous process, the creation of which he supports, would have freed about 200 detainees, instead of the 38 the CSRTs let go. In 50 of these cases, he guesses, that judgment would have reflected the actual status of wrongly classified detainees. In 150 additional cases, he suspects, the government had correctly identified detainees but would not have been able to prove a case adequately in a more court-like proceeding.[75] Other insiders believe this estimate high. But clearly, a fairer process that makes detention harder would generate less of it. Since the ARBs in any event sent home many of those whose detentions lay at the margins, those costs were probably not all that high in practice.

The administration's critics chronically portray the Guantánamo policy as lawless. This is the wrong vocabulary. The problems that plagued, and still plague, Guantánamo by and large did not stem from defiance of the law. They stemmed, rather, from a mismatch between the assumptions of the laws of war, which the administration tried to adapt for the task at hand, and the realities of that task, which required something more public, adversarial, and courtlike in character. This misunderstanding by administration critics of Bush's basic error led to a profound error in their own response: Instead of seeking to create a more appropriate regime, they went to court. In a perverse turn of their own, many critics actually came to *oppose* the creation of institutions better tailored to adjudicating war on terror detentions than the ones the administration had set up.[76] They came to see Congress, the one institution capable of delivering a system that might work better, as a device chiefly useful for giving judges free rein. And it was in those judges, not in the legislature, in whom they put their hopes.

Four

The Necessity and Impossibility of Judicial Review

To AMERICANS TODAY—particularly, but not exclusively, liberal Americans—any case against giving the courts a predominant role in setting rules to govern the war on terrorism involves a steep uphill climb. We live, after all, in an age of judicial power. Americans have grown comfortable with judges making all manner of decisions regarding contested, politically loaded questions. Judges decide abortion policy, the permissible use of race in university admissions and public school placements, whether gays can marry, how to count votes in elections, and countless other matters that affect Americans' day-to-day lives. Against this backdrop, it hardly seems a novelty that the courts might resolve questions arising over the legality of detentions, interrogations, and surveillance tactics—matters that lie at the core of any reasonable understanding of liberty and restraint on governmental power.

Yet the case against a dominant role for the judiciary in designing the legal architecture of the conflict is a strong one. The risks of a big judicial footprint in the war on terrorism are significant, far more significant than those who are keen to leverage judicial power as a counterweight to executive power acknowledge. What's more, the judiciary's capacity to design the kind of creative policies America needs in this conflict is exceptionally limited. Even as a check on the executive branch, the courts have proven erratic, useful more in spurring congressional action than in the restraint they have imposed themselves—for notwithstanding the popular mythology, they have not yet imposed much actual restraint. This is not to say that judges have *no* role in overseeing the legal architecture of the war. But their proper role is not every-thing that human rights advocates imagine it to be. And critically, it is not a leading role in the design of the architecture but, rather, an important one in the fabric of that architecture as designed by others.

Before turning to competing visions of what judicial review in this area ought to look like, let us step back for a moment and contemplate its reality to date—a reality that, more than six years after the September 11 attacks, has answered virtually none of the fundamental questions this conflict poses yet, in the very act of not answering those questions, has made the justices central players in counterterrorism policy. There is a yawning, though little-understood, chasm between the practical impact of the Supreme Court's deci-sions in this area so far and the potential implications of those decisions in the future—perhaps the near future—to justify more extensive judicial supervi-sion of war making. Taken on their own, the Court's pronouncements to date have been something less than dramatic. At the same time, they contain doc-trinal seeds of a far more aggressive judicial posture—one that several of the justices clearly regard as desirable. The Court, in other words, has loaded and cocked its gun, positioning itself for a veritable sea change in the relationship between the federal branches in wartime. Yet it has skillfully done so without closing off any policy options for either the executive branch or the legislature in the short term. It has not actually pulled the trigger.

Consider the manner in which the high court has decided the major en-emy combatant cases to date, particularly the *Rasul* case in 2004, in which it initially asserted jurisdiction over Guantánamo, and the *Hamdan* case in 2006, in which it struck down the administration's plans for military commis-sion trials there. In both instances, the Court's decisions operated at three dis-tinct layers simultaneously. On the surface, the rhetorical and most politically immediate level, the decisions represented a harsh rebuke of the administration and an attempt to rein it in. Go down a layer to the practical substantive importance of the decisions, however, and that rebuke looks like something of a feint—less than initially meets the eye. But still a level below that, at the layer of the tectonic plates of the relationship between the branches, the decisions paradoxically portend far *more* than meets the eye. All of these layers are real; all operate at once. And to understand what judicial review in the war on terror has been so far, its simultaneous triviality and momentousness, one needs to understand all three.

At the topmost layer, the one on which the press focused and which consequently dominated public understanding of the cases, the decisions operated as dramatic setbacks for the administration. The administration had, after all, urged the Court to refrain from asserting jurisdiction over Guantánamo, and the Court in *Rasul* did just that in unambiguous terms: "Aliens held at the base, no less than American citizens, are entitled to invoke the federal courts' authority." The administration fought tooth and nail for the proposition that an American citizen held domestically as an enemy combatant has no right to counsel and no right to respond to the factual assertions that justify his detention. The Court in *Hamdi,* however, held squarely that "a citizen-detainee seeking to challenge his classification as an enemy combatant must receive notice of the factual basis for his classification, and a fair opportunity to rebut the Government's factual assertions before a neutral decision-maker." It held as well that "[h]e unquestionably has the right to access to counsel" in doing so. The administration urged the Court once again two years later to refrain from asserting jurisdiction and to uphold the president's military commissions, yet the Court in *Hamdan* asserted jurisdiction again and struck down the commissions. These holdings led the *New York Times* to call the 2004 cases "a stinging rebuke" to the administration's policies, one that "made it clear that even during the war on terror, the government must adhere to the rule of law."[1] It declared *Hamdan* two years later a "victory for the rule of law" and "the latest in a series of rebukes to the Bush administration."[2] The three cases left the administration scrambling to alter its litigating positions, and they prompted changes in both law and administrative procedures.

One layer down, however, the rebukes appear somewhat less severe. Almost from the day *Hamdi* came down, in fact, a dissident analysis of the case of the Louisiana-born Taliban member saw it as a kind of victory for the administration dressed up in defeat's borrowed robes. As conservative commentators David B. Rivkin, Jr., and Lee A. Casey put it in the *Washington Post:*

> In the context of these cases, the Court accepted the following critical propositions: that the United States is engaged in a legally cognizable armed conflict with al Qaeda and the Taliban, to which the laws of war apply; that "enemy combatants" captured in the context of that conflict can be held "indefinitely" without criminal trial while that conflict continues; that American citizens (at least those captured overseas) can be classified and detained as enemy combatants, confirming the authority of the Court's 1942 [Nazi saboteurs case]; and that the role of the courts in reviewing such designations is limited. All these points had been disputed by one or more of the detainees' lawyers, and all are now settled in the government's favor.[3]

Even among those who celebrated the administration's defeat, this analysis had some resonance. The famed liberal constitutional theorist Ronald Dworkin, for example, began an essay on the cases by triumphantly declaring, "The Supreme Court has finally and decisively rejected the Bush administration's outrageous claim that the president has the power to jail people he accuses of terrorist connections without access to lawyers or the outside world and without any possibility of significant review by courts or other judicial bodies." But he then went on to acknowledge that the Court had "suggested rules of procedure for any such review that omit important traditional protections for people accused of crimes" and that the government "may well be able to satisfy the Court's lenient procedural standards without actually altering its morally dubious detention policies."[4]

Nobody would seriously argue that *Rasul* and *Hamdan* were secret wins for the president, but like *Hamdi,* the cases do, at this second level of analysis, have less bite than bark. In both, for starters, the Court acted on statutory, not constitutional, grounds, meaning that if Congress didn't like what the justices had to say, it could change the law. More importantly, in neither instance did the Court forbid the policy course the administration had sought to take by declaring the administration's substantive action unconstitutional.

Rasul, for example, was an entirely nonsubstantive decision. The Court asserted that, under then-current statutory authorities, it had the power to decide habeas corpus cases brought by detainees at the base. Nothing about the decision, however, precluded Congress from changing those authorities— narrowing the scope of the habeas statute to clarify that the administration had properly assumed in the first instance that no such jurisdiction existed. Indeed, this is precisely what Congress did in the DTA. Nor did the decision say anything about the answers to the legal questions that a court with juris- diction over those questions would ultimately have to address: what rights detainees might have or whether the government might be violating them. And the Court not only did not declare inappropriate military detentions of suspected terrorists, it declared in *Hamdi* precisely the opposite the very same day it handed down *Rasul.* In *Hamdi,* after all, a plurality of justices specifi- cally validated the military's authority to hold even an American citizen as an enemy combatant under certain circumstances.[5] *Rasul,* in short, said almost nothing about the executive's power to detain; it deals entirely with the judi- ciary's power to speak the final word.

The *Hamdan* decision had a similar flavor. Like *Rasul,* it conspicuously avoided forbidding the administration's proposed policy course: trial by tri- bunals lacking the full protections of traditional courts. Rather, the Court first found that it had jurisdiction to consider the military commissions question, notwithstanding the apparent bar in the DTA. It then ruled that the adminis- tration could not create military commissions without first going to Congress. Only the legislature, it ruled, could authorize the administration to contra- vene what the justices found to be the requirements of the Uniform Code of Military Justice and the Geneva Conventions. Once again, the Court conspic- uously avoided ruling that the Constitution precluded the military's policy—a holding that would have prevented the military from doing what it wanted. On the jurisdictional side, rather than ruling that Congress lacked the power to throw out cases from Guantánamo, it merely ruled that Congress hadn't in the DTA clearly ordered the courts to dismiss pending lawsuits, as well as prospective ones. As to the commissions, it held that they violated statutory and treaty law, but it stopped well short of either ruling that the Bill of Rights applied to these trials or that if it did, the commissions violated any of its provisions. So Congress felt at liberty to respond with the MCA, which addresses both of these points—clearly throwing out pending suits and authorizing military commissions with specific permission for derogations of conventional trial norms.[6] In other words, the administration's dramatic rhetorical setbacks in these cases amounted in practical terms merely to a few procedural hoops to jump through before doing as it wished.

The ultimate evidence that—at this intermediate level of analysis—the decisions do not do all that much is that notwithstanding these three highly publicized cases, all of the fundamental questions remain unanswered. If and when a new front in the war on terrorism opens and the military captures a new crop of detainees, any presidential administration will face very much the same quandaries as Bush faced in 2001 and 2002. Can the military warehouse at a military base abroad foreign citizens captured overseas without intrusive interference by American courts keen to protect their rights under either American or international law? What process must it grant to an American citizen it wishes to hold as an enemy combatant, and is that process different if the citizen is detained domestically by law enforcement rather than overseas by the military? Must such a person be granted immediate access to a lawyer or can he be held incommunicado for intelligence-gathering purposes? Are military commissions a viable form of trial in the modern age, given the last fifty years of developments in international law and American constitutional law? For all the court battles to date, none of these questions yet has an authoritative answer. And the courts have barely begun tackling second-order questions like how decades-old surveillance laws interact with powerful new technologies that permit the capture and processing of huge quantities of digital data traveling overseas. At this middle level of analysis, the Court's decisions aren't quite sound and fury signifying nothing, but they have signified a whole lot less than many people think.

But then there's the tectonic level, where the impact of the decisions is akin to the persistent grinding of plates deep within the San Andreas fault; the plates haven't slipped yet, but they're threatening to. Indeed, the Court's deepest impact to date has not lain in the substance of anything it has done but in its insistence on its own predominant role—the insistence that it has the final say. The decisions seem to threaten a completely different judicial posture in the war on terrorism, one that is a kind of mirror image of the executive power model the administration has adopted. Call it the judicial power model. Under this vision, which clearly attracts the Court's more liberal justices, the Court asserts the inherent authority to review executive military actions. It sets its own jurisdiction for such review without regard to the wishes of the two political branches or to the historical limits of judicial power. In the absence of clear substantive law to apply using that jurisdiction, the justices mold substantive rights for detainees out of international humanitarian-law principles the United States has either never embraced at all or never clearly implemented in its domestic statutes. And they claim that this power of review follows the American military wherever it goes around the world. This specter is not a paranoid conservative fantasy. It is one very plausible endpoint of the road on which the justices set off in *Rasul.* It would represent a tremendous shift in the balance of power among the branches of government during wartime—and a disaster for the institution of the presidency against which any reasonable executive-branch lawyer would try to protect his client. At this most speculative level of analysis, *Rasul* and *Hamdan* portend a rebuke even more extreme than the top-level beating the press understood.

The explanation for the disparity between the substantive and tectonic levels—the difference between what the Court actually did and the posture it threatened—lies in the specific manner in which it crafted its opinions. While the Court has so far acted on statutory grounds only, it also intimated without deciding in both *Rasul* and *Hamdan* that a more fundamental basis for its jurisdiction exists. In *Rasul,* for example, Justice John Paul Stevens, having determined that the habeas statute reached Guantánamo, added the following curious paragraph:

> Application of the habeas statute to persons detained at the base is consistent with the historical reach of the writ of habeas corpus. At common law, courts exercised habeas jurisdiction over the claims of aliens detained within sovereign territory of the realm, as well as the claims of persons detained in the so-called "exempt jurisdictions," where ordinary writs did not run, and all other dominions under the sovereign's control. As Lord Mansfield wrote in 1759, even if a territory was "no part of the realm," there was "no doubt" as to the Court's power to issue writs of habeas corpus if the territory was "under the subjection of the Crown." . . . Later cases confirmed that the reach of the writ depended not on formal notions of territorial sovereignty, but rather on the practical question of "the exact extent and nature of the jurisdiction or dominion exercised in fact by the Crown."

This paragraph is a kind of time bomb, a marker that did nothing in the short run but may do everything in the longer term. Scholars agree that the courts have some form of habeas jurisdiction as an inherent feature of their existence; the Constitution makes explicit reference to habeas, implying that it must exist in some form as part of the fabric of law the Constitution made indelible.[7] Case law and commentary alike suggest that this inherent jurisdiction coincides with the habeas reach of the courts at the time the new states ratified the Constitution—what lawyers call "at common law." So Stevens is here suggesting that if the habeas statute did not reach overseas detainees like those at Guantánamo, the Constitution might create jurisdiction over them anyway. Similarly, in *Hamdan,* the Court reserved the question of whether constitutionally based jurisdiction would have existed even had the DTA's jurisdiction-stripping provisions applied to the case. It once again altered the legislative status quo, making its own power a matter of statutory default and forcing Congress to write it out of the picture if it chose—even as it held out the possibility that such legislation might be futile and that the Court would then fall back on a more fundamental legal basis for intervention.

Whether the votes exist on the Supreme Court to go this extra step we will find out soon enough. In December 2007, the Court heard oral arguments in *Boumediene v. Bush,* which asked whether the MCA violated the Constitution in stripping the courts of all habeas jurisdiction over Guantánamo.[8] But this current round of Supreme Court decision making, like its two predecessors, will probably not finally resolve the basic questions. Even if the Court does assert a constitutional basis for its jurisdiction over Guantánamo—that is, a jurisdiction that Congress cannot take away—that would not necessarily imply that subsequent cases have any merit, that either American or international law gives detainees at the base any substantive rights the military is failing to honor. Saying that a court may *consider* a detention is quite different from saying that the detention at issue has some legal defect. Notwithstanding the efforts of lawyers for the detainees, the current round of litigation will likely leave unresolved the question of what rights detainees have and how to apply those rights.[9]

It is also likely to leave open the mother of all jurisdictional questions: whether the Court's overseas jurisdiction extends *beyond* Guantánamo. Because of the oddity of Guantánamo, an American military facility located permanently in a hostile country yet leased in perpetuity to exclusive American jurisdiction and control, the Court's decision regarding detentions there could well end up being more of a quirk of Guantánamo itself than anything else. The justices' flirtations with undertaking a major role in overseeing wartime detentions would be relatively insubstantial if their power ultimately depended on the peculiar status of the Cuban base. The administration could then simply weigh the inconvenience of subjecting detentions to the judicial review that would flow from that particular choice of detention site and, if it finds the prospect too onerous, bring no more detainees to the facility and use other overseas detention options instead.

Yet the justices have also laid the groundwork for a far more aggressive intervention in overseas military affairs. *Rasul* ever so carefully elided the question of whether its holding ultimately depended on any specific feature of Guantánamo itself, and the Court certainly left itself wide space to hold otherwise. "Petitioners contend that they are being held in federal custody in violation of the laws of the United States. No party questions the District Court's jurisdiction over petitioners' custodians," Justice Stevens wrote. The habeas law, "by its terms, requires nothing more." By this logic, the courts might hear cases from Iraq or anywhere else in the world as easily as from Guantánamo.

The Court's holdings, in short, do nothing and everything all at once. Read narrowly, they neither preclude nor require any particular policy. They do not create substantive rights for overseas detainees either based on the Constitution or based on international law (except in the sense, since altered by Congress, that *Hamdan* interpreted provisions of the Uniform Code of Military Justice as implementing a portion of the Geneva Conventions). They don't even require that judicial review be an operative feature of any set of legal rules. As Justice Stephen Breyer put it in *Hamdan,* "The Court's conclusion ultimately rests upon a single ground: Congress has not issued the Executive a 'blank check.' . . . Indeed, Congress has denied the president the legislative authority to create military commissions of the kind at issue here. Nothing prevents the president from returning to Congress to seek the authority he believes necessary." Taken at its word, the Court is merely interpreting statutes so as to force a measure of congressional involvement in policy making, a congressional okay before the president can do what he had previously tried to do on his own.

The Bush administration has consistently chosen to take the Court at its word, notwithstanding the judiciary's obviously shifting premises. As a consequence of his administration's ideological commitment to the executive power model for the war, Bush has developed an impressively long line of perverse refusals to hedge his legal bets against the assertion of judicial power by a court clearly contemplating a major expansion of its authority in this arena. He sought and received from Congress a law under which habeas corpus is tightly constrained and judicial review otherwise limited. He reconstituted his military commissions. He sought clarification from Congress that the Court's application of the Geneva Conventions to the conflict with Al Qaeda need not necessitate any change in interrogation policy and that all but the most severe violations of the conventions in any event do not constitute war crimes under American domestic law. And critically, confronted with a Court that openly flirts with an active posture in this conflict, he did little to ensure that the government's treatment of detainees warrants the kind of deference for which he asks.

It remains to be seen whether all of this will satisfy the Court. I, for one, very much doubt it will. At a minimum, Bush has played a very dangerous game for the future of the executive power his administration holds so dear. After all, it is hard for a court to defer when there is nothing, or little, to defer to. And under the architecture the administration has in large part built on its own and in small part won from Congress, detainees are coming before the courts having had only cursory hearings with no assistance from counsel, making allegations of horrific mistreatment, and facing the prospect of detention for life without a full opportunity to present their cases in court. Whatever inclination to restraint the Court might have—and it isn't much of one—will be sorely tested the more such cases the justices see.

THE BROAD VISION of judicial power in the overseas fight against terrorists has two interconnected sources. One involves the right of individuals detained to their day in court. The other involves the power of the courts themselves to review administrative action for compliance with legal norms the administration may be flouting. That is, judicial review of wartime detentions is seen, depending on the argumentative context, both as a means of holding government accountable to the law and as a means of vindicating and freeing innocent people who may have been erroneously detained. Both of these purposes have strong claims on the American conscience, for we are a society of law and a society whose specific vision of law historically emphasizes procedural justice. But neither purpose quite justifies the kind of pervasive judicial review we take for granted elsewhere in American life, in which a person aggrieved by a supposedly illegal or unconstitutional law or policy can haul the government into court to justify it and—if the government cannot do so compellingly—have it declared inoperative.

There is, for starters, the problem of the complainants—or victims, if you prefer—of the supposedly illegal actions under challenge. With a few isolated exceptions, they have all been aliens overseas. And one should pause at least a moment to consider by what right an alien with no connection to this country save the alleged desire to destroy it may haul its sovereign into its own courts to press legal claims. One can engage this question, as the federal courts are now busily doing, at the level of legal doctrine or consider it at a more philosophical level. Both approaches, in my view, should lead to the same conclusion: that no such right exists, and that we should therefore consider the scope of judicial review in this area as a matter of legislative policy, not a question of constitutional command, inherent judicial power, or the historical reach of the writ of habeas corpus. Based on the performance of the justices to date in *Rasul* and *Hamdan*, I fully expect the Supreme Court to reject my view.

The doctrinal question, for all the smoke thrown up around it, is not a hard one. As I noted earlier, the Supreme Court confronted the problem of federal court jurisdiction over enemy aliens overseas in 1950, when it considered the case of German prisoners of war convicted of war crimes by American military commissions. In that case, Justice Robert Jackson decisively rejected the notion that his Court's power extended that far, writing, as quoted earlier, "Nothing in the text of the Constitution extends such a right, nor does anything in our statutes." In *Rasul*, the Court backhandedly overruled this case, *Johnson v. Eisentrager*, on the statutory point, at least as to detainees at Guantánamo—holding that the habeas statute did grant it jurisdiction over those held at the base. The justices are now considering the constitutional question as well.

There was, to put it simply, nothing legally extraordinary about the administration's insistence in 2002 that the Court's jurisdiction has geographical boundaries; at least until *Rasul*, it was the Court's insistence as well. Indeed, it has become fashionable to tag the Bush administration with lawlessness for creating a "legal black hole" at Guantánamo, a place where no law reigns save the executive branch's will. But this reading has always seemed odd and more than a little ungenerous. In the genuine crisis that followed September 11, the administration relied on the clearly stated view of an esteemed personage of the Supreme Court's history, writing a majority opinion in a quite famous holding of the Court itself. It assumed, in short, that it could take the Supreme Court at its word. This tempting of fate by relying on *Eisentrager* so long was certainly foolish. But the administration's reading of the law was, doctrinally speaking, far from lawless; it was the reading most faithful to history and precedent.

This understanding of the law, moreover, reflects a philosophical understanding of the function of courts that warrants, in my opinion, something other than the opprobrium of all decent people. The Constitution is a social compact among the people and the states to create a national government to govern them. An American citizen is party to that compact wherever she goes in the world, and therefore retains a claim on the adjudicatory power of the courts when mistreated by her government abroad. The alien domestically is, to a lesser but still considerable degree, also party to the compact—subject to American law, entitled to many of its rights and protections, and therefore entitled as well to have its courts resolve her disputes with its sovereign. But not *everyone* in the world is a party to that compact. Indeed, it's hard to see why the Constitution promises people so wholly outside of the American social compact as Al Qaeda or Taliban operatives overseas any of its benefits. This is why Justice Jackson waxed so incredulous in *Eisentrager* when addressing the possibility that an enemy alien who had never set foot in the United States might have recourse to its courts. "[E]ven by the most magnanimous view," he wrote,

> our law does not abolish inherent distinctions recognized throughout the civilized world between citizens and aliens, nor between aliens of friendly and of enemy allegiance, nor between resident enemy aliens who have submitted themselves to our laws and nonresident enemy aliens who at all times have remained with, and adhered to, enemy governments.

Jackson was thinking in the terms of his era, when enemy aliens were citizens of enemy countries. But change the wording only a little and his point remains as pertinent today as it was more than five decades ago. Why, we should ask, should Al Qaeda and Taliban operatives abroad have the privilege of invoking the jurisdiction of American courts?

I can conceive of only two possible answers to this question, and they are closely related. The first is that the Constitution binds the executive branch wherever in the world it operates, and that judicial review must necessarily follow. The second is that judicial review somehow flows from the fact of detention by American forces. Someone who suffers injury at the hands of an America behaving illegally under its own or international laws, in other words, has a claim on its legal system that a normal foreigner abroad would not have. But both of these arguments, if accepted, would prove too much. The family of a person killed in an errant missile attack has suffered a great deal more than someone merely detained, and the victim of that strike has certainly been subject to the exertion of American power no less subject to the Constitution than the person detained. Yet at least under current doctrine, neither the alien's injury nor the illegality of the government's conduct that led to the tragedy—however egregious the illegality may have been—would induce the courts to entertain a wrongful-death suit by such a family. There are untold numbers of people abroad who might ascribe their misfortunes, real or imagined, to American governmental behavior alleged to defy legal norms. Why is this area so different that jurisdiction unthinkable in those instances is constitutionally required here?

I don't mean to make a camel's-nose-under-the-tent argument—that allowing habeas jurisdiction will lead willy-nilly to extensive judicial supervision of war planning. I don't doubt that the judiciary could open the door just a crack and entertain habeas claims but not others. The Court, for example, could tie its power to the unique situation of Guantánamo or it could hold that detention differs so fundamentally from other exertions of governmental power that the Constitution specifically limits the power of Congress to suspend habeas corpus. There would, however, be little principled reason to make these distinctions. To advocate that the courts treat detentions differently allows the extent to which the reach of courts to overseas detentions and interrogations is a policy question, and not—unless one is truly willing to open the floodgates—a question of principle. Those advocating the judicial power model for the war on terrorism merely wish to shift the forum for that policy judgment from Congress to the courts themselves.

A broad conception of judicial review in this conflict also suffers from an unrealistic assessment of judicial competence and capacity to evaluate military actions. This is true partly because of the limits of judges as people untrained in military matters and the limits of evidence collected in a fashion so far removed from the one to which judges are accustomed. Even when the military uses evidence it did not obtain through any untoward coercion, it will generally not have observed such standard law enforcement practices as preserving chains of custody of physical evidence. Society asks a lot of a judge who has never been to Afghanistan, who has never served in the military, and who has no intimacy with the day-to-day conduct of its overseas antiterrorism operations to decide not merely how to handle a morass of evidence of questionable probative value about a detainee who may pose an extreme danger if allowed to walk free but also to make up the rules and standards under which he will consider that evidence. The temptation among some judges in that situation, understanding their own limitations, will be to defer absolutely to the military's judgment. Other judges, like the carpenter whose only tool is a hammer and for whom every problem therefore resembles a nail, will try to apply criminal justice evidentiary standards to combat operations. The public should find neither reaction an appealing prospect.

There's a deeper problem still, one to which I have alluded before: International conflict resists the principled application of legal rules of the sort that judges are, at their best, adept at managing. We don't like to admit this. An entire vocabulary has grown up around trying to impose the civilized language of law on warfare and international operations more generally. Such vocabulary is useful, moral, worthy, and therefore important in its own way. Yet it also creates a certain confusion, for we don't mean quite the same thing by "law" here as we do in civilian contexts. The principles are fuzzier—tinged with caveats that amount to "except when we really have to" or "it's different when our guys do it." We embrace this kind of hypocrisy, because it's the least bad option. Is anyone genuinely sorry that the Allies did not free the Nuremberg defendants on grounds that their conduct was legal—even required—by the laws of their society at the time and that laws under which the tribunals condemned them were after-the-fact creations? Of course not. But neither does any democrat who believes in a civilized legal system want to import such a norm into the domestic justice system. Does anyone really believe that because the laws of war condemn the spies and saboteurs who operate covertly behind enemy lines, America should forswear the covert gathering of human intelligence during wartime? Of course not. But neither should we relish eroding the protections due to soldiers by accepting a norm in which people can fight out of uniform.

Then there's the small matter of Abraham Lincoln, savior of the Union, liberator of the slaves—one of the few Americans who accomplished the most for human freedom. Yet early in his presidency, Lincoln found himself in confrontation with the Chief Justice of the United States, Roger B. Taney, over the freedom of a single man—a secessionist sympathizer named John Merryman. Union troops had arrested Merryman in Baltimore, where restive Southern sympathizers had violently interfered with Lincoln's efforts to ship northern troops southwards to the front. Merryman's lawyers had gone to Taney for a writ of habeas corpus, whereupon the army had announced—on Lincoln's orders—that habeas corpus had been suspended in Maryland. Taney responded with a blistering opinion, accusing the army of tyranny and violating all manner of constitutional prohibition and demanding that the president do his duty and rein it in. Lincoln defied him.

Consider the two men's words side by side nearly a century and a half later. Wrote Taney:

> The Constitution provides . . . that "no person shall be deprived of life, liberty, or property, without due process of law." It declares that "the right of the people to be secure in their persons, houses, papers and effects, against unreasonable searches and seizures shall not be violated, and no warrant shall issue, but upon probable cause, supported by oath or affir-

mation, and particularly describing the place to be searched, and the persons or things to be seized." It provides that the party accused shall be entitled to a speedy trial in a court of justice.

These great and fundamental laws, which Congress itself could not suspend, have been disregarded and suspended, like the writ of habeas corpus, by a military order, supported by force of arms. Such is the case now before me, and I can only say that if the authority which the Constitution has confided to the judiciary department and judicial officers, may thus, upon any pretext or under any circumstances, be usurped by the military power, at its discretion, the people of the United States are no longer living under a government of laws, but every citizen holds life, liberty and property at the will and pleasure of the army officer in whose military district he may happen to be found.

In such a case, my duty was too plain to be mistaken. I have exercised all the power which the Constitution and laws confer upon me, but that power has been resisted by a force too strong for me to overcome. It is possible that the officer who has incurred this grave responsibility may have misunderstood his instructions, and exceeded the authority intended to be given him; I shall, therefore, order all the proceedings in this case, with my opinion, to be filed and recorded in the circuit court of the United States for the district of Maryland, and direct the clerk to transmit a copy, under seal, to the president of the United States. It will then remain for that high officer, in fulfillment of his constitutional obligation to "take care that the laws be faithfully executed," to determine what measures he will take to cause the civil process of the United States to be respected and enforced.[10]

Lincoln responded in a message to Congress on July 4, 1861:

Soon after the first call for militia, it was considered a duty to authorize the commanding general, in proper cases, according to his discretion, to suspend the privilege of the writ of habeas corpus, or, in other words, to arrest and detain, without resort to the ordinary processes and forms of law, such individuals as he might deem dangerous to the public safety. This authority has purposely been exercised but very sparingly. Nevertheless, the legality and propriety of what has been done under it are questioned, and the attention of the country has been called to the proposition that one who is sworn to "take care that the laws be faithfully executed," should not himself violate them. Of course some consideration was given to the questions of power, and propriety, before this matter was acted upon. The whole of the laws which were required to be faithfully executed, were being resisted, and failing of execution in nearly one-third of the States. Must they be allowed to finally fail of execution, even had it been perfectly clear, that by the use of the means necessary to their execution, some single law, made in such extreme tenderness of the citizen's liberty, that practically, it relieves more of the guilty, than of the innocent, should, to a very limited extent, be violated? To state the question more directly, are all the laws *but one* to go unexecuted, and the government itself go to pieces, lest that one be violated? Even in such a case, would not the official oath be broken, if the government should be overthrown, when it was believed that disregarding the single law, would tend to preserve it?[11]

How many human rights activists today realize they are deploying the same arguments that Taney, one of history's villains for his authorship of the infamous *Dred Scott* decision, deployed back then?[12] And would they wish in retrospect that their arguments had prevailed during his confrontation with Lincoln during the Civil War? Law has a big place in wartime, indeed a growing place. Lawyers play an ever-escalating role in the military, and this is not mere window dressing. Militaries in democratic societies feel increasingly bound by laws that operate as very real constraints on their behavior. All of this tends to disguise the facts that law can never fully regulate international conflict the way it regulates more civilized projects and that the process of applying law to warfare changes law as much as it changes warfare. Legal principles inevitably become a bit more malleable, a bit less like comparable legal principles in the civilian arena. Necessity breeds exceptions, situations in which principled rules don't apply because they can't apply—unless, that is, the principle in question is the ugly one that the ends justify the means. Judges are exactly the wrong people to ask permission to break the rules, either because they will refuse (as Taney did) in situations in which the president cannot honor the refusal or because they will acquiesce to steps that the judiciary ought not permit and certainly ought not cloak in the respectability of law. Such acquiescence is, in reality, more the norm than the exception in the history of warfare. The most famous example is the internment of Japanese Americans during World War II, whose legitimacy the Supreme Court, to its great shame, blessed.[13] But this is not the only example. The courts also tolerated the persecution of socialist dissenters during World War I, to cite another.[14] When judges oversee wartime executive action, they err in both directions—both by interfering with arguably necessary ugliness, as Taney did, and by blessing the most unholy of excesses.

Consider now the interrogations of Khalid Sheikh Mohammed and certain other high-value detainees. To subject such decisions to the broad form of judicial review that human rights advocates demand requires one of two steps. One can either truly subject them to principled rule, or one can ask judges to behave like consequentialists and validate with the imprimatur of law the ugly decisions the executive branch sometimes has to make. The first option is, in practical terms, not going to happen: What president, sworn to protect America from threats foreign and domestic, is really going to forgo the information the highest-value detainees may have stored in their brains? Presidents do not err on the side of restraint in those situations on which they believe that country's ultimate fate depends.

The second option, asking judges to okay those decisions, should be at least as uncomfortable as the possibility of a more modest conception of the judicial function in the current conflict. To go back to the capture of Auschwitz commandant Rudolf Hoess, would we really want a panel of judges, far from the action and with no conception of how vulnerable Hoess's wife might have been to more traditional interrogation, to declare that those British soldiers' agonizingly coercive interrogation of her was lawful? Would we really prefer that the interrogation had not taken place and Hoess gone free? Or are we perhaps content with what happened? The interrogation happened, the British caught Hoess, and no court anywhere had to stamp its approval on an ugly action. There is an honorable place for judicial silence—one that too-easy recourse to the courts obliterates—a place that neither precludes nor validates options. When the Supreme Court, as it has done since September 11, positions itself as a central actor in the design of the rules of the war on terror, it risks obliterating its capacity for silence. Those who cheer its incipient but growing role need to think hard about whether they want in the future the courts to be obliged—by the very nature of their role in society—to pronounce on the capture of Rudolf Hoesses.

Indeed, if we don't leave judges space for silence, we will end up either paralyzing our response to terrorism or corrupting the judiciary. We will have to decide as a society whether we want to prohibit highly coercive interrogation in all circumstances or to put judges in charge of it. If we are entirely honest, the answer to this question, which I address in Chapter 7, is that we don't want to prohibit it in all circumstances—but that we just as surely don't want to say that, much less write it into our laws. Insulating judges from such questions offers a measure of permission for a kind of constructive hypocrisy that allows us more restrictive rules than we could probably otherwise afford. The gaps let us ban torture and conduct just shy of it, and when we need to practice it anyway, protect those we ask to do the dirty work from branding as war criminals. That hypocrisy, so deplored by human rights groups, seems to me valuable. It's a messy marriage of the twin facts that, on the one hand, no society can survive in the long run while shrinking from the steps necessary to secure its survival and, on the other hand, that some of these steps are ones of which no democracy can be proud.

All of this, the liberal or human rights advocate will argue, is pretty speculative stuff. There is no evidence so far that judicial review has impeded the war on terrorism in any significant respect. This person might challenge us to identify any horror stories of intelligence lost or terrorists escaping capture because of the inhibitions imposed by judges—or self-imposed by the executive because of the fear of judges. Rather, she might point out, the effect of habeas so far has been salutary: sustained pressure on the administration to move toward a fairer and more accountable system. In contrast, abuses by the military and the CIA—Abu Ghraib, the secret prisons program, and waterboarding being the most infamous—are far from speculative. They are very real. Given this balance, it seems perverse to focus on hypothetical dangers posed by the judiciary, rather than actual dangers posed by the executive— dangers against which enhanced judicial power offers a check.

We should give this critique its due. Those critical of the administration's executive power approach to the war on terror can criticize only awkwardly the one governmental institution that has pushed back. With Congress content for so long to duck responsibility for policy choices the federal government had no choice but to make, the alternative to some assertion of judicial power may have been an unchecked executive—or, rather, one checked only by political constraints. In the face of that reality, perhaps even-handed, pox-on-both-houses criticism is unfair. What's more, a broad concept of judicial review could prove harmless to the executive's operational flexibility in the long run. Other countries, most notably Israel, have confronted terrorism with comparatively robust judicial oversight and have not tied their own hands unduly.[15]

Yet this critique is valid only because judicial review has so far amounted to so little in practical terms. Judges, as I noted earlier, have not foreclosed options to the administration, either by forcing the release of detainees or by indelibly imposing legal regimes that would actually inhibit robust action. And it is a perverse defense indeed of the practical workability of a robust conception of judicial review to point out that it hasn't, in fact, constrained executive action. Were judges to begin imposing real restraints—as the developing doctrine portends—we must anticipate that those restraints would carry consequences. While I do not doubt that the political impact of the judiciary's involvement so far has been constructive in a number of ways, we cannot ignore the threats it might carry. Unchecked judicial power poses a different threat to democratic government than does unchecked executive power. It can be hard to appreciate when judges are acting as the first line of defense against executive excess. But we ignore it at our peril.

Indeed, this critique ironically points to one other reason for skepticism of habeas review as a promising strategy for protecting innocent people swept up in the war on terror: It hasn't quite worked that way. Since the first detainees came to Guantánamo in the wake of the American intervention in Afghanistan, habeas litigation has proceeded continuously up and down all levels of the federal court system. Taken together, these hundreds of cases have produced orders to release zero detainees. They have admittedly served the important function of forcing the administration to moderate its policies, to pursue diplomatic options for repatriating detainees, to put in place administrative structures that more rigorously assess the detainee population, and to go to Congress to get certain rules written into law. The political pressures and the new administrative structures have, as we have seen, led to the release of hundreds of detainees. But it is important to identify what all of this litigation has not accomplished: For the person erroneously or unnecessarily detained at Guantánamo, access to federal courts has not meant freedom. It has at most pushed the policy process toward the creation of review procedures that have meant freedom. If one's goal is ultimately a legal architecture that more clearly and reliably separates the combatant from the noncombatant, it is on the integrity of those procedures that one should focus.

IF ONE TAKES the preceding analysis remotely seriously, one begins to understand the seductive temptation the executive power view of the conflict held for the administration. Why not simply treat the current conflict as, like previous wars, an executive branch affair different from the wars of the past only in requiring *greater* flexibility and creativity on the part of the president and his agents? Why not accept that the proper place of judicial review is, therefore, highly limited, perhaps even nonexistent? Why not accept that whatever legal structures ought to govern the conflict, they ought not involve the courts? The answer, to put it bluntly, is that this vision requires accepting the idea of war as an adequate legal model for modern counterterrorism. For the reasons described earlier, I do not accept this premise. The administration can kid itself that it is merely applying the laws of war, but as detailed in the previous chapter, something else is going on too: decisions as to the justice of long-term imprisonments based on facts alleged by the government and disputed by the accused.

And that is a subject that judges know something about.

In tacit recognition of the hybrid nature of the war on terror, the imperfect applicability of both the rules of warfare and the rules of criminal justice, the administration's position has actually moved considerably in recent years. Early on, it advocated a pure view of executive power, one in which the president wielded authorities inherent in his constitutional role as commander in chief of the military and required no congressional backing other than Congress's initial authorization to use force against Al Qaeda. In this view, the judiciary played no legitimate role at all.[16] Following *Rasul,* however, the administration accepted a limited form of appeal for detention-related judgments to the D.C. Circuit Court of Appeals. The result is that verdicts from military commissions are subject to judicial review, as are detention determinations by the CSRTs. These types of appeals are only just beginning. The commissions have so far convicted only one detainee, David Hicks, who accepted a plea deal and therefore waived his appeals. The other detainees pursued their habeas actions until exhausting that option before resorting to the D.C. Circuit appeals that Congress had given them to challenge their detentions. The vitality of this category of appeals, therefore, remains very much up in the air. Still, judicial appeals are now part of the system into which the administration and Congress have together stumbled. Some form of judicial review of detentions is now a matter of near consensus.

But the administration's acceptance of a role for the judicial branch is more of a grudging concession to political and jurisprudential reality than an effort to imagine the optimally effective judicial involvement. And the judicial oversight the law now contemplates is limited. Under the DTA, the courts may evaluate "whether the status determination of the Combatant Status Review Tribunal with regard to [the detainee] was consistent with the standards and procedures specified by the Secretary of Defense for Combatant Status Review Tribunals (including the requirement that the conclusion of the Tribunal be supported by a preponderance of the evidence and allowing a rebuttable presumption in favor of the Government's evidence). . . ." To "the extent the Constitution and laws of the United States are applicable," the law also allows the courts to examine "whether the use of such standards and procedures to make the determination is consistent with the Constitution and laws of the United States."[17]

Because the CSRT procedures are not especially rigorous, compliance with them is not necessarily comforting. The D.C. Circuit judges hearing the first round of CSRT appeals have indicated that they do not mean simply to sign off on CSRT findings, but see their review as relatively probing—a view that may trigger a new round of Supreme Court litigation.[18] Nonetheless, one can easily imagine a detainee slipping through a CSRT appeal as a result of bad intelligence he was unable effectively to rebut. The most basic deficiency is that under the DTA, the Court reviews the CSRT's record but hears no evidence itself. Given that the detainees have essentially no opportunity to present evidence to the tribunals, this structure leaves judicial review of the record closed too early. A lawyer for Guantánamo detainees concluded his arguments in *Boumediene* on behalf of restored habeas by using the case of Murat Kurnaz—the probably innocent German detainee discussed earlier—to make exactly this point:

> [Kurnaz] was told, two years after he was detained . . . he was told at his CSRT, as many of these individuals were not, that he was being held because he associated with a known terrorist. And he was told the name.
>
> He was told that he associated with somebody called Seljuk Bilgen [Selcuk Bilgin] who, the government contended, was [a] terrorist, who . . . had blown himself up while Mr. Kurnaz was in detention . . . in a suicide bombing; and all that Mr. Kurnaz could say at his CSRT where he had no lawyer and had no access to information was I never had any reason to suspect he was a terrorist. Well, when the government, in the habeas proceedings, filed its factual return in [Kurnaz's habeas case], it filed as its factual return the CSRT record. His counsel saw that accusation. Within 24 hours, his counsel had affidavits not only from the German prosecutor but from the supposedly deceased Mr. Bilgen, who is a resident of Dresden never involved in terrorism and fully getting on with his life. . . . [A]nd that evidence would not have been allowed in under DTA review. It wouldn't have been in the CSRT, and it won't come in under DTA review. And that's why it is inadequate.[19]

It's a serious problem with the current system. And since subsequent decisions by the ARBS are subject to no judicial review at all, the combined consequences of restricting habeas and creating only an emasculated alternative form of judicial review of CSRT judgments are very great indeed.

Nor is the authorization for the D.C. Circuit to review the CSRT procedures for compliance with American statutory or constitutional law terribly useful. It isn't clear what American law applies to aliens at Guantánamo; that fact is precisely what enabled the administration to make up its own set of rules in the first place. In fact, the D.C. Circuit has already declared that the Constitution provides *no* judicially cognizable rights to detainees at the base.[20] The absence of applicable law is, in fact, the heart of the entire problem. Merely authorizing the courts to apply whatever law may exist neatly avoided the admittedly difficult step that might have helped: legislating new rules to govern a novel situation. Judicial review without clear underlying rules can predictably serve neither the cause of separating the combatant from the civilian nor the cause of holding the executive to the rule of law. The rule of law, after all, presupposes some law to rule. The paucity of any completed appeals under this provision to date makes it unclear how, in practice, the mechanism will function. But the fear of human rights groups that it will not prove adequate seems at least somewhat justified. In the absence of any clear statutory standards, it could operate as a recipe for judicial deference to weak executive procedures—that is, unless judges grow uncomfortable and mold it into a device for freewheeling imposition of standards of their own choosing.

It is critical, however, to diagnose precisely the problem with this review mechanism. The central malady is neither the supposed lawlessness of the Bush administration nor the anticipated absence of habeas corpus as the front line of judicial review. It is, rather, that the entire structure is significantly underdeveloped. The badly conceived system of judicial review is only one feature of a larger review system crudely forged from an inadequate model. It is neither the system's main flaw nor will correcting it alone do much good.

As of this writing, the Supreme Court is poised to hand down its decision in *Boumediene,* likely in one form or another reasserting its power to hear habeas cases from Guantánamo—and it is mulling the related question of how substantial the D.C. circuit appeals really are. The day that *Boumediene* comes down, assuming the justices rule as expected, news stories the world over will announce once again the great defeat of the administration and the rebuke to its aggressive approach. These stories, however, will generally not discuss the mess the decision will leave—hundreds of habeas corpus suits proceeding even as direct appeals from CSRT judgments pile up in the federal courts, and all of this litigation taking place with no agreed-upon legal standards of review or substantive law guiding the key questions: Whom can the military hold? For how long? With what kind of showing? Under what evidentiary rules? America will, put bluntly, have come no closer to a coherent law of terrorism than it was the day detainees began arriving at Guantánamo. It will merely have declared—yet again—that the Supreme Court has the final word.

WE COME, then, to the question of what judicial review ought to look like in the war on terror if one accepts that it should exist more robustly than the administration prefers but should not be of an unbridled or general nature, as human rights advocates wish to see. The answer is conceptually simple, though devilishly complicated in operation: Judicial review should be designed for the relatively narrow purpose of holding the executive to clearly articulated legislative rules, not to the often vague standards of international legal instruments that have not been implemented through American law. Judges should have an expanded role in the powers of presidential preemption in the antiterrorism arena, for the judiciary is essential to legitimizing the use of those powers. Without them, the powers themselves come under a barrage of criticism which they cannot easily withstand. And eventually the effort to shield them from judicial review fails, and the review that results from the effort is more intrusive, more suspicious, and less accommodating of the executive's legitimate need for operational flexibility. Judges, in other words, should be a part of the larger rules the legislature will need to write to govern the global fight against terrorism. Their role within these legal regimes will vary—from virtually no involvement in cases of covert actions and overseas surveillance to extensive involvement in cases of long-term detentions. The key is that the place of judges within those systems is not itself a matter for the judges to decide. The judiciary must not serve as the designer of the rules.

Habeas corpus litigation is not a policy-making engine. In the presence of a reasonable policy, it also poses no great threat to the administration's legitimate needs. If Congress were to create appropriate procedures for administrative and judicial review of detentions, habeas would become largely superfluous even were it retained in some form. If, for example, habeas review remained available after a detainee had exhausted administrative and direct-review procedures, it would follow repeated determinations of the legality of the detentions in question by procedures legislated specifically to evaluate the integrity of those detentions. Depending on how Congress structured the regime, this could be needlessly duplicative or—as in the role habeas plays in the criminal system—a useful backstop check for egregious systemic failures. What makes no sense, however, is for habeas review to take place before any of these other procedures are even put to use and to thereby morph into a device for the design of the system itself. The proper place of habeas is at the back end of these cases, not as the front line of defense.

Judicial review cannot exist in a vacuum. In the common parlance, it often sounds like oversight by a council of elders. But for the institution to serve a useful function, the term "review" requires some flesh—that is, judicial review has to mean the review by judges *of something and pursuant to some known or recognizable law*. In the current habeas cases, all of this grows pretty fuzzy. For what exactly is under challenge? The ability of the military to detain the enemy? The ability of the military to detain the enemy as unlawful enemy combatants? The ability of the military to detain the enemy without pressing charges? For all the pious talk of the "rule of law," there is no clear law here. It only makes sense to decide what function judges should play in this process in the context of more basic decisions about what the process should look like. Put another way, one needs law—law made by Congress—if judicial review is to be anything more refined than simple judicial power.

Those who have spent the last seven years fearing the unchecked inherent powers of the president should not now push to supplant those powers with the unchecked inherent powers of the judiciary. For the development of imaginative new legal systems, the Supreme Court is a perverse address to which to turn. It is long past time we stopped neglecting that peculiar domed building across the street.

FIVE

The Case for Congress

T HE CONGRESS of the United States is an unlikely hero for any story these days. Its approval rating stands at a shocking 21 percent as of this writing, more than ten points lower even than those of the faltering President Bush.[1] Unlike the president and the courts, both of whom sizable groups of Americans see as natural leaders in the project of devising a new law of counterterrorism, the national legislature has no political base in the counterterrorism arena. Aside from a small group of commentators, nobody is clamoring for a pervasive role on its part in the war on terrorism.[2] In fact, the major voices on all sides seem to fear one. The administration fears congressionally imposed constraints, and while critics welcome a possible reversal of the curbs on habeas corpus, they tend to fear that legislation would do more to authorize the administration's course than to restrain it. Leaving the ambiguous status quo—in which Congress subcontracts its legislative function first to the executive branch and ultimately to the courts—gives all sides the fatalistic comfort of inevitability. We don't as a society have to choose our counterterrorism policies; we watch like sports fans for those policies to emerge out of a dialogue between a president and a court, one of whom we define as our "good guy" and the other our foe.

The affirmative case for Congress's playing a major role in the conflict would be easier had the legislature amassed some underappreciated record of accomplishment that one could unveil, reinterpret, or somehow present as justifying a greater level of respect than the legislature normally garners. Alas, Congress warrants only a little more admiration than it accrues. Its legislative record has been desultory, reactive, unimaginative, and every bit as caught in the intellectual traps of past precedents as has the executive's and, somewhat more forgivably, the judiciary's. Nothing Congress has done to date justifies particular faith. Designating Congress as an essential actor—perhaps *the* essential underperforming actor—in this conflict requires either a naïve leap of faith concerning its hitherto hidden capacities or a particularly realistic and level-headed understanding of the role it could play, who might induce that role, and how.

The case for Congress emerges not only from its own institutional virtues—and Congress does have some virtues—but from the default of the alternatives. The presidential power model has failed, and the judicial power model it triggered has not fixed and cannot fix the problems it created but, rather, promises new problems of its own. We are left in somewhat the same fix as Lord Byron, who found himself two centuries ago groping about for a hero for his epic poem and, finding all contemporary options unacceptable, finally settled on a classical image of licentious gluttony, cruelty, and selfishness. "I want a hero: an uncommon want,/When every year and month sends forth a new one," he wrote. "Till, after cloying the gazettes with cant,/The age discovers he is not the true one;/ Of such as these I should not care to vaunt,/I'll therefore take our ancient friend Don Juan."[3] Our age may not yet have discovered that the presidency and the judiciary are not the true heroes for the project of our time, but it will. If the goal is a long-term, stable set of legal structures for a conflict of indefinite duration against a novel adversary, neither the judiciary nor the executive can ultimately deliver. And Congress, an admittedly perverse and improbable hero, then has a vital role to play: Only Congress can remove the conflict from the paralyzing war-versus-law-enforcement divide and craft for terrorism new legal rules tailored to terrorism's own peculiarities. Only Congress can effectively constrain the executive in its exercise of the powers of presidential preemption and at the same time constrain the courts in their ambitions for a greater role in foreign and military affairs. Only Congress can ultimately write the law of this long war.

John Yoo and other executive power enthusiasts treat the notion of a major congressional role in the war with contempt. "Critics," Yoo wrote, "usually look to Congress as the main engine for the development of terrorism policy. Critics claim that Bush has violated the law, or acted as if he were above the law. They place all of their hopes in Congress. If only Congress would pass a law regulating terrorism policy, all would be right with the world."[4] This, he claimed, is naïve. "It should come as no surprise that Congress has not enacted a grand statute regulating all facets of terrorism policy. There wouldn't be much political upside and, if they choose rules that turn out to be mistaken, it might come back to haunt them at the ballot box."[5]

The skeptics of congressional leadership certainly have a point. The legislature cannot possibly take the lead among the three branches of government in counterterrorism policy. Unlike the presidency, Congress is not a unitary actor, but a sharply divided one—divided among two major political parties, divided among several regions of the country with differing attitudes towards government and liberty and different exposure to terrorist threats, and divided among hundreds of individual egos. The legislative process moves slowly and unpredictably, making Congress unsuited to lead in a crisis. Because of the requirement of sixty votes in the Senate to move legislation to a vote, legislative efforts can often end in paralysis. The compromises necessary to produce new law often mean that nobody gets exactly what he or she wants. And the whole machinery is subject to pressure from interest groups whose concerns don't extend beyond their particular parochial desires. What's more, Yoo is quite correct that Congress as an institution has little incentive to try its hand at leadership in matters of foreign conflict. As the great constitutional scholar John Hart Ely once put it, the shift of war powers to the executive branch over the course of the twentieth century is often styled "a usurpation, but that oversimplifies to the point of misstatement. . . . In fact, . . . the legislative surrender was a self-interested one: Accountability is pretty frightening stuff."[6]

The executive, in contrast to the legislature, speaks with one voice. The president wields a veto, giving him a powerful weapon to deflect legislation he dislikes. Perhaps more important, Congress largely depends on him, as the actor who implements policy on the ground, for its information about his needs and the problems that give rise to them. The constitutional system structures the presidency, not the Congress, for leadership in foreign policy in general and particularly so in times of crisis.

In other words, it is most unlikely that Congress will suddenly arise from a long slumber and begin energetically writing imaginative new laws, forcing them down an unwilling president's throat, and stunning the federal courts into deference. It is more likely that some president will go to Congress, ask for help, and propose a legislative scheme, probably one conceived of and drafted in the executive branch. Congress will likely modify that scheme, attach more conditions to it than the president wants, and limit his freedom of action somewhat. But precisely because of its penchant for ducking accountability, it will ultimately give the president what he wants—or, at least, what he needs. Voting this way shields members from almost any eventuality. It lets them claim a share of credit for success; they voted for the law in question, after all. It also lets them deflect blame for failures, which members can pin on the manner in which the president used authority they gave him. As a general rule, in other words, Congress will muster in response to the president's call.

That rule, in turn, implies that the prerequisite for a constructive congressional role is a somewhat different conception of power on the part of the executive branch—one that resembles Jamie Gorelick's tendency during the Clinton administration to see the presidency's power and prestige as enhanced by congressional backing, not David Addington's tendency during the Bush administration to see any congressionally imposed restraints as an attack on presidential prerogatives. To a president willing to accept that working with Congress is not, as Addington put it, "giv[ing] away the president's power" but enhancing it, Congress can offer something priceless: actions that, unlike unilateral presidential acts, can build comprehensive legal systems and do so *in the name of the political system as a whole.*

BEFORE IMAGINING what Congress ought to do, it is useful to take a closer look at what the legislature has already done. While Congress has not performed impressively, it has not been entirely idle either. It has engaged in oversight over the administration's conduct of the conflict—anemically prior to the Democratic takeover of Congress after the 2006 elections, aggressively since then. It set up the 9/11 Commission and conducted its own thorough investigation of the intelligence failures that preceded the attacks.[7] And its committees held hearings at times that have helped shape public debate. It also passed a huge amount of legislation bearing on the war on terrorism. This legislation has done everything from authorizing the use of force in Afghanistan to reorganizing the executive branch bureaucratically to appropriating vast sums of money for intelligence, the military, and law enforcement to creating any number of new criminal laws. Only a small number of these changes, however, alters the fundamental legal authorities of the government to interact with the enemy.

The first of these changes was the USA PATRIOT Act, which the administration sought and obtained in the immediate aftermath of the attacks.[8] Seeking the PATRIOT Act seems, in retrospect, entirely out of character for the administration. Here it did not "go it alone"; it behaved, rather, more or less as it should have approached legal constraints generally. It took existing law seriously enough to recognize that, to do as it believed necessary to confront Al Qaeda, it needed changes. It identified the changes that it thought it needed, and it asked Congress for them. With only a few exceptions, none of them terribly significant, it got what it asked for.

The PATRIOT Act, however, did not embody anything like a cohesive vision of what powers the state ought to have in order to confront the problem of global terrorism. It represented, rather, a set of prospective guesses about what new authorities the intelligence community would likely need in an augmented confrontation. Because of the prospective nature of these guesses, they were a little like firing a shotgun at a dart board. Some of the pellets hit

the bull's eye; some proved largely irrelevant; a few went far astray. For example, one section that attracted particular controversy at the time Congress
considered the act authorized the attorney general to lock up those aliens he
suspected of being terrorists for up to seven days without either filing criminal
charges or initiating deportation proceedings.[9] This provision, as passed,
actually watered down somewhat the administration's request, which had
sought the power to detain such people without the seven-day limit.[10] Yet
while the proposal sparked particular anxiety in the fall of 2001, it proved
almost entirely redundant of other immigration detention authorities and,
as a consequence, has never become a significant tool in the government's ar-
senal. Because of earlier immigration reforms, locking up people while attempting to deport them is easy, so the provision, along with the controversy
surrounding it, proved wholly unnecessary. Other provisions generated un-
controversial changes to money-laundering statutes and expansions of the
criminal law.

The major significance of the PATRIOT Act from the standpoint of the
powers of presidential preemption lies in a dense and widely misunderstood
set of provisions involving what the act terms "Enhanced Surveillance Procedures." These changes, broadly speaking, broke down the so-called wall that
had inhibited the sharing of information between intelligence and law enforcement agencies in the years before the attacks. The PATRIOT Act allowed
sharing of certain grand jury information with intelligence agencies, and clarified that spies and cops should not keep the information they collect from one
another in the kind of bureaucratic apartheid that had developed under prior
law.[11] It also permitted what are called "roving wiretaps" under the FISA—
that is, wiretaps that are not limited to a single communications device but
follow the targeted individual whatever communications equipment he might
use.[12] And it altered FISA's so-called primary purpose standard, in which the
government could only get a wiretap order under FISA—which is easier than
under the criminal law—when its primary purpose was intelligence gathering,
not law enforcement. Under the PATRIOT Act, the government could make
use of the FISA court whenever intelligence was a "significant purpose" of the
surveillance.[13]

The PATRIOT Act also allowed for delayed notice of search warrants in circumstances under which a "court finds reasonable cause to believe that providing immediate notification of the execution of the [search] warrant," which is the usual practice, "may have an adverse result."[14] In a provision that became particularly controversial because of opposition from librarians, it allowed "access to certain business records" in national security cases on order of the FISA court.[15] The law also expanded the use under FISA of pen register and trap-and-trace devices—systems that can track what numbers a phone is calling or from which it receives calls without capturing the contents of those calls—from telephone communications to comparable addressing information for Internet traffic as well.[16] Numerous other technical provisions of the PATRIOT Act were designed to grease the wheels of national security surveillance. The result was both to facilitate collection of information domestically and to ensure the availability of that information within the government to those officials who needed it.

This was a substantial series of architectural changes, an integration of the intelligence and law enforcement functions of government that law and particularly practice had rigorously separated in the wake of the Watergate era. The separation, which grew out of a period in which the security agencies had all too routinely deployed the surveillance apparatus of the state against political dissenters and others, made sense when America's major adversaries were foreign countries. While the line between intelligence and law enforcement became tricky sometimes in espionage cases, it was a pretty good rule of thumb that the American government has no business spying on its people domestically except when they are "agents of a foreign power" and therefore legitimate foreign intelligence targets. That line breaks down a bit in terrorism cases, as the run-up to September 11 displayed so tragically. Sometimes a suspected terrorist can't quite be linked to a foreign group, as happened with Zacarias Moussaoui. The CIA grossly failed to inform the FBI of the entry into the United States of two Al Qaeda operatives who ended up on airplanes on September 11—a disastrous missed opportunity that stemmed, in large measure, from the wall's inhibiting the sharing of information.[17] In terrorism cases, investigators often don't know whether they're first and foremost investigating a crime or gathering information for some other legitimate purpose—identifying other terrorists abroad or at home, for example. The PATRIOT Act, along with an additional FISA amendment that followed shortly after it, added flexibility to joints that had stiffened with age.[18]

Congress's second major round of legislative activity sought to reorganize the American government so as to confront terrorism more effectively. The most important developments were the creation of the Department of Homeland Security and the intelligence reform act that created the director of national intelligence.[19] These were hugely significant bureaucratic steps, ones with great impact on the organizational capacity of the government to effectuate counterterrorism policy—though in which direction is a matter of some dispute.[20] They were, however, oddly unimportant to the architecture of the war itself. After all, to the person spied upon, it matters very little whether the director of the CIA is also the head of the intelligence community more broadly or whether he is merely the director of an agency within it. To the immigration detainee locked up because he may pose a security risk, it matters no more whether the agency detaining him is named the Immigration and Naturalization Service and resides within the Department of Justice or if it is called U.S. Immigration and Customs Enforcement and resides within the Department of Homeland Security. This type of legislation does not substantially alter the powers of government, merely the efficiency with which it can use those powers.

In contrast, the DTA attempted to alter substantially the powers of presidential preemption, both in terms of their substance and in terms of the judiciary's role in supervising them. The act came amid much acclaim and criticism, often from the same people, because its different provisions seemed to pull in opposite directions. On the one hand, it attempted to overturn the *Rasul* decision and strip the courts of habeas jurisdiction over Guantánamo Bay. On the other, it sought to impose apparently significant restrictions on interrogations, both by the military and by the CIA.

Yet the architectural changes of the DTA have proven of limited impact. The Court-stripping language, as discussed earlier, did not survive *Hamdan*. The interrogation restrictions, likewise, have not in practice prevented the president from authorizing coercive tactics. This surprised and angered many people, because the DTA seemed so firm. It forbade military personnel from using "any treatment or technique of interrogation not authorized by and listed in the United States Army Field Manual on Intelligence Interrogation."[21] And it specifically required that no detainee, "regardless of nationality or physical location, shall be subject to cruel, inhuman, or degrading treatment or punishment"—an effort to stop the CIA from using highly coercive interrogation tactics that approached the legal definition of torture.[22] It defined "cruel, inhuman or degrading treatment" as including treatment "prohibited by the Fifth, Eighth, and Fourteenth Amendments to the Constitution of the United States."[23]

But in practice, these restrictions had only modest effect. In the case of the military, as I explain in greater detail in Chapter 7, tough interrogations had two sources: unauthorized practices by people in the field and a few deviations from the Army Field Manual that had taken place with high-level consideration and approval. It was, therefore, a relatively easy matter to keep on the right side of the new law. The Army Field Manual was clarified and made more specific to give better guidance to interrogators.[24] The new provision served to put the force of law behind Pentagon policy and to forbid future instances of deviations from that policy when particular detainees proved less compliant than interrogators hoped.

In the case of the CIA, the administration interpreted the law exceptionally narrowly. While the casual reader might understand the DTA's text as banning any interrogation tactic that would not be permitted in a police station for being "degrading," the administration read it under case law only as precluding those tactics that "shock the conscience." It read this test as creating a permissive and flexible standard, since it takes a lot more to shock the average person's conscience when a major terrorist attack looms than under more typical civilian circumstances.[25] Attorney General Michael Mukasey has confirmed that the CIA discontinued the most coercive technique used prior to the DTA—waterboarding—in the wake of its passage, yet the government does not consider it categorically barred under the new law, either, and other tough tactics, in any event, continued.[26] The DTA did not result in a shutdown of the

CIA's secret prisons program. Considerably after it went into effect, President Bush described the interrogation "procedures" deployed in that program, saying they "were tough, and they were safe, and lawful, and necessary."[27]

The DTA also contained the first—and so far the only—attempt to regulate the detention procedures themselves. The attempt was perfunctory. Congress required that the Pentagon submit to the congressional oversight committees its procedures "for determining the status of the detainees held at Guantánamo Bay or to provide an annual review to determine the need to continue to detain an alien" and the comparable procedures for detainees in Afghanistan and Iraq. And it required that CSRT and ARB procedures "shall, to the extent practicable, assess . . . whether any statement derived from or relating to such detainee was obtained as a result of coercion; and . . . the probative value (if any) of any such statement." It also required an annual report to Congress describing the number of detainees whose status was reviewed and the procedures used.[28] These requirements were window dressing.

Conceptually speaking, the most important change in the DTA was among the least noticed at the time. In his eagerness to get rid of the proliferating habeas cases, Bush made a fateful architectural concession: that some form of judicial review would cover detentions at Guantánamo. The legislation, therefore, includes the authorization for the D.C. Circuit Court of Appeals to review CSRT and military commission judgments.[29] This decision represented the administration's first formal acknowledgement that it was not operating in a pure law-of-war environment. In warfare, after all, the detainee does not get access to the civilian justice system. This provision, though the administration pretends otherwise and human rights groups downplay it as an inadequate substitute for habeas, stands as an acknowledgment in law that detentions in the war on terrorism are something different from either war or criminal justice and that they require legal arrangements that will hybridize the two.

The MCA, passed in the wake of *Hamdan,* represents by far the most ambitious congressional effort to write the rules of the war on terrorism. The law took on several interrelated issues, all served up by the Supreme Court. It authorized military commissions explicitly and clearly in statute and spelled out the procedures for them in considerable detail; it spelled out as well the war crimes that these tribunals could try. The procedures were notably more generous to the accused than were the administration's earlier procedures—though those too had come a fair distance from their earlier incarnations. The law also forbade the invocation of the Geneva Conventions as a source of law in American civil litigation, an effort to prevent detainees from complaining to the courts about treatment that violates treaties and to prevent the courts from expounding on broadly worded treaty protections by way of crafting restrictions of their own.[30] It defined narrowly those "grave breaches" of Common Article 3 of the conventions, which prohibits inhumane treatment, that should be subject to criminal prosecution. The Court had declared that Common Article 3 applied to the conflict, so Congress made clear that only the most brutal violations of it are subject to prosecution as war crimes. The new law delegated to the president the authority to regulate and define conduct that, short of a grave breach, also violates the treaties.[31] It immunized retroactively CIA personnel who, relying on the administration's legal opinion that the article did not apply to the conflict, may have inadvertently run afoul of Common Article 3 in conducting war-on-terrorism interrogations.[32] And it once again sought to remove the habeas corpus jurisdiction of the federal courts.[33]

The MCA, in other words, bit off a lot of meat: It specified how it wanted enemies tried, what role it wanted the courts to play in that process, and how it wanted international law and domestic law to interact. It did all this in an obnoxious sort of way—with a crude political power play by the administration in the run-up to the 2006 midterm elections. Both because of that power play and because many of the judgments embodied in the legislation were controversial, the act has emerged with a bad odor among many Democrats. Some of the complaints, no doubt, have merit. The act was thrown together hastily, sloppily in spots, and some of its more controversial provisions could certainly have borne more debate and improvement. Moreover, because the statute focused not at all on the rules for the detentions themselves and sought to cut off judicial review of those detentions, it fueled the fire over habeas and ginned up the next round of litigation. Instead of building a structure from the bottom up—focusing first on what the government needs to do to lock someone up and only then on what the rules should be for trial—it worked backwards. First, in the DTA, Congress established the appeals mechanism for the trials and the detentions. Then, in the MCA, it authorized the trials themselves. It still, however, has never grounded the detentions in law—meaning that the entire edifice, controversial and rickety at this stage, stands on a bed of sand. By cutting off all of the habeas actions, or attempting to, Congress insisted that this absurd structure be immune from the judicial scrutiny most readily available. That this policy judgment now dominates discussion of the MCA is hardly a surprise.

It is, however, a shame, for Congress in many respects took a genuine step forward with the MCA. The trials it authorizes meet the minimum standards that key liberals articulated when they criticized the administration's original regulatory commissions. In 2002, for example, Neal K. Katyal and Laurence H. Tribe wrote that

> the Constitution at least requires, at a bare minimum, that offenses be defined in advance by positive legislation, that the judicial branch be open to test whether any given individual is properly subject to the jurisdiction of the tribunals at issue and whether the system of tribunals as a whole comports with constitutional commands, and that appeal to some body independent of the president as the convening and prosecuting authority be available to test whether any conviction and sentence handed down by one of the president's tribunals is supportable in law on the evidence presented.[34]

The MCA commissions arguably meet all of these standards and would do so inarguably were even a modest version of habeas corpus available to supplement the review the DTA creates. While it is possible to imagine unfair trials being conducted under the new statute, one can easily imagine trials of impeccable fairness taking place under it as well. There is, in other words, a baby in all of this bath water—one that, in all of the anger over habeas corpus, Guantánamo, and the Geneva Conventions, risks getting flushed. Congress got a fair bit right in the MCA on which it might reasonably build in the future.

Since then, Congress has passed one additional piece of architecturally significant legislation, albeit on a temporary basis. In the summer of 2007, the legislature passed—with a six-month sunset provision—a major change to the FISA that set off a firestorm of protest. The *New York Times* blasted it as an "unnecessary and dangerous expansion of President Bush's powers" and warned that it would "allow the government to intercept, without a warrant, every communication into or out of any country, including the United States."[35] The *Washington Post* called it "reckless" and fretted that "the government will now be free to intercept any communications believed to be from outside the United States (including from Americans overseas) that involve 'foreign intelligence'—not just terrorism. . . . Instead of having the Foreign Intelligence Surveillance Act court ensure that surveillance is being done properly, with monitoring of Americans minimized, that job would be up to the attorney general and the director of national intelligence."[36] Both newspapers attacked congressional Democrats for bowing to pressure from the administration and allowing such an unacceptable law to pass.

The provision is, truth be told, hard to assess rigorously without access to facts that remain stubbornly classified. And the law certainly has some problems, a subject to which I shall return in Chapter 8. But as a short-term stopgap, it was something far less than outrageous. Indeed, as I explain later, to consider beyond the pale this sort of warrantless wiretapping of communications between targets overseas and Americans at home, one would have to be outraged at much more than Congress's changes to the FISA but at the FISA itself. All the horrors the *Times* and *Post* feared in the new law were permitted by the original one it supposedly gutted. The gist of the new law resided in a single sentence: "Nothing in [FISA's] definition of electronic surveillance . . . shall be construed to encompass surveillance directed at a person reasonably believed to be located outside of the United States."[37] This was an effort to undo a drift under which the 1978 law, intended to regulate domestic wiretapping, had increasingly come to cover much overseas intelligence collection as well. The FISA modernization bill is a significant architectural development if a version of it becomes permanent, as seems likely. If not, it's a kind of blip. As of this writing, the temporary law has lapsed but a consensus seems to have developed that something like it should remain on the books. For all the sturm and drang over the temporary law, the Democratic alternatives to it are not all that different.[38]

All in all, Congress's performance has been patchy and erratic. With respect to FISA, the legislature has been oddly specific and detailed. With respect to military trials, it has been fairly comprehensive, albeit belatedly so and only after the Supreme Court forced it to act. With respect to detention, it has maintained virtual silence. The major theme of congressional action to date has been its lack of initiative and its insistence on responding to the executive's requests and to court judgments rather than generating policy of its own. Indeed, of the major congressional actions to date, only the interrogation restrictions within the DTA have enacted congressional, rather the executive, ideas. The result of Congress's scattershot approach is that while individual pieces of legislation have been architecturally significant, what has emerged is not really a building. It is a shanty assembled in a junkyard out of whatever scraps were available—with little attention paid to how those scraps would interact. Some are elaborately sculpted and painted, some are bits of plywood slapped together. The styles vary, and yet it isn't always clear where one ends and the next begins. Some are oddly invisible or exist only in hazy outline. And it is from a chair in this hut that the president of the United States wields his powers of preemption, apparently imagining it a palace that could stand no improvements.

THE PROJECT of imagining and designing a functional structure for the powers of presidential preemption is, in some respects, more akin to the writing of a constitution than to conventional statutory draftsmanship. Richard Posner once quipped that the Constitution was in this area "a sieve."[39] He meant, I think, that the document answers authoritatively many fewer questions than Americans like to pretend, which is to say that it permits a great deal more in

the way of policy making. Because the rules we write and the decisions upholding or rejecting them will tend to acquire a certain critical mass over time,
however, they will become a kind of constitution for the war on terrorism. If
writing such a document sounds daunting, it should. The questions America
is debating here are fateful ones in which the stakes are high and which carry
grave risks on both sides. Are we more afraid of a broad and relatively unconstrained governmental power to detain the enemy than we are of those detainees a more constrained power would release? Are we more afraid of coercive
interrogation than of the information the refusal to use it in all circumstances
would forfeit? Are we more afraid of pervasive electronic surveillance than of
missing intelligence out of caution? Posner overstates the matter a little; the
slate is not entirely blank. But there is a lot of room on it still to fill.

The good news is that we are not writing with indelible chalk. One of the
virtues of not writing the constitution for the war on terror into the Constitution itself is that it allows for trial and error, for shifting regimes over time,
and for ongoing public debate and calibration in the face of a fluid geopolitical situation and ever-shifting technology. It also allows for great specificity;
whereas constitutional language tends towards broad generalizations like
"due process," statutory language can spell out policies in precise details. FISA
offers an imperfect example of both these virtues. Since its original passage, it
has undergone repeated amendment in an effort to keep it current, and the
scheme it lays out is not some general set of principles but a highly detailed set
of rules and procedures. While it protects constitutional values, it need not
exist at the level of inspirational constitutional rhetoric but is unapologetically
technical. The law of the long war requires something of the same sensibility,
the sense at once of providing clear, well-understood, specific rules of the road
that preserve confidence in the rule of law yet, at the same time, remain
amendable in response to a fast-changing world. And like the FISA, the law of
terrorism in general will live in its details. Because the issues are so complicated, grand statutory arrangements can founder on a word, a phrase, or a
mischievous punctuation mark.

Nonetheless, there are certain high-altitude principles that ought to guide the building of a legal system for this conflict. Curiously, these principles are also ideas that only Congress can meaningfully bring to bear on the powers of presidential preemption.

The first is that it is, in fact, a system that we're building. Its parts are interconnected and affect one another. Legislators cannot ignore the often perverse incentive structures legal rules create between and among these parts. If the rules in federal courts make it too difficult to try a terrorist suspect, that creates an incentive to try him in a military commission instead. If the rules of military commissions make trial there too difficult, those rules create an incentive to hold him without trial as an enemy combatant—a status that currently requires only a small quantum of evidence that he has a limited opportunity to rebut. If the rules for detention at places like Guantánamo that are outside of the theater of combat become too stringent, they create an incentive to keep people detained in the field—which can be far more dangerous—or to turn them over to foreign governments that may treat them more brutally. If detention itself becomes too difficult, that creates the worst incentive of all: not to take prisoners in the first place. Congress needs to understand its legal apparatus as an organism of sorts, one in which any given intervention has ripple effects through the larger operation of the system.

The second general guidepost is that the purpose of this system is to both authorize and regulate the global conflict against terrorism. It is not an attempt to shape the law of war more generally. Nor is it meant to influence the criminal justice system. Indeed, one of the reasons to write this body of law in the first place is to *avoid* seepage of legal doctrines devised for terrorism into domains that already have coherent bodies of law of their own. We don't want the lessened standards for detention in these cases to infect the domestic criminal justice system. Nor do we want the heightened standards we should impose here relative to the laws of war migrating back towards more conventional military conflicts, where standards for detention ought to be low. We don't want the decisions we make in trying terrorism defendants to become precedents for more routine criminal trials. And we don't want the nastiness we may sometimes tolerate in interrogations in this conflict to become acceptable treatment for American service members caught by foreign nations under the laws of war. We need to imagine ourselves as writing a law of terrorism, a set of rules that while influenced by and related to other bodies of law, nonetheless exists on its own, not as an appendage to any body of law derived for other purposes.

Another basic principle is that this system must be at once a creature of American domestic law and somehow harmonizable with international treaties to which the United States has bound itself. The war on terrorism is inherently an international project. That means that on a routine basis, the United States needs to work with allied governments. Just as the executive branch cannot wisely "go it alone" in its relations with the other two branches of government domestically, the United States cannot in the long run have no meeting of the minds with its allies regarding what tactics are acceptable in the war on terrorism. This does not mean that Congress necessarily needs to forswear the death penalty or other policies on which European opinion has turned its back. Nor does it mean that the United States must move decisively towards the law enforcement model of counterterrorism that Europe has so consistently embraced. That said, the United States has taken on—in the case of the Geneva Conventions even championed—certain international commitments. And it does itself enormous harm when it presents the war on terrorism as in conflict with those commitments. To some extent, America and Europe simply fail to see eye to eye on the appropriate legal structures for terrorism and should adopt a live-and-let-live approach. To the extent that Congress can pass legislation that implements and interprets America's obligations under international law, it can at once bridge these differences to a degree by enacting America's commitment in domestic law and ensure that they have enough give in the joints so as not to paralyze counterterrorism.

A good example here lies, ironically, in one of the most controversial provisions of the MCA, the section that dealt with Common Article 3 of the Geneva Conventions. Common Article 3 provides a baseline standard of humanitarian treatment of detainees, including a vague ban on "outrages upon personal dignity, in particular, humiliating and degrading treatment."[40] Opinion as to what precisely this language bans differs markedly, but it's certainly hard to square it with interrogation tactics like waterboarding—the kind of simulated drowning the CIA used on the detainees in its secret prisons. The administration initially contended that the restriction did not apply in this conflict at all, but the Supreme Court in *Hamdan* disagreed. Because federal criminal law made breaching the treaty prosecutable, the question of what precisely this language meant suddenly took on great significance.

The MCA, as discussed above, defined Common Article 3's meaning in American law. The act has been lambasted for forswearing America's obligations under the conventions and creating exceptions to those obligations, but on its face it actually does neither of these things. Rather, it defines those "grave breaches" of the article that constitute war crimes for purposes of American criminal law: torture, certain cruel or inhuman treatments, medical experimentation, murder, maiming, rape and sexual assault, hostage taking, and intentionally causing serious injury. For lesser forms of degradation and abuse, it instructs the president to issue an executive order outlining those "violations of treaty obligations which are not grave breaches" and thus not subject to prosecution as war crimes. And it asserts that these steps "fully satisfy" America's obligation under the conventions.[41] This language has accrued a lot of unwarranted derision from human rights advocates, but it was actually quite deft. In one step, Congress did several things. It managed to honor a treaty America has long supported, for the new language permits nothing the treaty forbids but merely clarifies which violations are war crimes, as opposed to lesser misconduct. It also gave the administration the flexibility it insisted upon, allowing it to effectuate its own interpretation of the treaty for all but the most obvious and severe violations of it. And it gave those conducting interrogations guidance concerning what red lines they must not cross. While I would draw somewhat different lines, the argumentative structure of the MCA's Geneva Convention implementation seems exactly right. Congress need not posture the United States in opposition to international law, as the administration did at the outset of the conflict; acting creatively, it can generally work within it credibly.

Flexibility is itself another important principle. The administration has feared going to Congress because of the concern of being bound by new law. But law need not mean rigidity. In this context, it is critical to build executive discretion and agility into any statutory regime—not by way of giving the president a blank check but in recognition that a fluid and dynamic conflict sometimes requires ugly actions that the legislature may not want to bless but may also not want to preclude in all circumstances. Many observers since 2001 have criticized governmental failures under both the current and former administrations to take bold, aggressive, and creative action to confront Al Qaeda.[42] Adding more law to an already rich tapestry of restrictions—a tapestry that contributes to risk aversion and institutional conservatism—involves some risk of pushing the bureaucracy in exactly the wrong direction. At the end of the day, we need law that permits the government to spy on, catch, and interrogate the bad guys and that encourages a measure of creativity in doing so.

Finally, and perhaps most importantly, the law of terrorism must at once restrain and empower the executive branch. It must restrain it from actions we don't want it to take, or at least inhibit it from taking them. Yet it must simultaneously authorize and spur the president to take bold actions that may be just short of those it precludes. With a few notable exceptions, for example, most Americans do not want their government engaged in torture. They do, however, want their government aggressively interrogating the enemy. And they will not forgive the officials who fail to take aggressive but legal steps in interrogations when their consequent failure to garner information frustrates their efforts to prevent the next attack. Americans don't want their government spying on American citizens without good reason; they do want their government spying aggressively on Al Qaeda suspects and will not forgive failures of surveillance owing to timidity about lawful steps rooted in the desire not to cross the legal limits. In other words, American law somehow has to at once define the lines of acceptable governmental conduct, push the government to approach those lines, and prevent it from stepping over them. To have a prayer of accomplishing anything like this acrobatic feat requires significant clarity in statutory design.

The ultimate goal for a law of terrorism is to reassure Americans in an ongoing fashion that rules exist, that we know what they are, that the government follows them, and that they permit a robust confrontation with the enemy. This point may seem obvious, but it is ultimately what separates a legal regime that spreads accountability for tough decisions around the three branches of government from either a blank-check regime in which the executive branch does as it pleases or from one in which legalisms pervasively hamper governmental pursuit of a goal that nearly all Americans support. Only Congress, consisting as it does of elected officials from every part of the country and representing cumulatively the people as a whole, can deliver this framework and the legitimacy it will convey to the presidency in the exercise of his awesome powers of preemption.

With those preliminary thoughts, let us turn now to what a law of terrorism might look like across the range of areas in which we so desperately need it.

Six

The Twin Problems of
Detention and Trial

ALMOST FROM THE BEGINNING of the war on terrorism, the problem of detention has dominated the debate over the broad push and pull between liberty and necessity. First, in the aftermath of the attacks, American political culture divided over the immigration roundup and deportation of nearly eight hundred Arab and Muslim men. Then it argued over President Bush's military commissions order, then over his decision not to apply the Geneva Conventions to captives in the conflict. This debate somehow evolved into a broader one about whether American forces should be locking up enemy combatants at all. This development was surprising in one sense, since as a strictly legal matter, the power to lock up the enemy is a matter of black-letter law written on pure white paper with indelible ink. As a social matter, however, it is not surprising at all, for a grave anxiety about noncriminal detention itself has lain beneath the debate from the outset.

And rightly so. With the exception of battlefield killing, no action the government takes in this conflict more impinges on human freedom than does long-term incarceration. At the same time, no action more encumbers terrorist ambitions than the incapacitation of a group's leadership and operational cadre. Detention thus tugs hard on the bell pulls of both liberty and security.

Without a strong capacity to lock up the enemy, America merely awaits the next attack. Unless Congress designs that regime carefully, however, it will—like the current system—bring ongoing discredit to the United States and threaten to permit the long-term detention of innocent people this country should not be holding.

Unfortunately, public debate on the subject has shown an unerring instinct for the capillaries, not the heart, of the issue: the geographical location of America's highest-profile detention facility and the timing of judicial review of detentions there. While both these questions are, in their own way, significant, they are emphatically not the central issues at hand. They are a pair, rather, of very small tails wagging a very big dog. That dog is the detention policy itself.

As I argued earlier, habeas corpus review of detentions is only significant in the absence of some other cohesive system for evaluating their legality. In the normal criminal justice system, habeas review shows up only as a stopgap against injustice. It never operates as the front-line defense against wrongful conviction. Only after the accused has been convicted at trial and exhausted all of his direct appeals can he attack in state courts the processes that yielded his conviction and sentence. And only after state-level habeas review has availed him nothing can he take up the matter in federal court. What's more, because the criminal justice system is a fully developed one whose integrity our political system generally regards highly, the courts conducting habeas review treat its results with great deference—disturbing them only when substantial constitutional error plagues the outcome, and not always even then. Habeas law in the criminal context is both well developed and dense; courts know what standards to apply and authorities know how to conduct criminal trials so as to survive habeas review. If the military were operating a strong, stable, and fair detention regime, habeas review would become much less significant—whether the federal courts retained habeas jurisdiction or not. If it were entirely clear as a matter of law that the government were entitled to hold a given detainee, that detainee would have no successful habeas action to file.

The reason habeas actions present such a headache for the administration these days is that the status of detainees in the war on terror is very much disputed. Nobody knows for sure what rights the federal courts will grant under international law, the U.S. Constitution, or federal statutes to alien detainees captured abroad in murky factual situations in a potentially perpetual conflict. Their situation is sufficiently novel that the mere fact of habeas jurisdiction creates significant uncertainty concerning the government's power to detain the enemy—or those it believes to be the enemy. Debating the vitality of habeas jurisdiction is a poor substitute for making policy choices concerning how these cases ought to be governed.

The debate over Guantánamo likewise skirts the core of the problem. The public diplomacy difficulties created by the facility are real. Guantánamo has become a symbol around the world, fairly or unfairly, of excess in America's response to terrorism. It has come to symbolize injustice and arbitrary detention. But simply closing it will not repair the damage, which arises not because of the peculiar features of the base—which is, after all, just another naval base—but because of the peculiar status of the detainees held there. Even in the face of an aggressive effort to repatriate, resettle, and prosecute detainees, the United States will end up holding some number of Al Qaeda and Taliban fighters outside of the criminal justice system for some time to come—and we hope to capture more. So if the military closes the detention operation at Guantánamo, it will simply have to re-create it somewhere else. As long as there is no accepted procedure for making detention decisions, the public diplomacy woes that plague the base will continue to plague any future detention site—which will become, in the public mind, Guantánamo by some other name. Debating Guantánamo in the absence of a larger discussion of detention policy is really an exercise in debating the setting for a policy in lieu of discussing the policy itself.

To put it simply, if America gets the underlying system right, the problems of habeas corpus and Guantánamo will take care of themselves. Habeas will, one way or another, prove a nonproblem—either because it will not be necessary at all or because its existence will not encumber detention operations. Guantánamo will either grow less controversial as detention policy improves or it will be closed and a new facility opened without the taint of its history. On the other hand, if America fails to get the system right, neither restoring habeas rights nor closing Guantánamo will compensate for that failure. One step will merely inject judges into the confusion. The other will require the costly construction of a new facility and the movement of detainees to it in order to shift the focus of international agitation from one military base to another. The right approach is to focus on the law of the detentions themselves.

This project would have been easier closer to the outset of the conflict. The distance between the administration and its critics has widened over the years, largely because the position of the critics has been something of a moving target. When the military opened the Guantánamo facility the winter after the attacks, the criticisms from human rights groups were relatively modest. They too saw the conflict in terms of the laws of war and its permissive standards for detention, arguing only about a narrow range of questions related to conditions of confinement for detainees, the status of Taliban fighters, and the necessity of holding cursory tribunals before denying any fighters treatment as POWs. Human Rights Watch, for example, did not question the authority of the military to hold the detainees. It did not even question the legitimacy of holding many of them as *unlawful* enemy combatants. It insisted, rather, that the Third Geneva Conventions applied to the war on terrorism, that Article 5 of that convention required that a "competent tribunal" determine whether detainees were entitled to prisoner-of-war status, and that Taliban soldiers— as fighters for the de facto government of their country—were entitled to treatment as prisoners of war. It also objected to the metal cages in which the military initially held the detainees.[1] Rhetoric aside, the distance between this view and the administration's was not great.

Over time, the administration has moved substantially towards Human Rights Watch's view of things. While it never accepted an obligation to afford POW treatment to Taliban detainees, it did hold the CSRTs, which in all other respects greatly exceeded the promise of Article 5. But in a kind of mission creep, the human rights groups refused to take "yes" for an answer. Their position moved too—and moved quite fundamentally. Human Rights Watch, for example, no longer clearly accepts the Geneva Conventions as the governing law in this conflict. In a letter to President Bush in June 2007 urging the immediate closure of Guantánamo, it objected far more broadly to "the continued detention of approximately 375 men at Guantánamo Bay, without charge and without any meaningful review of the legal basis of their detention. . . ."[2] Along with other human rights and civil liberties groups, it signed a letter blasting an admirable effort by Armed Services Committee Chairman Carl Levin to bolster the procedural protections of the CSRTs and to codify the process in law: "if Congress tinkers with the CSRT process in a way that gives it a greater veneer of due process respectability," the letter warned, "it will be seen by some as an adequate substitute for habeas corpus, and the critical effort to restore habeas rights to detainees will flounder."[3] Charges, meaningful legal review, and habeas corpus are not features of the Geneva regimes. Between 2002 and 2007 the baseline of legitimacy for detentions had shifted for the human rights groups from rigorous compliance with the Geneva Conventions to criminal charges and extensive judicial involvement.

To reach anything like a legislative consensus with all this water under the bridge, both sides will have to move considerably. Human rights and civil liberties groups are going to have to acknowledge the necessity—or at least the legitimacy—of some noncriminal form of detention and some trial mechanisms that stop short of the norms prevailing in American federal courts. The administration, for its part, is going to have to be far more candid about the fact that some war-on-terrorism detentions will have constitutional roots outside of the laws of war—in some body of law that confers greater procedural protections, involves both defense lawyers and the judiciary more, and involves a higher burden of proof for the government.

It only makes sense to think about detention and trial in counterterrorism as an integrated system. That system begins on battlefields or in civilian settings abroad or at home and can end in military detention or in prosecution in American federal courts, military commissions, or theoretically in some alternative trial venue. The system is in total disarray. While the vast majority of aliens who fought for or conducted operations on behalf of Al Qaeda have ended up in military detention, some—like attempted shoe-bomber Richard Reid—have ended up facing indictment as civilians in federal court. One American citizen—John Walker Lindh—who allied himself with the Taliban was prosecuted and pleaded guilty in federal court and sentenced to twenty years in prison. Another, Yaser Esam Hamdi, did substantially the same thing yet was held for three years in military detention and was then, after the Supreme Court decision that bears his name, sent home to Saudi Arabia. (Oddly, in retrospect, most civil libertarians were more concerned about Hamdi's detention than Lindh's incarceration—though Lindh has since petitioned for executive clemency arguing that the seventeen additional years he will spend in prison while Hamdi is free is unfair to him.[4]) Meanwhile, the so-called Lackawanna Six—a group of young Muslim men from upstate New York who trained at a terrorist training camp in Afghanistan and then returned home and did little else—pleaded guilty in federal court and received sentences ranging from seven to ten years.[5] Australian former Guantánamo detainee David Hicks pleaded guilty before a military commission.[6] Alleged twentieth hijacker Mohammad Al-Qahtani was detained at Guantánamo for years without charge before facing military commission charges in February 2008.[7] Alleged twentieth hijacker Zacarias Moussaoui went through a circus of a trial in federal court in Virginia.[8] And alleged twentieth hijacker Ramzi Binalshibh was held and interrogated by the CIA in its secret prison, then transferred to Guantánamo and ultimately charged alongside Qahtani.[9] Jose Padilla faced detention first in civilian custody and then in military custody for three years, and he then faced trial and conviction in federal court.[10] There is no rhyme or reason to who ends up in what system, save the convenience of the executive branch at any given time.

Part of the reason for the chaos has been the administration's nearly total failure so far to establish military commissions as a viable trial mechanism. This failure has greatly increased the number of detainees who have faced no trial at all but languished instead in Guantánamo accruing victim status among the cognoscenti. It has also put pressure on civilian courts to handle these cases, and the civilian courts—particularly in Moussaoui's case—have not looked especially up to the task.

Part of the reason, however, is a certain lack of attention at the policy level to the detention and trial system as a system. When detention standards are depressed, and trial standards elevated, the combination creates an enormous incentive to rely on detentions instead of criminal trials. This makes perfect sense in the conventional war setting, where the sole purpose of detention is to disable the enemy from fighting, and trying soldiers for crimes (other than war crimes) is prohibited altogether and certainly never a priority. In the struggle against Al Qaeda, however, this incentive structure is perverse. Many detainees, after all, *have* committed crimes. Doubt *does* attend the circumstances of their capture and the reality of their belligerency. And both domestically and internationally, doubt also attends the legitimacy of their long-term detentions in the absence of criminal charges. To the extent that American authorities can allege and prove criminal charges using a reasonable set of trial procedures, each detention would then rest on stronger ground. In addition, the relationship between detention and trial in global antiterrorism is more complicated than the comparable relationship in traditional criminal law, where the authority to detain derives entirely from the authority to prosecute and has no vitality apart from the prosecutorial power. In antiterrorism, interrogation and intelligence gathering are key governmental objectives; detention alone can often satisfy these objectives, while criminal charges can perversely frustrate them when detainees exercise the right against self-incrimination that attends all civilized trials. In global counterterrorism, we somehow want a relationship between these powers that facilitates interrogations, intelligence gathering, and the neutralization of dangerous enemies while not discouraging their timely prosecution under rules at once fair and reasonably tailored to the difficult problems terrorism trials present. We cannot square this circle completely, for the objectives in question exist in considerable tension with one another. The question is how close we can get.

THE INITIAL PROBLEM in imagining an administrative detention scheme is justifying its necessity—which many Americans have come to doubt as the conflict has worn on. The idea that we don't need administrative detention of any kind comforts the civil libertarian conscience, for it asserts a total congruence between our circumstances and our professed values as Americans: We don't lock up people without charge and we don't need to, either. The statement of values is simplistic, and the assertion of congruence almost certainly delusional. Just how delusional remains murky. While CSRT transcripts offer some window into the dangerousness of certain detainees, they give little sense of which detainees might plausibly face trial. The result is that we won't know the number of people too dangerous to set free yet impossible to put on trial until America has an administration as bound and determined to charge everyone it can as the incumbent one is complacent about detaining people without charge. The number, however, is certainly not zero and may not even be small. Pentagon officials have estimated that a total of around 80 Guantánamo detainees could, under the right circumstances, face criminal charges in military commissions.[11] Yet the second round of ARB review yielded 273 judgments that detainees required continued detention. And while that number continues to decline, a gap will remain. America will have to close that gap either by transferring detainees to foreign governments that might either free them or do terrible things to them, or by acknowledging some kind of authority on the part of the American government to hold them itself. The next president of either party is most unlikely to forswear such an authority.

To understand the need for some form of administrative detention apparatus, consider the case of a Yemeni man named Bashir Nasir Al-Marwalah—whom two ARB reviews have considered too dangerous to release yet whom the military has never designated, at least not publicly, for military commission trial. At his CSRT, Al-Marwalah frankly acknowledged attending the Al-Farouq training camp in September 2000 and being trained there on the "Kalashnikov, RPK Machine gun, and Seminov Rifle." He learned the skills of a sniper. He went to Afghanistan, he says, "to train" in order to fight in Chechnya and ended up with the Taliban retreating from what he termed "the back lines" of the fight with the Northern Alliance. He insisted that he "was not fighting, nor did I want to fight Americans," who "did not do anything to give me a reason to fight them." At the same time, when asked point blank if he was "a member of al Qaida," he responded: "I don't know. I know I am an Arab fighter."[12]

On this public record, one can imagine a criminal case against Al-Marwalah based only on an attenuated theory of some kind of conspiracy to kill Americans.[13] But such a case is by no means a sure thing: His own statements are far less than a crystalline confession of war crimes. And even assuming the now-classified evidence against him is overpowering, it may not be admissible even under the relaxed standards of a military commission. Material collected in the rough-and-tumble of warfare does not always meet the stringent criteria of courtroom evidence; interrogations conducted, sometimes coercively, to acquire short-term intelligence may often produce information that ought not be admitted. A criminal case would, in any event, be something of a pretext. The reason to detain men like Al-Marwalah, after all, is not that in taking up the cause of America's enemies in the past, they violated some specific criminal law. It is, rather, that trained "Arab fighters" who "don't know" if they're Al Qaeda members pose a prospective menace to American lives.

Guantánamo has many detainees either who openly place themselves in this category or who—the government claims—are placed there by reliable classified evidence. What are we to do with a man like Ghassan Abdallah Ghazi Al Shirbi, who concluded his CSRT by shouting, "May God help me fight the infidels" and who, despite his willingness to admit to all manner of Al Qaeda activity, the military has not successfully brought to trial? Should he walk free in the meantime?[14] Are we comfortable with the fact that, as a gesture to our British allies, the military released a British national named Feroz Ali Abbasi, who in a lengthy handwritten statement to his CSRT taunted: "Do not be fooled into thinking that I am in any way perturbed by you classifiying me as a (non-sensical) 'enemy combatant.' In fact quite to the contrary I am humbled that Allah would honor me so"? Abbasi went on, while denying he had ever pledged loyalty to Osama bin Laden, to acknowledge that he had traveled from Britain to Afghanistan after determining that "military struggle . . . was an individual obligation upon me"; he intended "to either join [the] Taliban or fight for the sake of Allah in Kashmir." Once there, he wrote, he attended a meeting of senior Al Qaeda operatives, though he claimed he had no idea who they were prior to the meeting. And in response to the government's contention that during this meeting, he stated his intention to "take action against Americans and Jews," he wrote that his interrogators had gotten it wrong. He and "Abu Hafs"—a nom de guerre of Al Qaeda bigwig Mohammed Atef—had been discussing the fight against "THE Americans and

THE Jews." The missing definite article, he went on, signifies only "militar[ily] aggressive Americans and Jews" such as "American troops in Saudi Arabia and Israeli troops in Palestine."[15]

Do we really want a rule in which such people walk free, as Abbasi did on January 25, 2005, if prosecutors cannot prove a criminal offense beyond a reasonable doubt using admissible evidence? If Congress does not want such a maladaptive rule, a rule under which publicly sworn military enemies of our country must walk free in the absence of criminal charges, why should it not stand up and say so and define the situations under which such people might remain detained?

Congress, in fact, accepts the need for such a system. It has legislated around the periphery of the CSRTs, requiring disclosure of their procedures, for example, and providing for appellate review of their judgments, and it has never tried to prevent the military from holding detainees outside of the criminal justice system. But neither has it ever explicitly blessed the system, much less tailored it.

The first challenge in that project is figuring out the universe of detainees to which to apply an administrative detention regime. The United States holds tens of thousands of people in its overseas military activities, as of this writing approximately 26,000 in Iraq alone.[16] Only a small minority of these detainees plausibly require new law. Most detainees in U.S. custody are locked up in relatively conventional theater conflicts—situations in which the military fights regionally-specific wars of limited duration. Some of these, like the initial invasion of Iraq, are indisputably covered by the Third Geneva Convention. In others, like the current American presence in Iraq—which is no longer a formal occupation and is therefore not technically covered by the Fourth Geneva Convention—the military applies the convention as a matter of policy. While the laws of war generally require some updating, these conflicts pose no fundamental challenge to their vitality. The laws of war quite obviously represent the relevant body of law to apply, and they are, by and large, adequate for the detention of enemy fighters picked up in those contexts. Sometimes the war on terrorism looks a lot like pure warfare, and where it does, the Geneva Conventions remain the appropriate legal framework for the struggle.

The problem only arises with a subset of detainees for whom application of the norms of warfare permits the government at once too much latitude and too little. This subset comprises those detainees for whom release at the termination of hostilities is something of a fiction—those who, even if they have committed no crime, American forces cannot set free without mitigating their individual menace. The defining feature of these detainees is that they somehow transcend their theater of conflict. The international jihadi captured in Afghanistan differs from the local Taliban fighter; the latter will presumably demobilize when his movement surrenders, negotiates a peace, or gets wiped out. The former, by contrast, is part of a global struggle against the United States and the Western world more generally and may well move on to the next combat arena when the fight against the Taliban winds down. As we have seen, moreover, this person can be much harder to identify accurately than the traditional theater detainee. So relying here on the laws of war produces at once too low a threshold for the detention itself and paradoxically a requirement for release that is quite unsuited to a global fight with a nonstate actor.

The hallmark of this type of detainee is that one regards him as dangerous not merely as an arm of a particular military force but *in his individual capacity as well*—and that one cannot imagine relinquishing custody of him without some mechanism to manage the danger that he poses. Many, though by no means all, of the non-Afghan Guantánamo detainees probably meet this test, as do some detainees in Iraq. The latter group certainly exceeds the Guantánamo population in size, but is masked within a far larger population of more conventional theater detainees. Because the military applies the Geneva Conventions in Iraq, this group currently has a viable legal framework for its detention. But that framework won't last forever. There will come a time when the military will release large numbers of the detainees in Iraq because either the fighting ends or American troops are ready to leave the country. This subpopulation will then look suddenly like orphans of the laws of war, which will provide scant support for their continued detention. Yet notwithstanding that fact, their release will still seem like a terrible idea. If the military cannot arrange for the Iraqi government to take responsibility for them—perhaps by trial, perhaps by some other means—they will become indistinguishable from the Guantánamo population.

The group of detainees whose incarceration does not, in fact, depend on any particular state of armed conflict but flows from their individual menace as terrorists requires new law—both to tighten the standards and procedures for the detentions themselves and to justify those detentions to the public and the courts for as long as need be. This law needs to be severed from the laws of war, for its premises differ fundamentally from those of wartime detentions. As such, the reviewing body should be a civilian federal court assessing whether each detainee meets a legislatively prescribed standard, not a military panel assessing whether or not the detainee meets the definition of an "unlawful enemy combatant." At the same time, fully civilizing the detention and trial system, for reasons I will explain, would likely put at risk the ability to conduct criminal trials that don't sport the full panoply of rights and protections of the American criminal justice system. As a result, the trial system will probably have to retain some military influence. It will be, in other words, a hybrid that will unapologetically draw on both the military and civilian law enforcement traditions.

THE CONSTRUCTION of any administrative detention apparatus for the war on terrorism begins with the frank truth, described at length in Chapter 1, that the American legal system tolerates indefinite detention in a number of settings less compelling than the disabling of overseas terrorists with no connection to the United States save the desire to kill its nationals. A responsible administration and Congress would treat these detentions openly and candidly for what they are: preventive incarcerations designed to keep extremely dangerous individuals from acting on their deeply held murderous beliefs and instincts.

This is a psychological Rubicon we simply need to cross. Preventive detention seems so anti-American, so characteristic of regimes we detest, that many people prefer the comfort of the myth that our justice system does not countenance detention for things other than crimes. That the mythology is, well, mythological does not neutralize its power. Yet the result is perverse: the use of proxy detention powers far less suited to the task at hand and, ironically, less protective of the rights and interests of those locked up than a well-crafted administrative detention law would be. The federal government detained more Arab and Muslim men domestically in the immigration system after September 11 than have ever set foot in Guantánamo; it barely bothered to mask the preventive nature of some of those detentions. When an admitted Al Qaeda member states that he means to "kill Americans at the first opportunity upon his release from prison," we can kid ourselves that such a person is detained because he is an "enemy combatant"; the real reason we hold him, however, is no more his allegiance to the other side in a war than it is some crime prosecutors may or may not be able to prove against him. It is the menace he poses.[17] The psychological barrier to preventive detention has roots in the most laudable American values, but in the war on terrorism policy makers need to understand the limits of the principle.

Once we cross that threshold, we confront a practical problem: designing a scheme capable of isolating alien terrorists in a fashion that is as fair and accurate as possible. This task requires, first, an effort to define the population subject to administrative detention. At a minimum, this category should include overseas fighters who are not members of any uniformed military but have engaged in hostilities against the United States or its allies. It should also include individuals who have purposefully planned or have knowingly and materially supported those hostilities. It should not, however, include everyone who has ever aided or worked for the enemy, not even necessarily those who have ever fought for the enemy, but only those who pose a demonstrable prospective threat to American national security. These terms will require careful legislative definition; nobody wants American forces going around the world locking up pious old ladies who give a few dollars to charities. The core of the authority should more or less track the domestic power to lock up the insane: A person should be subject to administrative detention if he is both a member or associate of opposing forces *and* dangerous for that reason.

Defusing the controversy over such detentions requires the creation for each detainee of what does not exist today: a rigorous set of factual findings and a documentary record, available to the public and the press to the maximum extent possible and reviewed by an independent judicial body. As such, any legislative scheme requires a few core elements not present in the CSRTs, all designed to make the process more adversarial and courtlike and to produce an outcome that speaks with enough authority to support a detention in the public and judicial arenas.

The first of these is an impartial finder of fact—namely a federal judge. CSRT panels are made up of three military officers, none necessarily trained in law and all part of the normal chain of military command.[18] The military modeled this arrangement loosely on the Article 5 tribunals required by the Third Geneva Convention before an army can deny a captive treatment as a prisoner of war. For the more delicate fact-finding necessary to determine whether the government has competent evidence that a captive is detainable as an alien terrorist, however, the CSRTs are wholly inadequate. Indeed, if we make these judgments outside of the laws of war, there is no compelling reason for these tribunals to reside within the military at all. The military might capture alien terrorists. But so might domestic law enforcement. So might the intelligence agencies. While one can plausibly consider all such people military detainees under the laws of war, it makes just as much sense to consider their cases in a civilian context, as we do the mentally ill or the illegal alien with a criminal record. This strategy has a number of decided benefits. The most important is that it puts the prestige of the federal judiciary behind each detention judgment.

The detainee should also receive representation from competent counsel. The "personal representative" under current rules, who has no obligation to keep conversations with the detainee confidential and who is not charged with zealously representing the detainee's legal interests, is simply no substitute for professional assistance in either challenging the government's evidence or presenting the detainee's own story. As we have seen, many detention cases do require a resolution of disputed issues of fact. Asking judges—or the military, for that matter—to resolve these questions in the absence of a professional presentation on behalf of the detainee is asking for error. To enable a reasonable presentation on a detainee's behalf, lawyers for the detainees should be cleared to see the evidence against their clients, including classified information and all exculpatory materials. The detainee himself should be given a more detailed summary of the evidence against him, one sufficiently specific to provide a fair opportunity for rebuttal. The detainee should also receive a more meaningful opportunity to present evidence, obtain witnesses, compel testimony, cross-examine witnesses against him, and respond to evidence admitted against him.

At the same time, the standards for admissibility of evidence ought to be relatively low. The law should bar the Court considering a detention from admitting statements obtained by torture or conduct just short of it. But beyond that, probative material—even hearsay or physical evidence whose chain of custody or handling would not be adequate in a criminal trial—ought to be fair game. While the government should carry the burden of proof and that burden should be relatively exacting in comparison with combatant detentions under the laws of war, the rules should not preclude the government from using certain intelligence data that it could never introduce in federal court. Rather, they should permit the use of secret material, attacked in closed session by the detainee's counsel, and they should be open to all evidence probative to a reasonable person.

Finally, the Court must retain jurisdiction over each detention for as long as it persists to ensure that detention remains necessary and that the conditions of detainees' confinement are humane. The government should be obliged on a regular basis to argue for the continued necessity of detention, and counsel for each detainee should have the opportunity to argue that, for one reason or another, his client no longer meets the statutory criteria for detention: that, as an alien terrorist, he poses a substantial threat to the security of the United States.

The best way to implement such a system would be through some kind of specialized national security court, an idea others have proposed with varying

levels of specificity.[19] Modeled on the special court that authorizes surveillance in national security cases, the FISA court, such an arrangement would
maximize the public and international legitimacy of detention decisions. Having such a specialized court in this arena would put detentions in the hands of
judges with all the prestige of the federal court system, yet with particular expertise applying rules designed to protect classified information and manage
legitimate security concerns.

A somewhat less ambitious alternative would be legislation along the lines
proposed by Senate Armed Services Chairman Carl Levin in 2007.[20] This approach would bolster statutorily the procedural rights a detainee would receive within the CSRTs, beefing up the existing military panels but leaving the
first-line judgments in the hands of the military—not the civilian—justice
system. The function of the federal courts in this model would be to review
these judgments in much the same way that federal courts routinely review
actions by federal administrative agencies. This model's advantage is that it
would be far easier to harmonize with current practices, as it builds on the
system that already exists, under which detainees can appeal CSRT judgments
to the D.C. Circuit Court of Appeals. The major disadvantage, however, is
that it would still leave the power to detain rooted in the laws of war and the
detention decision itself in the hands of the military. This would forfeit the
unique power of judicial fact-finding to justify detentions in the minds of
the public. Its proximity to a discredited prior policy also may give such a
system—perhaps unfairly—the taint of executive detention with a judicial
rubber stamp. By not separating war-on-terror detentions clearly from more
traditional wartime detentions, moreover, it would retain the current policy's
conceptual and legal peculiarity of providing for law-of-war detentions in a
conflict that lacks defining attributes of warfare.

The regime I have sketched here contains real risks, about which I wish
to be candid: One is the risk of injustice, another the risk of making necessary detentions too difficult. The distance between the detention norms in
the criminal justice system and under the laws of war is so vast that any effort to hybridize them necessarily involves accepting some of the ills against

which these systems evolved to protect. The criminal justice system protects—imperfectly—against punishment based on wrongful accusation. Water down the evidentiary threshold for incarceration, allow in evidence the criminal justice system would not admit, and permit a measure of secrecy in considering certain evidence, and the result will be an increased error rate over that which the criminal justice system would tolerate. Some of these errors will trigger real injustices.

The flip side of this coin also presents genuine dangers. Detentions under the laws of war are designed to facilitate the disabling of enemy fighters without killing them. Give such fighters lawyers, raise the evidentiary bar, and put a substantial burden of proof on the government to justify each detention, and the result will be that some very dangerous people will go free and do bad things. That has already happened with some releases from Guantánamo; some number of released detainees have gone back to the fight.[21] The more courtlike and fair procedures become, the more likely nasty characters are to benefit from that fairness. And those errors too have human rights consequences, albeit ones that human rights groups tend to ignore. Releasing fighters bent on killing civilians is a dubious triumph for human liberty.

At least in my judgment, however, the balancing of risks in a carefully crafted administrative detention scheme makes more sense than either the system of wartime detentions that has evolved since September 11 or the reversion to a purer law enforcement approach to locking up the bad guys. The latter option would simply turn loose large numbers of dangerous people. Ironically, the current system may have the effect of doing the same thing. It has the courts breathing down the administration's neck. Presidential candidates in the 2008 race promised to abandon it. America's allies hate it, and the U.S. population neither admires nor understands it. Its very secrecy and permissiveness guarantee its vulnerability—and its vulnerability creates huge political pressure to release or transfer detainees who in fact ought not go free. Guantánamo is steadily depopulating, and America will, I fear, come to regret some of the releases the Pentagon now races to effectuate. Only a system enshrined in law and requiring of the executive enough restraint to command respect for the detentions it permits can create the kind of sound basis for long-term imprisonments that will permit them to take place when needed and for as long as necessary.

THE IDEA OF CREATING civilian legal authorities for holding those detainees whom the laws of war fit badly paradoxically complicates—rather than simplifying—the project of trying detainees for crimes. Ideally, one wants to maximize the size of the group that will face trial, since the more incarcerations America can justify with credible convictions for serious crimes, the fewer people it will have to hold without trial in a system struggling to acquire domestic and international acceptance. Yet ironically, the desire to conduct a large volume of criminal trials presents strong reason to stick with some form of military tribunal, even as the detention function migrates to a civilian agency—presumably the Department of Justice. Trying terrorists in federal court is a tricky business. Yank people out of the military system and treat them as civilians and it is suddenly no longer clear by what authority the government can depart from the letter of two hundred years of case law concerning trials under the Bill of Rights. Honor every bit of that case law, however, and conducting actual trials will become so difficult that the available pool of defendants for whom it presents a viable option will likely decline dramatically. The perverse result will be, in the name of the human rights and civil liberties of terrorist suspects, to place greater weight on a system of indefinite detention that grants them fewer protections than even the meanest military trial. By contrast, America has a long tradition of military commissions, and the Supreme Court has always tolerated the idea that the government might mete out stiff penalties—including death—based on military procedures that deviate from the trial norms of civilian courts. As recently as *Hamdan,* in fact, the justices took it as a virtual given that military commissions, properly authorized, could be lawful.[22]

Yet military commissions too have problems. By their very nature, they are limited in jurisdiction to the trial of war crimes and, specifically, to trials of unlawful enemy combatants for those war crimes. Treat detainees as civilians for purposes of detentions and it is no longer clear by what authority the military may try them. The alternative is a most peculiar hybrid: holding people in civilian detention yet subjecting them to military trials.

The simplest unraveling of this gnarly knot would be to dispense with trials altogether—which is, for all practical purposes, what the Bush administration has done. It has, to be sure, completed a few trials (and for all its talk of military commissions, all but one of them in federal court). Most suspected terrorists, however, have ended up in administrative detention and simply stayed there. Both federal court trials and military commissions have, in practice, proven largely hypothetical options with respect to most detainees captured. Even high-value detainees like Khalid Sheikh Mohammed and Ramzi Binalshibh, those whose trials would presumably pay the biggest public relations dividends, went unprosecuted for years before the government finally got around to filing charges in 2008—and the public hardly clamored in discontent. The idea may shock the civil libertarian conscience, but it is worth asking whether, if the country's administrative detention apparatus were more satisfying and credible, America could sever counterterrorism incarceration from the criminal process altogether. Unless we understand *why* we try terrorism suspects, the answers to questions like *when* and *how* we do so will tend—as they have during the Bush administration—to gravitate towards convenience. And because convenience will almost always militate against bothering with a trial, criminal charges will almost invariably tend to look like an unnecessary and resource-intensive assumption of risk. After all, what happens if you try a high-value detainee you could not possibly release, and a court acquits him?

With traditional crime, we try suspects in part because trial represents the only means at the government's disposal to incapacitate criminals from further damaging society; the preventive function and the punitive function are intimately bound up with one another. With most counterterrorism captures, by contrast, detention fully satisfies the need to protect society against the detainee, so the added value of any trial is comparatively small. The major reason to hold a trial is a kind of legal public relations: Trials have more public acceptance than administrative detentions. They fit in better with the values of a democratic, rule-of-law society. Many European countries harbor deep discomfort with detention without criminal trial—though their own criminal justice systems often grant their governments far greater detention and other investigative powers than does America's.[23] The more people whose long-term incarcerations the government can tie specifically to criminal verdicts, the less friction and controversy those incarcerations will incur. This benefit, while real, is far from overwhelming given the difficulty of terrorism trials, and it doesn't provide a tremendous incentive to bring criminal cases against a baseline of comparatively easy detention.

Yet having no working trial system is dangerous. An administration that wanted to alleviate this country's alienation from its allies by maximizing the acceptability of its war on terrorism policies literally could not do so without letting dangerous people go free—for it has established neither federal court trials nor military commissions as reliably viable trials options. The administration has wanted to bring charges in military commissions against a substantial number of Guantánamo detainees for some time, yet has failed to do so. As the intelligence value of detainees declines and the desire to mend fences with allies increases, the attractiveness of trying detainees will likely increase along with it—at least somewhat. The more functional an option our trial system presents at that point, the more often the government will choose to use it.

This is the main reason the human rights groups are so misguided in their contemporary insistence that terrorism trials require no special rules or deviations from traditional trial norms. To demand, as Amnesty International repeatedly does, that detainees face normal trials in U.S. federal courts is really to demand that, in practice, fewer of them face trial at all.

The most successful American terrorist prosecutions took place during the 1990s, when the FBI broke up the cell surrounding Sheikh Omar Abdel Rahman in the years that followed the first World Trade Center bombing. One indicator of the inadequacy of federal court procedures for trying terrorists is the fact that neither the judge in that case nor the prosecutor emerged as advocates for normal criminal trials for such defendants in the future. The lead prosecutor, Andrew McCarthy, recently coauthored a paper arguing for congressional establishment of a "National Security Court" to create "an appropriate forum for fairly detaining and trying terrorists no matter how long the war on terror ensues" and for thereby "removing from our criminal justice system cases for which it was not designed and the handling of which necessarily reduces the quality of justice afforded by the system."[24] The judge, who later went on to preside over the litigation surrounding the initial phases of Jose Padilla's detention, was Attorney General Michael Mukasey. The Second Circuit Court of Appeals on appeal described in effusive terms Mukasey's handling of the case, which involved numerous defendants in addition to Rahman, saying he had "presided with extraordinary skill and patience, assuring fairness to the prosecution and to each defendant and helpfulness to the jury. His was an outstanding achievement in the face of challenges far beyond those normally endured by a trial judge."[25] If anyone's work has demonstrated that civilian justice can handle international terrorism, it is Mukasey. Yet shortly before his appointment as attorney general, he wrote that far from demonstrating the adequacy of the civilian justice system for handling terrorists, Padilla's conviction demonstrates that "current institutions and statutes are not well suited to even the limited task of supplementing what became, after Sept. 11, 2001, principally a military effort to combat Islamic terrorism." Ideas like McCarthy's, Mukasey argued, "deserve careful scrutiny by the public, and particularly by the U.S. Congress. It is Congress that authorized the use of armed force after Sept. 11—and it is Congress that has the constitutional authority to establish additional inferior courts as the need may be, or even to modify the Supreme Court's appellate jurisdiction."[26]

The problem, put simply, is that criminal trials in the federal system give defendants a bonanza of procedural opportunities to gouge sensitive information from the government and to force the government to choose between the vitality of its prosecution and other crucial interests. Terrorism trials consume immense resources. They can offer defendants a platform from which to command public attention and communicate with confederates. Perhaps most important, the fundamental mismatch between the manners in which intelligence officers collect information and in which criminal investigators amass evidence can paralyze prosecutors who inherit defendants from intelligence investigations.

Moussaoui's case put all of these problems on vivid display—though, in sharp contrast to Mukasey, the presiding judge in that trial emerged as an impassioned advocate of federal court terrorism trails.[27] The government ultimately obtained a conviction, but it also lucked out. Moussaoui, the only person to face criminal charges in federal court in this country in connection with September 11, may have been a dangerous terrorist, but he was also a nutcase who tried to represent himself, filed crazed pleadings, and made ludicrous courtroom speeches in which he repeatedly compromised any potential defense by admitting to key elements of the charges against him—for example, that he was a member of Al Qaeda, pledged to attack America. For months, he refused to cooperate with his court-appointed lawyers, and when the judge took away his ability to act as his own counsel, he pleaded guilty—thereby relieving the government of the burden of proving a tricky case.

Despite the lucky breaks, Moussaoui's conviction took an extraordinary effort: nearly five years of litigation up and down the federal appellate ladder, millions of dollars, and a docket so long that a mere computer listing of the public documents filed in the case takes up more than two hundred pages.[28] The case required the handling of massive volumes of classified information, even more than is typical in national security cases. And more particularly, it involved potential witnesses whose testimony Moussaoui sought yet whom the government was holding and interrogating in its high-value detainee program overseas and refused to produce for security reasons. A defendant more inclined to demand his rights and less inclined to turn the Courtroom into a circus could have made these proceedings far more difficult than Moussaoui did, and the question of the availability of overseas detainees to such trials still lacks a definitive answer. It is, therefore, no surprise that after Moussaoui, noncitizen Al Qaeda suspects have not shown up in American courts if the government can avoid bringing criminal cases. Prosecutors dropped one such case, that of an Al Qaeda suspect named Ali Saleh Kahlah al-Marri, and turned the defendant over to the military as an enemy combatant.[29] Even as the government claimed Moussaoui's case a victory, it has avoided testing these waters again.

Other problems with federal court terrorism trials are less visible. Perhaps the most important of these is that the criminal process can remove interrogation from the table. Consider the cases of Ramzi Yousef, the mastermind of the first World Trade Center bombing, and would-be shoe-bomber Richard Reid. The Justice Department prosecuted both men in federal court. Reid pled guilty without a plea bargain requiring his cooperation. Yusef was convicted at trial. As a result, government agents did not have the opportunity to interrogate them as they would a military detainee—or a civilian detainee under the system I have outlined above. Indeed, rules of legal ethics affirmatively *prohibit* lawyers from contacting people known to be represented by lawyers but require instead that attorneys go through one another in negotiating with clients.[30] And, of course, criminal suspects famously have a right to remain silent and to have an attorney present at questioning. So unless a plea bargain facilitates a defendant's cooperation, the information he possesses can elude authorities.

In short, to rely on normal federal court processes for terrorism trials would likely mean in practice very few trials—and, as a consequence, either a lot of administrative detention if that is available or dangerous people walking free if it is not. With respect to citizens, federal court trial represents the only viable option for now, so the rare case like Padilla's will still end up in federal court. With respect to foreigners, however, the huge gulf between the difficulty of trial and the ease of detention by other means ensures that if we rely on this system, we make the trial option hugely unattractive. It's not that they can't be done, but they can't be done easily enough to make them worth the marginal benefit they promise.

To some degree, the use of general courts martial might bridge the gulf. Courts martial, the tribunals in which the military tries its own personnel, offer a highly developed trial system conducted in a somewhat more controlled environment than a federal court. Many observers, including numerous military lawyers, believe that trials under the Uniform Code of Military Justice (UCMJ) present a viable trial option from which the military need not have departed in order to conduct successfully orderly trials that reasonably protect sensitive material and proceed in a secure and controlled environment. To be sure, courts martial would partially alleviate the problem. I suspect, however, that they would alleviate it far less than advocates of trials under the UCMJ believe. With rights that have come to mirror closely those promised in federal court, a UCMJ trial system would—though perhaps less than federal court proceedings—create a significant disincentive for trying people at all. And just as with federal court trials, this incentive structure will operate as a kind of inverse function: The more difficult trials are to conduct, the fewer of them there will be. To get as many of them as possible, Congress should aim to make trials, at least of non-Americans, as pared down as it can reconcile with fundamental fairness and due process. The UCMJ, and particularly the case law under it, promises more than America owes to suspected alien terrorists.

The alternative is to try these individuals using modestly depressed standards. The goal here is not, as the administration aimed to do with its initial military commission order shortly after the advent of the war, to make the ideological point that America need not give detainees a full-fledged trial, that the executive branch can determine on its own what rules to use, and that the rest of the world—and the courts—can be damned if they don't like it. The goal, rather, is narrow and practical: a trial regime that gives detainees enough due process to satisfy the commands of the Constitution and garner international tolerance, if not quite admiration, yet at the same time facilitates the maximum number of criminal trials, thereby lessening the burden that any system of administrative detention will have to bear.

Vituperative rhetoric aside, the MCA is not a terrible place to start. The actual deviations it authorizes from standard practice in courts martial are not dramatic. As the administration's regulatory commissions went through numerous revisions and finally through the legislative process, they grew a great deal closer to the normal military justice system. The commissions offer the government considerable flexibility in protecting classified information, though unlike earlier proposals, they would not permit anyone's conviction on the basis of material he cannot see and challenge.[31] They offer somewhat relaxed rules of evidence, under which commissions may admit material "if the military judge determines that [it] would have probative value to a reasonable person." The law specifically allows the admission of hearsay unless the military judge decides that the threat of unfairness it poses outweighs its probative value.[32] And this is, to be sure, more permissive than the federal rules of evidence or their counterparts in courts martial.[33] Discovery rules have similar flex in the joints. And, most controversially, the MCA does not categorically bar statements given under duress. While it prevents any statement obtained by torture from serving as evidence, it allows the admission of statements obtained by coercion short of torture if the military judge finds that the statement is reliable and would be probative to a reasonable person.[34] While these standards certainly deviate from contemporary American practice, the tolerance of hearsay is actually quite similar to the rules of international tribunals that human rights groups tend to admire and the justice of whose verdicts they don't contest. Assuming judges treat allegedly coerced statements conservatively under the rules, there is, in other words, no good reason to believe that fair trials that meet accepted international standards could not take place under MCA-like procedures.

That said, Congress could not simply import the MCA's standards into civilian courts; the Bill of Rights promises a jury trial, to cite only one rather fundamental problem. So the question is how to justify constitutionally the sort of modest deviations from federal court practice that might facilitate a great many more trials.

One possibility is to rely on Guantánamo. Aliens abroad, at least as of this writing, have no constitutional rights. Guantánamo remains technically abroad, and Congress can therefore do as it likes there—until the Supreme Court says otherwise. This option has certain superficial attractions, but it would be shortsighted. For one thing, holding terrorist trials offshore because they would not meet domestic legal requirements would send exactly the wrong message about what America seeks to accomplish. The task of putting America's enemies before the bar of justice is not some illicit tax shelter or some Internet gambling scheme, for which one runs off to a nearby Caribbean island that has some nominal sovereignty and convenient laws. America should have a trial system of which we can stand proud before the world, one in which trials could take place as lawfully in Washington as in Cuba. While one can muster strong operational reasons for keeping detainees at Guantá-namo, hiding from the Constitution is not one of them. The second problem is that current doctrine, under which detainees at the base have no constitu-tional rights, probably has a short future anyway. The courts, as discussed earlier, clearly contemplate applying American law to the base—either as part of some larger assertion of extraterritorial application of constitutional rules or, more modestly, because of its peculiar international status. Relying on the present state of the law, therefore, just asks for trouble down the line, when the high court will treat that doctrine with the same disrespect it has already shown related precedents.

The alternative is to harness the long tradition in constitutional law of tol-erating deviations from conventional trial practice in the particular context of military commission trials. That means that, unlike the detention procedure, the trials will still need to be rooted in the laws of war: One cannot hold mili-tary commissions for civilian offenses, only for war crimes. These trials, how-ever, should not have roots *only* in the laws of war. Military commissions have a nasty sound, in large measure because of their long disuse, the rough justice they have sometimes administered in the past, and the crudeness with which the administration sought to revive them. If they have a future—and, in my view, they must if criminal trial is to represent a significant feature of the war on terror—Congress will have to create an elegant marriage between them and certain civilian trial norms so as to give the more relaxed procedural di-mensions of the MCA some of the public legitimacy of federal court trials.

The DTA and MCA already started down this road to a degree, providing civilian court review of military commission procedures. And McCarthy and his coauthor sensibly proposed taking this logic a big step further and adding a federal judge to the existing military commission format, thereby "com-bin[ing] features of military commissions, which give pride of place to na-tional security, with the stewardship of Article 3 judges independent of the executive branch."[35] Convicts could appeal their convictions directly up the federal appellate ladder. Congress might incorporate other elements of civil-ian trials as well: a unanimous verdict for purposes of conviction, for example, or perhaps even a civilian jury. The basic rule of thumb should be that procedures for trying those accused of terrorism will in spots require special flexibility but ought to look as much like standard federal court practice as possible.

Such a hybrid trial scheme should pass muster constitutionally if designed carefully. The Supreme Court in *Hamdi* specifically upheld the military's authority to detain unlawful enemy combatants in this conflict. It has upheld military commissions in the past and strongly implied in *Hamdan* that, with an appropriate act of Congress, it would regard them as proper now, too. The Court's having said all this, it would be exceptionally odd for it then to object to tribunals modeled on commissions yet with procedural protections *added* to make them fairer and more like regular courts.

The key to maintaining the constitutionality of this scheme is that these courts—whatever Congress chooses to call them—must have jurisdiction only over war crimes and only over unlawful enemy combatants. That way, the government will be able to defend them, wherever it convenes them, as traditional military commissions with enhanced new protections and judicial review, rather than as a diminution of the rights guaranteed in federal court.

There is, as I noted earlier, admittedly a tension between holding detainees in civilian custody and trying them using a military process. The tension, however, ought to be surmountable as long as Congress makes clear that the status of "alien terrorist" under American domestic law and the status of "unlawful enemy combatant" are not mutually exclusive categories. Under the MCA, for example, a person qualifies as an unlawful enemy combatant— and therefore for trial before a military commission—if he "has engaged in hostilities or . . . has purposefully and materially supported hostilities against the United States or its co-belligerents [and] is not a lawful enemy combatant (including a person who is part of the Taliban, Al Qaeda, or associated forces)."[36] While this definition could certainly bear some tightening, even its current text illuminates how a regime based on military commissions might coexist with a civilianized detention scheme. A person, after all, can meet this definition while in civilian custody. As long as prosecutors can demonstrate facts adequate to trigger military trial jurisdiction, the law should not

preclude the use of a procedure that might fall short of constitutional acceptability for an American service member but dramatically exceeds what the
Supreme Court has accepted for unlawful combatants in the past. Nor should
it preclude the addition of civilian trial elements that ought to significantly
reassure public and international opinion. Under such a regime, even many
alien terrorists captured domestically could face trial under streamlined rules.

AMERICAN CITIZENS and permanent resident aliens, for a variety of interrelated reasons, should not face such trials. The Constitution might theoretically tolerate a military commission for an American citizen. It has in the past
and the best reading of case law suggests that it could again in the future.[37] But
the administration has wisely declined to test this proposition. Citizens and
permanent resident aliens are unambiguously part of the American social
compact, and we can therefore expect courts to show far more solicitude for
their rights than they will show to nonresident aliens. This is not just a function of judicial adventurism; there exists a big difference between Khalid
Sheikh Mohammad and Jose Padilla, and it's not just that one is an Al Qaeda
kingpin and the other a lesser figure. It's that Padilla has deep ties with American society. He grew up on its streets and spent time in its prisons. If our justice system does him unjust injury, it injures the American body politic. This
feeling, to some degree, finds a home in American law. But far more than that,
it will find a home in the hearts of judges who hear criminal cases. And if
American law does not treat this country's nationals and permanent residents
as a distinct class with privileged rights in the justice system, the solicitousness
the courts will show their plight could well destroy any ability to relax trial
and detention standards for those outside of its social compact.

Congress, rather, needs to posture the law so as to ensure that when the
courts confront a detention and trial scheme for the war on terrorism, they do
not confront a slipperly slope in which what they approve for Khalid Sheikh
Mohammad today the government will use for someone like Jose Padilla to-
morrow, a minor drug offender next week, and a political dissenter five years
from now. The legislature needs to force the courts to confront the question

differently: Does the Constitution disable the legislature in the absence of a federal court trial from authorizing the detention of a foreigner who allies himself with the enemy? Does it prohibit the legislature from tailoring a trial regime for such people and thereby perversely *mandate* that the military hold them without charge? The answers to these questions will prove different if Congress does not keep American citizens out of the stew.

Fortunately, the number of American citizens involved in terrorism has so far proven miniscule. They fit relatively neatly into three categories: battlefield detainees, those easily subjected to trial in federal courts, and the singular, high-profile, and deeply disturbing case of Jose Padilla.

America should generally treat those captured on traditional battlefields or in theaters of active combat as it does other detainees caught under similar circumstances. There will surely be slight differences. Because Americans are entitled to receive habeas corpus review wherever in the world the military might hold them, they need to have liberal access to counsel. But as long as the United States is applying the laws of war and envisions releasing detainees when hostilities end, an American fighting for the other side is little different from a Saudi fighting for the other side. The great error the administration made in Yasser Esam Hamdi's case lay not in capturing or holding the young Saudi man who happened to have been born in Louisiana. It lay in making a spectacle of him by bringing him to the United States and trying there to frustrate judicial review of his detention. In similar cases involving detainees in Iraq, the military has not repeated its error.[38]

For long-term detention of American citizens outside of traditional law-of-war situations, no substitute for trial should exist. As long as the numbers remain so small, the justice system can manage the burdens associated with federal court trials. The Justice Department reached plea agreements with John Walker Lindh, a battlefield detainee of whom, unlike Hamdi, the government wished to make an example. It reached plea deals as well with the Lackawanna defendants, who had trained at an Al Qaeda camp in Afghanistan, and it has successfully prosecuted a few other citizens as well. Using federal courts for American citizens could become more difficult if the number of Americans wrapped up with Al Qaeda were to grow substantially, or if

Americans began emerging as the kind of senior Al Qaeda leaders or operatives whose trials would profoundly test its system. Over time, if Al Qaeda begins actively recruiting Americans because of their ease of entry into the United States and their ability to navigate its culture, we may have revisit this question. But as long as the number of Americans involved in jihad against their country in any way is a rounding error on the detainee population, the traditional justice system—difficult as it may sometimes be—seems the way to go.

The truly hard category has only one member: Padilla. It has become somewhat fashionable to describe Padilla—the man held for years as an "enemy combatant" after his arrest at O'Hare International Airport in Chicago, Illinois, and finally convicted by a jury in Florida of crimes unrelated to the menace he allegedly posed—as a small-fry victim of governmental overreaction, or to insist that his ultimate conviction showed that the criminal justice system is adequate for the job of neutralizing people like him.[39] The truth is that when Padilla arrived in Chicago, he presented the government with a very hard case.

Intelligence agencies had learned of him through the coercive interrogations of high-level Al Qaeda operatives overseas. He had a serious criminal record—as a juvenile, he had even been involved in a murder—and they had information that he was on his way here to conduct devastating terrorist attacks. Then, only eight months after September 11, 2001, he showed up in the United States. Law enforcement agents initially detained him as a material witness in a terrorism investigation. But Padilla was no Lindh or Hamdi. He was a genuine thug who had allegedly developed high-level Al Qaeda contacts and had been sent here to conduct operations. It is too easy, years after the fact, to dismiss him as a nothing. In 2002, no responsible government official could have regarded him as anything other than a most extreme threat.[40]

The government, however, had a problem: It couldn't make a criminal case against Padilla. Its evidence consisted of intelligence that was both too sensitive to use in court and obtained by coercive means against other detainees. And Padilla himself wasn't talking. The decision to designate him as an enemy combatant and transfer him to military custody was an effort not merely—or even chiefly—to aggrandize executive power but to prevent his release and to create a detention status under which agents could interrogate him and find out what he knew.

In accomplishing this, the administration made several critical errors. For starters, then–Attorney General John Ashcroft dramatically announced the arrest as the foiling of a dirty bomb plot—an allegation from which the government later had to back away and which greatly diminished its credibility. More fundamentally, the decision not merely to hold Padilla but to keep him from contact with his lawyers and to frustrate any legal process for him was both unfair and self-defeating. These errors, however, should not obscure the genuine difficulty of the situation the administration faced—and will likely face again. It probably needs a narrow statute to allow some short-term detention power for such cases, when they arise in the future.

The model for such a law ought to be civil commitment of the dangerously mentally ill—with two big differences. The first is that the law must allow the Court to consider classified material and intelligence information that might not meet traditional evidentiary standards. The accused would not have access to this classified evidence; his lawyers, to whom he would have access, would be encouraged to attack it vigorously. The second major difference is that detentions under this regime would have strict time limits. This model would serve not as a system of indefinite preventive detention, but as an emergency stopgap to neutralize an imminent terrorist threat posed by an American citizen who—for one reason or another—the criminal justice system cannot incapacitate. As such, it would require the government, over a relatively brief period of time, to put up or shut up. Had Jose Padilla wished to blow up apartment buildings because of delusions associated with schizophrenia, American law would tolerate his commitment for as long as necessary to secure the public from him. Surely, the fact that he wished to blow up those buildings on assignment from Abu Zubaydah should not preclude a fixed, say, six-month period of detention so federal authorities can protect the public, interrogate him, and try to either build a criminal case against him or correct their misapprehensions about the danger he poses.[41] After the massacre at Virginia Tech in 2007, many commentators criticized Virginia law for not having confined killer Seung-Hui Cho, who had shown obvious signs of violent mental illness.[42] Would this argument have been less compelling had Cho acted for ideological reasons, having displayed similarly obvious signs of violent jihadism?

Our system has deep ideals. It is not, however, pure—and never has been. Constructing a detention and trial regime for the war on terrorism is a project in mining those impurities. Congress ought not feel ashamed of this project. Those impurities are our system's nods to unpleasant realities—and we face such realities now. We have preserved these unpleasant legal principles for use at such an hour.

SEVEN

An Honest
Interrogation Law

M ANY YEARS AGO, at least 20, maybe more, I was in Jerusalem and had an interview with Jacobo Timerman," began former *New York Times* columnist Anthony Lewis at a 2004 forum on torture and the road to Abu Ghraib. Timerman, Lewis explained, "was a prisoner in Argentina who was tortured." After his release, he immigrated to Israel. "Timerman and I were talking about a lot of things one day, and we got onto the subject of torture. He started asking me questions." Timerman told Lewis, "Suppose you had a prisoner, and you knew that he knew that there was a bomb about to go off in a crowded city. . . . Say you knew that it was going to happen within two or three hours. And that you thought that if you tortured this man, you could find out where the bomb was, and you could prevent the terrible loss of life. Would you do it?" Lewis tried to avoid the question, but Timerman pressed and he finally acknowledged, "Well, I am reluctant, but I guess I would." Timerman responded, shouting, "No! You cannot start down that road!" Lewis told his audience that he has "never forgotten that moment. You cannot start down that road. That is what I believe about torture."

Actually, it's not quite what Lewis believes about torture, as a single question from the forum's moderator quickly made clear. "Are you so sure that

Timerman was right?" Lewis initially seemed to try, once again, to avoid the question, calling it unfair. Most of the time the government "thinks it knows that people know something, it is wrong," he argued. But then he answered it, and it turns out that Lewis's answer had not changed all that much in the two decades since Timerman had spoken those words he never forgot. "If I actually believed . . . that somebody who was a prisoner under my control knew where there were weapons of mass destruction, nuclear weapons . . . that were going to be used shortly, I might change my view. Yes, I might."[1]

So maybe, under certain circumstances, you can start down that road after all.

Few issues provoke the kind of high-minded moral rhetoric that interrogation does, and with good reason. Torture is one of the hallmarks of totalitarianism, antithetical to liberty and consequently corrosive of democratic values. Yet dig deep enough—and it often does not take much digging—and the most categorical opposition to coercive interrogation gives way to consequentialism. Often it's the so-called ticking time bomb case. Said Senator John McCain, author of the DTA's interrogation restrictions and a torture victim himself, when confronted with the question of what the president should do if he learned that Al Qaeda had hidden a nuclear bomb in New York and he had a suspect in custody: "You do what you have to do." McCain doesn't think what you "have to do" should be legal. But he doesn't urge shrinking from it either.[2] He makes clear as well that if an interrogator can through such tactics "save an American city or prevent another 9/11, authorities and the public would surely take this into account when judging his actions and recognize the extremely dire situation which he confronted."[3] Jessica Montell, executive director of the Israeli human rights group B'Tselem, which campaigns against coercive interrogation practices, put the matter just as bluntly. "If I as an interrogator feel that the person in front of me has information that can prevent a catastrophe from happening," she said, "I imagine that I would do what I would have to do in order to prevent that catastrophe from happening. The state's obligation is then to put me on trial, for breaking the law . . . and then the Court decides whether or not it's reasonable that I broke the law in order to avert this catastrophe."[4]

There are, of course, principled opponents of coercive interrogations, people who like Timerman object in *all* circumstances to physical or mental coercion and who insist on maintaining that position however dire the consequences may be. Law professor David Luban, for example, dismissed the ticking time bomb scenario as "an intellectual fraud" that is "proffered against liberals who believe in an absolute prohibition against torture. The idea is to force the liberal prohibitionist to admit that yes, even he or she would agree to torture in at least this one situation. Once the prohibitionist admits that, then she has conceded that her opposition to torture is not based on principle" and is left "haggling about the price." Luban compared this tactic intellectually to "Getting the vegetarian to eat just one little oyster because it has no nervous system. Once she does that—*gotcha!*"[5] Others confront the hypothetical more directly. Kenneth Roth, executive director of Human Rights Watch, declared that "the prohibition on torture is one of the basic, absolute prohibitions that exists in international law. It exists in time of peace as well as in time of war. It exists regardless of the severity of a security threat."[6] Philosopher Henry Shue wrote that were he capable of saving the lives of dozens of children on an airplane by authorizing the torture of a suspected terrorist to find out on which plane he had planted his bomb, "I honestly believe that I would have said, 'Let's risk it—let's gamble that we can honor our principles and that the children . . . will not only not die but will live in civilized countries.'"[7]

But as the Lewis and McCain examples show, there are not many truly principled opponents of all coercion in all interrogations at all times. And whatever rhetorical pose politicians adopt, categorical opposition to coercive interrogation is not a tenable position for anyone with actual responsibility for protecting a country. The real question is not whether coercion is ever appropriate but how much coercion, how rarely, and with what, if any, degree of legal sanction. Judge Richard A. Posner, with typical indelicacy, spoke for a broad and cross-ideological swath of opinion when he wrote in approving paraphrase of law professor Alan Dershowitz: "If the stakes are high enough, torture is [morally] permissible. No one who doubts that this is the case should be in a position of responsibility. If torture is the only means of obtaining the information necessary to prevent the detonation of a nuclear bomb in

Times Square, torture should be used—and will be used—to obtain the information."[8]

The currently contested terrain in the battles over interrogation policy only secondarily involves torture itself, for the administration no longer asserts the legal propriety of torturing people—as its earlier memoranda seemed to do. It now merely argues about what conduct counts as torture. And to be fair, many of the coercive techniques used in the war on terrorism clearly do not qualify under federal law's strict definition. Other tactics, particularly waterboarding, straddle the line, but the use of waterboarding has been discontinued. In practice, the contested legal ground mostly involves a lesser category of illegal abuse: "cruel, inhuman, and degrading treatment." And it poses three distinct yet interwoven questions: Where should the legal lines in interrogations lie? When, if ever, should we permit transgressions of those lines? And how readily should the law tolerate circumvention of the legal rules using foreign proxy intelligence services? For clarity's sake, I use the word "torture" to refer only to conduct that violates the federal antitorture statute: an "act committed by a person acting under the color of law specifically intended to inflict severe physical or mental pain or suffering . . . upon another person within his custody or physical control."[9] Acknowledging that lesser tactics might still reach most people's colloquial understanding of torture, I use the term "coercive interrogation" to describe physical or mental pressures that do not meet this threshold.

In a fashion that parallels the relationship between detention and trial, the rules for interrogation and the rules for covert actions and renditions operate as a system. Make it too hard for the military or civilian officials to interrogate people held openly, and you increase the attraction of a secret program in undisclosed sites where unpleasant interrogation tactics can take place quietly. Tie the hands of CIA interrogators too tightly in such a program, and you create an incentive for rendition to countries that lack Western scruples about interrogation tactics. On the other hand, allow the military too much leeway in interrogations and you pay enormous costs both in its public image and in its internal discipline. Allow the CIA to play "bad cop" while the military plays nice, and you project to the world an image of hypocrisy—an image you accentuate even further if you use Syrian or Egyptian interrogators in lieu of the CIA's own. No magically cost-free formula will deliver an interrogation policy that at once optimizes information flow and America's image and decency. The administration, however, made some particularly unfortunate choices in this area.

THE FLEXIBILITY the administration truly required in questioning Al Qaeda suspects concerned the very point that few people doubt in their hearts: that the rules against physically aggressive interrogations must—notwithstanding their absolutist language—sometimes give way when the stakes run high enough and more civilized options prove unavailing. Yet the administration claimed a great deal more flexibility than that. By reading laws written to restrict coercive interrogations so as to permit them, it claimed in effect that these laws had little or no meaning—not just that it had to operate outside them in a few extreme cases but that they actually *allowed* behavior the law was never intended to allow and should not allow. What's more, by conducting its covert CIA interrogation program in quasi-public—that is, by announcing that it had captured people like Khalid Sheikh Mohammed and then making them disappear into "black" detention sites—it effectively announced a policy of coercive interrogations, which President Bush ultimately did openly in September 2006, when he finally shipped the CIA prisoners to Guantánamo. The administration, in other words, did not merely insist either that the rules must have exceptions or, like McCain, that interrogators might sometimes have to breach them. It announced, rather—all the while strenuously denying that it ever engaged or would ever engage in torture—that the law *allowed* physically coercive interrogations and that it conducted them, at least sometimes, as a matter of policy.

For its part, Congress has played a particularly slippery game on interrogation. It has passed two laws articulating flat bans on vaguely defined categories of abuse: torture and cruel, inhuman, and degrading treatment. The absoluteness of the bans gives members the ability to argue that they have authorized nothing untoward in any questioning of anyone. The vagueness, meanwhile, gives the administration enough interpretive latitude to authorize some pretty extreme tactics—waterboarding being only the furthest out on the limb. Members, therefore, need not take responsibility either for the intelligence failures associated with insufficiently vigorous interrogations or for the excesses of those interrogations, particularly when their fruits do not end up justifying their brutality. President Bush vetoed Congress's one serious effort to give clear guidance to the CIA about where the lines really lie. And the legislature has never tried passing meaningful restrictions and creating exemptions for certain emergency situations. On the books, therefore, is an absolute injunction not to do anything too mean—leaving far too open the question of what meanness is and how much of it is too much.

The result is a terrible conundrum for interrogators in the field: We want them to be aggressive, to walk up to the line of legality in an effort to get information that will stop the next attack. If any space remains between their conduct of interrogations and that line, the next 9/11 Commission will devote a chapter to the "missed opportunity" the interrogation represented; their timidity will become an "intelligence failure" worthy of study. Yet while most people accept that there are circumstances in which interrogators must cross even that line, on the other side of it lies criminality. And we refuse as a society to draw the line clearly or to promise that it won't move. We are, in short, asking men and women in the service of their country to live their professional lives standing on and leaning over the border of criminal conduct we lack the courage to define precisely.

It is an unforgivable abdication.

Fortunately, the actual dispute is far narrower than it seems, and a more sensible and honest legislative framework is readily available. Between the DTA and a new Army Field Manual on intelligence gathering, Congress and the administration, as I shall explain, have largely solved the problem of military interrogations. The remaining problem, the standards used by the CIA, involves a tiny number of people. Sensible legislation would tighten the baseline standard of treatment for these detainees, while tolerating departures from those standards in extremely limited circumstances with the highest levels of political accountability.

TORTURE AND OTHER highly coercive interrogation tactics present an unusual, perhaps unique, problem in modern law. Torture is unacceptable. It erodes American moral leadership. Its use presents a deep conflict with the self-image of a country that, after all, wrote a right against self-incrimination into its Constitution more than two hundred years ago. Coercion can also produce bad information, as subjects will sometimes say anything—specifically what they think their interrogators wish to hear—to make the abuse stop. What starts as a program for extremely limited circumstances tends not to remain cabined in those circumstances. It spreads, and as it spreads it corrodes. It creates a culture of torture. Yet sometimes coercive interrogation is also necessary—or, at least, perceived as necessary by virtually every government, even democratic governments, that has faced the problem of urgent, truly high-stakes interrogations.

In the debate over torture, people on both sides tend to parody this problem as the ticking time bomb case—a situation that, at least in the American context, does have an unreal, cinematic flavor. The true ticking time bomb situation has occasionally arisen in Israel, where the security services have sometimes busted terrorist cells after plots have already reached an advanced operational stage.[10] Given the infrequency of attacks in this country, however, it is exceptionally unlikely that authorities would capture someone here after a bomb has already been planted with near certainty that he knows where it is and in a situation in which a timed fuse makes every second count. The situation that truly tests our country's commitment to an absolute prohibition against coercive interrogation is not the ticking time bomb scenario. It is Khalid Sheikh Mohammed, and it is not a hypothetical scenario at all but a very real one.

In a technical sense, KSM, as various government agencies have dubbed him, does not present the pure ticking time bomb case. At the time of his capture, for one thing, authorities did not know of any particular bomb that was ticking or even that had been planted. KSM was, after all, not a cell leader but an overall director. His potential importance lay not in his knowledge of any single impending attack but in his knowledge of the organizational structure of Al Qaeda and its plans for *many,* presumably future, attacks. In the literal sense, in other words, he presented something less than the true ticking time bomb suspect; the bomb would not go off in three hours if he didn't break. In a larger sense, however, KSM is far *more* than a single ticking time bomb. He is all of the bombs, in various stages of imagination and construction. While the United States has not captured many such people, KSM was not the only one. And for leaders and operatives dedicated to protecting the country from further attack, failing to get all information potentially available from such people is simply not an acceptable outcome.

I have no doubt that once one opens the door to coercive treatment of such people, the category itches to grow. If we accept it for the Al Qaeda mastermind, do we also accept it for the cell leader? If we accept it for the cell leader, why not also the person who can lead us to the cell leader? The slope is slippery, indeed. But let's be candid that it is circumstances, and not just policy choices, that have put us on that slope. We did not end up there because of lawlessness. We ended up there because we caught people like KSM and—to borrow the formulation B'Tselem's Montell used—the interrogators felt "that the person in front of [them had] information that [could] prevent a catastrophe from happening" and felt obligated to "do what [they had] to do in order to prevent that catastrophe from happening."

We will face that situation again—and failure to find out what that subject knows will be no more acceptable than it was when we captured KSM. This is, I suspect, what Posner means when he not only defends the moral propriety of torture in emergency situations but predicts as an empirical matter that torture "will be used" at such times. In truly exigent circumstances, the logic of those circumstances tends to govern.

How reassuring it would be to square the circle by assuring ourselves that coercion never works anyway and that the logic of those extreme circumstances, therefore, requires no deviations from our values. Unfortunately, as least as the evidence stands now, we can't do that—or, at least, we can't do that without resort to ideology.

The idea that torture produces no information worth having has become a kind of conventional wisdom in the years since Abu Ghraib. And it has a distinguished pedigree. The eighteenth-century pioneer of criminology, Cesare Beccaria, wrote that

> The impression of pain, then, may increase to such a degree, that, occupying the mind entirely, it will compel the sufferer to use the shortest method of freeing himself from torment. His answer, therefore, will be an effect as necessary as that of fire or boiling water, and he will accuse himself of crimes of which he is innocent: So that the very means employed to distinguish the innocent from the guilty will most effectually destroy all difference between them.
>
> It would be superfluous to confirm these reflections by examples of innocent persons who, from the agony of torture, have confessed themselves guilty: innumerable instances may be found in all nations, and in every age. How amazing that mankind have always neglected to draw the natural conclusion![11]

In most senses, Beccaria's argument has obvious merit—one of several reasons the criminal justice system looks with extreme skepticism at evidence obtained under duress. And while the ambitions of intelligence gatherers seeking useful information differ notably from those of the justice system's agents—who want evidence that will stand up in court—Beccaria's arguments find direct parallels in the modern anticoercion absolutism. In his encyclopedic recent work, *Torture and Democracy*, Darius Rejali rejected any suggestion that coercion can work effectively in the intelligence context:

> Torture cannot be scientific. It is unlikely interrogators can torture in a restrained manner. Technology does not help them in this respect. Torture has strong corrosive effects on professional skills and institutions. Clean, selective, professional torture is an illusion. This is true regardless of whether one uses torture to intimidate, interrogate, or extract false confessions.

> For harvesting information, torture is the clumsiest method available
> to organizations, even clumsier in some cases than flipping coins or shoot-
> ing randomly into crowds. The sources of error are systematic and inerad-
> icable. . . . In short, organized torture yields poor information, sweeps up
> many innocents, degrades organizational capabilities, and destroys inter-
> rogators. Limited time during battle or emergency intensifies all these
> problems.[12]

Many professional interrogators echo these ideas—and virtually all interrogators seem to agree that the best intelligence comes by noncoercive means.
Chris Mackey (a pseudonym), who ran field interrogations for the army in
Afghanistan, wrote that "One of our biggest successes . . . came when a valuable prisoner decided to cooperate not because he had been abused (he had
not been), but precisely because he realized he would not be tortured. He had
heard so many horror stories that when he was treated decently, his prior
worldview snapped, and suddenly we had an ally."[13]

But as Mackey's riveting account of his work in Kandahar and Bagram
showed, there is another side to this argument. Mackey was appalled by Abu
Ghraib and the abuses in Iraq and Afghanistan that took place after he came
home. But he also wrote candidly about how his training in especially gentle interrogation techniques left him and his colleagues wholly unprepared
for Islamist terrorists. "The early story of the war in Afghanistan was one of
frustration and failure for us. Many Al Qaeda prisoners had been trained to
resist, and our schoolhouse methods were woefully out-of-date."[14] As time
went on, however, interrogators began using more coercive tactics, though
Mackey emphasized that they "never touched anyone."[15] They often used the
threat of repatriation to countries that routinely torture people as leverage in
interrogations—in one incident even dressing an interrogator up as a Gulf
state officer and walking him through the detention area to survey those he
would take charge of after an imminent, though fictitious, transfer.[16] In particular, they began using sleep deprivation, creating a rule under which they
could keep an interrogation subject awake as long as the interrogator himself
could stay awake. They called this "monstering."[17] And Mackey conceded that

it was part of a drift that led to harsher tactics later. "By the time we left Afghanistan, we had come to embrace methods we would not have countenanced at the beginning of the war. And while those who followed us at Bagram dismissed much of the so-called wisdom we sought to pass on, they took to monstering with alacrity. Indeed, as we left, it was clear they did not regard this as a method of last resort but as a primary option in the interrogation playbook. What was an ending point for us was a starting point for them."[18] But Mackey also contended—in contrast to the conventional wisdom—that the more aggressive tactics worked: "Our experience in Afghanistan showed that the harsher the methods we used—though they never contravened the [Geneva] Conventions, let alone crossed over into torture—the better the information we got and the sooner we got it."[19]

Mackey is not alone in his judgment that, at least in some circumstances, ratcheting up the pressure can produce useful results. The very damning independent panel report on Pentagon detention operations—the so-called Schlesinger Report—likewise noted, amid its disturbing history of the way certain harsh interrogation tactics migrated from Guantánamo to Iraq, that in the controlled atmosphere of Guantánamo those tactics helped: "At Guantánamo, the interrogators used those additional techniques with only two detainees, *gaining important and time-urgent information in the process.*" [Emphasis added.][20] A separate review of allegations of abusive interrogations at Guantánamo found that the particularly fierce interrogation plan in the case of alleged 20th hijacker Mohammed Al-Qahtani "ultimately provided extremely valuable intelligence."[21]

The Israeli experience suggests something similar. Until the High Court of Justice struck down the practice, the Israeli government had long contended that what it termed "a moderate degree of physical pressure" on terrorism suspects was critical to intelligence gathering. Even in declaring such coercion unlawful in 1999, the Israeli court never questioned its effectiveness but rather cited several instances in which coercive interrogations had produced lifesaving intelligence. The justices went so far as to acknowledge that their decision would complicate the "harsh reality" of fighting terrorism in Israel. "We are aware that this decision does not ease dealing with that reality," the justices wrote. "This is the destiny of democracy, as not all means are acceptable to it, and not all practices employed by its enemies are open before it."[22]

Nor should we blithely dismiss President Bush's own account of the intelligence gathered in the CIA's coercive program. In his speech announcing the transfer of the CIA's high-value detainees to Guantánamo in September 2006, Bush laid out in some detail what authorities had learned from the high-value program—which used interrogation methods he described as "tough, and . . . safe, and lawful, and necessary." According to the president, a few months into the conflict, "we captured a man known as Abu Zubaydah. We believe that Zubaydah was a senior terrorist leader and a trusted associate of Osama bin Laden." After recovering from wounds sustained on capture, "Zubaydah was defiant and evasive," but authorities "knew that [he] had more information that could save innocent lives." So the CIA "used an alternative set of procedures. . . . Zubaydah was questioned using these procedures, and soon he began to provide information on key Al Qaeda operatives, including information that helped us find and capture more of those responsible for the attacks on September the 11th. For example, Zubaydah identified one of KSM's accomplices in the 9/11 attacks—a terrorist named Ramzi Binalshibh. The information Zubaydah provided helped lead to the capture of Binalshibh. And together these two terrorists provided information that helped in the planning and execution of the operation that captured Khalid Sheikh Mohammed." KSM's questioning, in turn, resulted in "information that helped us stop another planned attack on the United States." It also led to the capture of another man, Zubair, whose interrogation "helped lead to the capture of Hambali," the leader of Al Qaeda's particularly violent Southeast Asian affiliate, Jemaah Islamiyah. Further questioning of KSM at that stage led to the capture of Hambali's brother "in Pakistan, and, in turn, led us to a cell of 17 Southeast Asian 'J-I' operatives. When confronted with the news that his terror cell had been broken up, Hambali admitted that the operatives were being groomed at KSM's request for attacks inside the United States—probably using airplanes." "KSM," Bush said, "also provided many details of other plots to kill innocent Americans"—attacks on buildings in the United States, for example. And, to top it off, Bush said that

KSM also provided vital information on Al Qaeda's efforts to obtain biological weapons. During questioning, KSM admitted that he had met three individuals involved in Al Qaeda's efforts to produce anthrax, a deadly biological agent—and he identified one of the individuals as a terrorist named Yazid. KSM apparently believed we already had this information, because Yazid had been captured and taken into foreign custody before KSM's arrest. In fact, we did not know about Yazid's role in Al Qaeda's anthrax program. Information from Yazid then helped lead to the capture of his two principal assistants in the anthrax program. Without the information provided by KSM and Yazid, we might not have uncovered this Al Qaeda biological weapons program, or stopped this Al Qaeda cell from developing anthrax for attacks against the United States.[23]

The reader can dismiss this account in any number of ways. For one thing, other accounts of the CIA's use of coercive tactics against the high-value detainees make them seem far less productive. Journalist Ron Suskind and some FBI officials involved in the case, for example, described Abu Zubaydah as a crazy split personality whose importance the government had dramatically overstated and whose interrogation sent agents on numerous wild goose chases.[24] And Suskind described the brutal interrogations of Ramzi Binalshibh and Khalid Sheikh Mohammed as producing little of value. "What had they learned? 'There was a grudging professional admiration for how hard these guys were,' [CIA official A. B.] Krongard recalled later. 'They were real soldiers. They went through hell, and gave up very, very little.'"[25] Indeed, Bush could have exaggerated or even lied. He may have been misled by a CIA keen to justify its alternative program. The intelligence gathered in the program might have been, as he claimed, first-rate yet all obtainable by gentler means had the agency shown more patience. The intelligence may have been all—or mostly—faulty. Perhaps a less brutal program would have produced, as Suskind suggested, *better* information.[26] All of this is possible.

Yet one should pause as well and consider the possibility that the president of the United States may be telling the truth and that America would be giving up a lot of intelligence of titanic importance if it forswore all coercion in all circumstances. One of the CIA officers who participated in Abu Zubaydah's interrogation, John Kiriakou, later described it in detail in an interview with ABC News—and his account largely backs up Bush's. (Kiriakou declined to participate in the coercive phase of the interrogation.) Zubaydah, he said, was "unwilling to give us any actionable intelligence" before the introduction of the new techniques, which "included everything from what was called an attention shake . . . all the way up to the other end, which was waterboarding." While Kiriakou expresses great discomfort with the use of waterboarding, he also insisted that it had a dramatic effect in the case. Zubaydah held out for thirty-five seconds, he said, but the following day told his interrogators that "Allah had visited him in his cell during the night and told him to cooperate because his cooperation would make it easier on the other brothers who had been captured." After that, he was "completely cooperative" and gave interrogators information that "disrupted a number of attacks, maybe dozens of attacks." Asked about the effectiveness of the CIA's palette of techniques—which also reportedly included stress positions, extended sleep deprivation, loud music, and temperature manipulations—Kiriakou was emphatic: "Yes, they do work."[27] Director of National Intelligence Mike McConnell is no less so. "Have we gotten meaningful information? You betcha. Tons! Does it save lives? Tons!" he said in one interview. "We have people walking around in this country that are alive today because this process happened." While McConnell seemed to acknowledge that waterboarding pushed the torture line, he also insisted that Khalid Sheikh Mohammed would not have broken without a harsh interrogation. "He would not have talked to us in a hundred years. Tough guy. Absolutely committed. He had this mental image of himself as a warrior and a martyr. No way he would talk to us."[28]

The point is that putting aside all moral considerations for a moment, it is simply not clear that the optimal level of coercion in intelligence gathering is zero. It is possible that, as Mackey put it, "If a prisoner will say anything to stop the pain, my guess is he will start with the truth."[29]

Here's the simple reality: We don't know how well, if at all, coercive interrogation works relative to other practices in the narrow band of cases for which coercion represents a morally plausible option. We don't know whether it gets more, less, or the same amount of true and useful intelligence from un-willing subjects. We don't know whether its marginal benefits—if they exist at all—exceed the costs we pay in international opprobrium and diminished professionalism within our security and intelligence services. And we don't know the set of tactics that optimizes the ratio of valuable intelligence ex-tracted in emergency situations to coercive force exerted—which seems, at least to me, the morally essential ratio. The American debate over interroga-tion, rather, is an argument in moral philosophy and anecdote, not an argu-ment in science. Those who have used conventional interrogation tactics successfully believe them optimal. Those who have used more coercive tactics successfully believe them optimal. There has been surprisingly little study of the relative efficacy of different modes of interrogation. We know hardly any-thing about what really works.

If you doubt this bold statement of our collective ignorance—either out of some certainty that toughness must work because everyone has a break-ing point, or out of certainty that nothing good can come from an evil like torture—consider a 2006 report of the Intelligence Science Board entitled *Educing Information: Interrogation: Science and Art.* The collection of papers included in the volume attempts to describe the state of our understanding of the extraction of information from uncooperative subjects. "[T]here is little systematic knowledge available to tell us 'what works' in interrogation. *We do not know what systems, methods, or processes of interrogation best protect the nation's security,*" stated the first paper.[30] A remarkable finding of the second paper asserted that we do not even understand the efficacy of *long-authorized* interrogations techniques: "U.S. personnel have used a limited number of interrogation techniques over the past half-century, but virtually none of them—or their underlying assumptions—are based on scientific research or have ever been subjected to scientific or systematic inquiry or evaluation." As to coercive alternatives, "[t]here is little or no research to indicate whether such techniques succeed in the manner and contexts in which they are ap-plied. Anecdotal accounts and opinions based on personal experiences are mixed, but the preponderance of reports seems to weigh against their effec-tiveness."[31] The report concluded with an admonition that "it is imprudent to base assessment only on the subjective feedback of interrogators" and urged "objective, scientific research" to help distinguish between valid and invalid lessons from field experience.[32]

Given the ethical constraints on studying torture, one struggles to imagine a serious research agenda in this area, though *Educing Information* concluded with an admirably serious set of suggestions towards one. And as long as we lack the fruits of such inquiry, we must take with a grain of salt both Rejali's insistence that highly coercive CIA techniques yielded only noise and Bush's insistence that those sessions mined gold the Geneva Conventions would have left in the ground. Rather, without a rigorous understanding of whether coercion works under any circumstances and, if so, what those circumstances look like, we have to accept at least the possibility that it *might* work in situations in which all else fails and that reasonable officials might feel, in certain situations, that they have run out of civilized alternatives.

That fact leads inexorably to a certain degree of toleration of the notion that in situations of extreme pressure, the government will sometimes attempt it—because when the stakes get high enough "might work" looks a whole lot better than standing by and waiting for a catastrophe. In these situations, security services simply will not resolve doubts about the efficacy of an interrogation tactic in favor of restraint. They are not going to say, with Henry Shue, "Let's risk it." Instead, they will risk a certain level of opprobrium. The real question is not whether they will—or should—do so. It is whether they should do so within the law or extralegally and, if the latter, what the contours of that extralegal action ought to look like.

THE ORIGINS of the military's interrogation problems lay in the reality that its interrogation policies assumed a different kind of conflict. The military crafted these policies for wars against an enemy more overt than Al Qaeda, an enemy against which human intelligence would therefore play a lesser role than it did after September 11. The policies assumed an enemy less committed in its hatred of the West than Al Qaeda operatives—and therefore more apt to gentle persuasion of detainees that aiding American efforts was in their best interests. Interrogators trained in the questioning of prisoners of war in conventional conflicts found themselves confronting captives trained to resist their inquiries, telling virtually identical stories, and not budging much from those stories under conventional pressures. "When prisoners were questioned, everyone's name had been 'lost' to fragile memory," wrote Mackey. "There were no identifying features, no addresses, no telephone numbers. In the recesses of our minds, where logic ruled, we knew it was impossible for so many prisoners to have forgotten so much. But we were confounded by the utter directness of the lies. It wasn't a kind of cocktail party fib, easily seen through, easily peeled away. It was the mindless refutation of the obvious."[33] When the military captured an Al Qaeda training manual that taunted the West for its refusal to use torture, it had the ring of truth for Mackey, who described its "core diagnosis" as "dead-on: The Americans would keep you in a cage eating halal [Meals Ready to Eat] and giving you showers a couple of times a week. But when it came down to it, you could lie to them, refuse to talk, switch your story from one session to the next, and there wasn't anything they could do about it."[34]

The blue-ribbon investigative panels that looked into the Abu Ghraib abuses tell a similar story. "It is clear that pressure for additional intelligence . . . resulted in stronger interrogation techniques. [It] did contribute to a belief that stronger interrogation methods were needed and appropriate in their treatment of detainees," the Schlesinger Report said. The old Army Field Manual dated from 1992, and its vagueness on many points left open questions as to how far interrogators could go. It authorized a series of interrogation procedures, but defined them in general terms—and without a lot of specific guidance concerning the "dos and don'ts" of implementation.[35] Its precise status was also squishy, for while it represented military doctrine, it did not carry the force of law. With the military suddenly fighting a war that put an unprecedented premium on collecting intelligence against an enemy unusually resistant to offering it, questions quickly arose over what exactly the Field Manual allowed and whether interrogators could breach that line.

In the fall of 2002, interrogators at Guantánamo grew frustrated with the recalcitrance of Mohammed Al-Qahtani, whom they believed to be directly involved in the September 11 plot. Qahtani had tried to enter the United States shortly before the attacks, but immigration officials had not admitted him. Mohammed Atta, it later turned out, was waiting for him at the Orlando airport into which he flew.[36] Yet Qahtani refused to talk, insisting he had come to the United States to deal in used cars and that he later went to Afghanistan to indulge his passion for falconry.[37] As an internal Army report later put it without naming him, Qahtani's "ability to resist months of standard interrogation in the summer of 2002 was the genesis for the request to have authority to employ additional counter resistance interrogation techniques."[38] That request, sent on October 25, complained that "despite our best efforts, some detainees have tenaciously resisted our current interrogation methods" and suggested three tiers of additional tactics to "enhance our efforts to extract additional information."[39]

The first category involved relatively benign behaviors: yelling at detainees and using deceptions. The second category involved more aggressive tactics: forcing detainees to stand for a maximum of four hours, using fake documents, isolating detainees for up to thirty days, interrogating detainees "in an environment other than the standard interrogation booth," depriving detainees of light and sound, hooding them during interrogation and transportation, interrogating detainees for twenty hours at a time, removing comfort items, taking detainees off of hot rations, removing clothing, forcing grooming and shaving of beards, and using detainee phobias like fear of dogs. The request also sought permission for a third category of tactic to be used only by special permission and only "for a very small percentage of the most uncooperative detainees (less than 3%)." These included "the use of scenarios designed to convince the detainee that death or severely painful consequences are imminent for him and/or his family," "Exposure to cold weather or water (with appropriate medical monitoring)," "Use of a wet towel and dripping water to induce the misperception of suffocation," and "Use of mild, noninjurious physical contact such as grabbing, poking in the chest with the finger, and light pushing."[40]

In response, the Pentagon's general counsel, William J. Haynes II, wrote a memo to then–Defense Secretary Donald Rumsfeld. Haynes advised that Rumsfeld approve the use of the first two categories and "the fourth technique listed in Category III." While the other techniques "may be legally available," Haynes wrote, "we believe that, as a matter of policy, a blanket approval of Category III techniques is not warranted at this time. Our Armed Forces are trained to a standard of interrogation that reflects a tradition of restraint." Rumsfeld agreed in early December, though he scrawled on the bottom of the memo, "However, I stand for 8–10 hours a day. Why is standing limited to 4 hours?"[41] Rumsfeld authorized the new techniques for use at Guantánamo only.

Even this limited permission lasted barely a month. In response to concerns raised by the Navy's general counsel, Rumsfeld rescinded the authorization for most of the new techniques, and required his personal sign-off for use of the remainder—something interrogators never sought and he consequently never granted. Instead, he asked Haynes to convene a working group to study interrogation techniques. The working group recommended a different list of aggressive tactics.[42] Rumsfeld approved only some of these in an April 2003 memo. The new list included a kind of "good cop, bad cop" interrogation, isolation of detainees, feeding them Meals Ready to Eat instead of hot rations, environmental manipulations like temperature adjustments, changing detainee sleep schedules, and the use of false flag interrogations.[43]

Even as this debate was playing out, interrogators in the field were conducting experiments of their own. The Schlesinger Report noted that "In Afghanistan, from the war's inception through the end of 2002, all forces used [the field manual] as a baseline for interrogation techniques. Nonetheless, more aggressive interrogation of detainees appears to have been on-going." This began with the relatively modest "monstering" described by Mackey, but as he noted, the drift once begun was hard to stop—particularly as techniques developed for the relatively controlled atmosphere of Guantánamo began migrating to Afghanistan and Iraq.[44] In Iraq and Afghanistan, detainees actually died in custody in incidents the military deemed homicides—though none of the interrogation tactics used in these cases were authorized.[45]

The combination of pressure for actionable intelligence, uncertainty in the field as to where precisely the lines lay under the field manual, and fast-shifting guidance from the Pentagon created a toxic stew. It unjustly oversimplifies matters to blame the high-level relaxation of interrogation policy at Guantánamo for the abuses at Abu Ghraib, which involved behavior far beyond the line of anything permitted by any policy. But it surely didn't help that the rules had become fuzzier. As one official report on intelligence activities at Abu Ghraib put it, "Confusion about what interrogation techniques were authorized resulted from the proliferation of guidance and information from other theaters of operation; individual interrogator experiences in other theaters; and, the failure to distinguish between interrogation operations in other theaters and Iraq. This confusion contributed to the occurrence of some of the non-violent and non-sexual abuses."[46]

The combination of policy changes and freelancing in the field led to some brutal interrogations. The most famous of these, both because of its intensity and because a portion of the interrogation logs leaked into the public domain, involved Qahtani, who—as an Army report later wrote—was subjected to a "creative, aggressive, and persistent" plan involving "160 days of segregation from other detainees, 48 of 54 consecutive days of 18 to 20-hour interrogations, and the creative application of authorized interrogation techniques." These included, "Requiring the subject . . . [to] be led around by a leash tied to his chains, placing a thong on his head, wearing a bra, insulting his mother and sister, being forced to stand naked in front of a female interrogator for five minutes." Interrogators brought in a dog to "growl, bark, and show his teeth" at Qahtani. They called him a homosexual and made him dance with one of the male interrogators.[47] Qahtani was repeatedly hydrated intravenously when he refused to drink water—and interrogators also poured water he declined to drink on his head. They restricted his ability to pray at times and controlled his access to the bathroom. A female interrogator straddled him to make him sexually uncomfortable.[48] And he eventually broke, giving what the government described as important intelligence and identifying roughly thirty fellow Guantánamo inmates as Al Qaeda operatives. Some time after the interrogation ended, when he got the chance to meet with his lawyer, he recanted everything, leaving many detainees to argue that he had implicated them only as a result of torture.[49]

FBI agents at Guantánamo complained about highly aggressive interrogation techniques such as these, and the Army investigated. It determined that interrogators had used techniques designed to humiliate detainees sexually—having female interrogators rub them, run their hands through their hair, and invade their personal space. In one instance, "a female interrogator told a detainee that red ink on her hand was menstrual blood and then wiped her hand on the detainee's arm." Interrogators played loud music and yelled at detainees, on some occasions leaving them alone with loud music and strobe lights for long periods of time. They cranked up the air conditioner to discomfort detainees. In one instance, they quieted a detainee by taping his mouth shut with duct tape. On a couple of occasions, they "short shackled" detainees to the floor—that is, chained not merely the detainees' feet but also their hands to the floor, "requiring the detainee[s] to either crouch very low or lay in a fetal position on the floor." Investigators determined that many of these tactics were authorized, some not. In Qahtani's case, they determined that the "cumulative effect" of a series of individually lawful techniques was "degrading and abusive treatment."[50]

In the end, the military's experience since September 11 supports to some degree claims both of the need for and the dangers of more flexibility in interrogation practices. The rules of detainee interrogation had clearly ossified and required modification, but the rethinking of those rules just as clearly spun out of control—particularly on the ground—and with sometimes tragic results. The military needed clearer, somewhat more permissive lines, much better defined, and with the force of law behind them.

And that, in an unusually happy coda to the story, is exactly what the combination of the DTA and the rewritten Army Field Manual gave it. Congress's elegantly simple contribution to this coup—the McCain Amendment—required a single sentence: "No person in the custody or under the effective control of the Department of Defense or under detention in a Department of Defense facility shall be subject to any treatment or technique of interrogation not authorized by and listed in the United States Army Field Manual on Intelligence Interrogation." The law gave the military, within the parameters of more general requirements of humane treatment, great latitude to set its own rules, requiring only that it publish and follow them.

This the military then did in a revised Army Field Manual released after an exhaustive internal discussion in September 2006. The new field manual offers a limited degree of new flexibility over the old one. It permits the use of the "good cop, bad cop" routine and gives interrogators permission to trick detainees by posing as people other than military intelligence personnel. It also allows, in the case of unlawful combatants and with specific authorization, segregation of individual detainees from the general population to prevent coordination of stories among interrogation subjects. Just as important as the new flexibility, it contains a great deal more specificity about all of the interrogation tactics it authorizes than did the prior version, so that interrogators have a better of sense of what exactly it allows and disallows. And it spells out in considerable detail what tactics are *not* permitted.[51] It complies with the Geneva Conventions. And as the military can amend it at any time, interrogation policy can remain fluid, even as it remains accountable under the law. It is a mark of how successful—if largely unnoticed—the policy changes have been that not even human rights groups today complain much about contemporary military interrogation policies. The complaints about coercive interrogations by the military, however justified, are all retrospective. Today, the military proudly brings guests to Guantánamo and bristles with frustration that public perceptions of its interrogations have not caught up with their now mundane reality.

THE MILITARY'S PUTTING its interrogation house in order ironically puts greater weight on the CIA's more secretive program, the exact parameters of which have never fully come into focus. The whole purpose of this program was to create a mechanism with permission to do those nasty things the military could not undertake. Bush has been all but candid on this point. He has described the "small number of suspected terrorist leaders and operatives" detained and questioned by the agency as "dangerous men with unparalleled

knowledge about terrorist networks and their plans for new attacks" and insisted that "The security of our nation and the lives of our citizens depend on
our ability to learn what these terrorists know." He has described the techniques of extracting that information from them as "tough" and "safe" and
"lawful" and "necessary." If we agree as a society that we need to insulate the
military from engaging in such tactics but also hypothesize that they will
sometimes prove necessary—or, at least, that leaders during crises will *per-
ceive* them as necessary and therefore feel compelled to try them—it follows
that the burden on the CIA's secret program will grow as the military's rules
become more restrictive.

Yet it was in the CIA's secret program, not in the military, that the administration dug itself the biggest hole, the one in which it has remained trapped.
The problem arose not from the administration's essential ambition: a stopgap mechanism for emergency interrogations under rules more permissive
than the norm. It arose, rather, because of two fundamental and grave errors
in the conception of this mechanism, errors not merely of law but of philosophy and concept. Only by understanding and correcting these errors can we
hope to imagine a sensible legislative policy for this hardest group of interrogations.

The first and most important error was the confusion of the need for occasional deviations from the rules with the nature of the rules themselves. The
fact that the CIA feels the need—rightly or wrongly—to use a particularly aggressive interrogation tactic in a particularly important case does not make
that technique legal. It is somewhere between difficult and impossible to
square waterboarding, for example, with the terms of the torture statute,
which forbids any "act committed by a person acting under the color of law
specifically intended to inflict severe physical or mental pain or suffering . . .
upon another person within his custody or physical control."[52] Waterboarding is specifically intended to induce the impression of drowning, and the torture law explicitly includes within its ambit the "prolonged mental harm
caused by or resulting from . . . the threat of imminent death."[53] The United
States has prosecuted as torture variants, albeit more extreme variants, of waterboarding for a century.[54] Even if the practice somehow doesn't cross the

torture line, federal law also prohibits "cruel, inhuman, or degrading" acts specifically so as to proscribe brutal treatment that falls short of the demanding threshold of torture but comes close to it. Given the proximity of waterboarding to that threshold, reading this lesser category not to include it when the stakes are high would seem to render the category itself something of a null set in those situations.

Yet that is more or less what the administration appears to have done. Instead of acknowledging these restrictions as real and meaningful but requiring occasional breaching, it generally read them in a fashion laughably narrow. Administration officials always insisted that the United States does not torture, and emphasized that torture violates the law. Yet the argument was absurdly circular. Having defined torture and torture lite so narrowly as to permit the activities they deemed necessary, they ended up defending brutal coercion even in the course of condemning it. And because they had *interpreted the law* as allowing this—rather than acknowledging the occasional necessity of crossing the line, as McCain does—they ended up defining down torture and other inhumane treatment for *everyone,* not merely for those few detainees whose seniority and real-time operational importance may actually have justified a measure of coercion. When President Bush stood before the nation and defended the CIA's interrogations of the high-value detainees, he insisted not merely that the "tough" techniques, including waterboarding, had been "necessary," but that they had been "lawful" as well.

When the White House, the attorney general, and the CIA all acknowledge that the agency has used interrogation tactics like waterboarding, when they will not concede that it and other repugnant conduct is out of bounds, when the vice president in fact publicly declares that a "dunk in the water" is a "no-brainer," and when the president signs the McCain Amendment's restrictions with the chest-thumping if meaningless statement that he will interpret them "in a manner consistent with the constitutional authority of the president to supervise the unitary executive branch and as Commander in Chief and consistent with the constitutional limitations on the judicial power," it matters little whether officials also piously intone that the United States does not torture and that it always treats detainees humanely.[55] The president is, after all, declaring that he has permitted and still permits highly coercive tactics that meet most people's colloquial understanding of torture and that he considers these tactics legal and, at least in some situations, appropriate. The public can draw its own conclusions about whether or not they are humane. This is a kind of double-talk that denudes law of meaning and renders the presidency morally laughable. And if its purpose was not to normalize coercive questioning but merely to create a zone of exception for truly unusual circumstances, it was unnecessary to boot.

To flesh out the administration's second error—the failure to keep covert actions covert—let us return for a moment to Al Gore's remark, quoted in Chapter 1, in response to legal objections to snatching a terrorist suspect abroad in 1993. "That's a no-brainer," he said. "Of course it's a violation of international law, that's why it's a covert action. The guy is a terrorist. Go grab his ass." The line may bring a smile to the reader's lips, in part because it reflects a genuine sophistication about the relationship between law and covert activity. Gore did not try to pretend that kidnapping a person and spiriting him to the United States for indictment violated no principles of international law. Rather, he assumed that this represented the very *reason* one would want to do it secretly, rather than in the open. Covert action, like hypocrisy, is a homage that vice pays to virtue; it is the respect a democracy can pay to law it feels compelled to violate. To conduct such operations in the open is to assert that we feel no shame about them. To refuse to do them at all, when more palatable options do not exist, is to deny the realities of leadership. The compromise position is to do them when absolutely necessary, but to do them both quietly enough to avoid undermining the law and one's moral position in the world and sparingly enough to avoid unjust and embarrassing errors. The Clinton administration conducted dozens of renditions. Neither the European nor the American public ever cared, in part because neither ever knew about them and in part because none of the people snatched turned out to be innocent.

The Bush administration, in contrast, so ramped up the use of rendition that it began to make errors—drawing public attention to a program that has to operate in the shadows to maintain plausibility. The administration did not limit its use of rendition to circumstances of countries without functioning judicial systems capable of neutralizing terrorists by more savory means or countries with whom the United States lacked extradition treaties. It went after suspects in, among other countries, Italy.[56] It also shifted the purpose of the program from disabling terrorists and delivering them to countries that wanted to punish them to interrogating them in the CIA's own custody, thereby requiring the agency to hold suspects for extended periods of time and engage in protracted coercive interrogations. Most critically, it did not merely fail to keep these operations quiet; it sometimes actually boasted of them. It thereby did violence to Gore's very sensible idea that when you have to violate international norms of behavior, you can avoid rendering those norms as laughingstocks by not flaunting it. It's the difference between the secret philanderer, whose discretion somehow respects his wife even as he desecrates the institution of marriage, and the open one, who humiliates his wife by letting the world know of his conquests.

In practice, this means having the maturity to make choices. And when you capture Khalid Sheikh Mohammed or some other high-value detainee, you face a choice: You can either hold and interrogate him in secret for a time *or* you can claim a great victory in the global war on terrorism. You cannot do both. Human rights advocates would, I am sure, object in principle to delaying announcement of a capture to give the CIA time for a discreet interrogation using, within reason, such means as the situation may require. I would not—just as I cannot confess to any profound wish that British troops had gone easier on the wife of Rudolf Hoess. Had KSM shown up in Guantánamo a month or two or three after his capture with no explanation of when or how we caught him, few people would have manned the barricades in protest. But to acknowledge that you're holding someone in secret, particularly over a protracted period of time, is to announce that you've made him disappear in order to use interrogation practices that you refuse to discuss in public and that likely would not pass muster under the Geneva Conventions or under any other relevant law.

This is what the United States did when it captured KSM, Abu Zubaydah, and Ramzi Binalshibh. In all three cases, officials publicly announced the arrests, which took place in raids in Pakistan. In all three cases, officials made little secret of having obtained custody of the captives, and in all three cases, the detainees then vanished to an "undisclosed" location.[57] In each case, public announcement of the arrests followed leaks or Pakistani disclosures, and it may be that, given Pakistan's role, keeping the arrests quiet was impossible. But that only means that conceiving of the detention as covert was a mistake. The result of pretending otherwise was that the United States ended up publicly holding people in secret—and it maintained this untenable stance for a long time. When Zacarias Moussaoui sought access to KSM and other high-value detainees during his criminal trial, prosecutors resisted, arguing up and down the appellate ladder that they should not have to provide such access. In a concession to the "secrecy" surrounding the detentions, the Court decisions quaintly redacted the detainees' names from the published opinions. But everyone knew, and in writing about the decisions, the newspapers published the names.[58]

In combination with one another, these two errors spoke louder than any disavowal of torture could possibly speak. The government simply cannot hide people in order to interrogate them under relaxed rules while publicly arguing that the known rules impose little restraint without effectively articulating a policy of torture. Given the small number of detainees for whom the government required extraordinary interrogation techniques—CIA director Michael Hayden has described it as fewer than thirty-three over the life of the CIA's program—this was as unnecessary as it was corrosive of American law and moral leadership.[59]

WITH RELATIVELY SIMPLE statutory changes, Congress can do a great deal to correct this problem. It can emphasize that the law represents a serious set of restrictions—a real requirement of humane treatment—yet build into it a certain degree of flexibility for the true emergency. The framework, in essence, should aim to tighten the baseline rules for CIA interrogations, making them more restrictive and accountable, yet at the same time create a stopgap mechanism for extraordinary cases. Congress should insist, in other words, that the exceptions are just that—exceptions to the rules, not the cases that define them.

The model established by the DTA for the military makes a great deal of sense for the CIA, too: Within the confines of the existing legal strictures on interrogation, the legislature should permit the agency the use of any technique to which it willingly attaches its name. That is, the CIA should have its own list of approved techniques, amendable at any time, to which the law binds its compliance. This list, in fact, already exists, but as in the military prior to the DTA, it exists purely as policy, not as law. The idea is to bind the agency to it and to use the political heat associated with sunshine and congressional oversight to smooth its roughest edges.

Congressional Democrats and some Republicans have pushed a superficially similar idea: obligating CIA interrogators, like their military counterparts, to follow the Army Field Manual.[60] But this idea goes too far. Even a completely responsible palette of procedures for the CIA would probably differ in some respects from the list in the Army Field Manual, which has to create rules not merely for the unlawful combatant but for routine interrogations of protected people like prisoners of war and, therefore, should not even approach the legal limits of interrogation roughness. As the agency will never have custody over such privileged belligerents and will generally, in fact, hold only those unlawful combatants deemed (correctly or erroneously) the most dangerous in the world, a CIA field manual might properly permit more than the Army Field Manual does. The Army document, after all, is used in zones of active combat by thousands of young soldiers with limited training; by contrast the CIA has many fewer interrogators subject to much more detailed training. The agency can probably get away with allowing more without letting things spin out of control, and it therefore might reasonably contemplate the judicious use of some of the enhanced techniques the military ultimately rejected in its rewrite of the field manual. Whatever one might think, for example, of yelling at detainees, removing comfort items, and denying hot rations, these acts surely come nowhere near the *legal* lines of a proper interrogation. Even techniques like stress positions, sleep deprivation, and temperature manipulations, which can be torturous in some iterations, can also be merely unpleasant and harassing in others. The CIA might with perfect propriety draw its policy lines in a different spot than the military, and Congress should tolerate its going deeper into the gray area than the military does.

Ideally, Congress would insist that this document, like the Army Field Manual, be openly disclosed, so that all approved interrogation techniques available under the law could withstand debate and scrutiny. This will no doubt prove a more difficult sell with the CIA than it did with the military—which contemplated but finally rejected including a classified appendix to its new field manual.[61] The administration, even in the face of leaks about the techniques deployed at its "black" sites, has generally refused to discuss the precise techniques the agency has used. For years it perversely refused even to confirm that it no longer permits the use of waterboarding, though this was something of an open secret, and officials ultimately confirmed in 2008 that the CIA had used it only three times prior to the passage of the DTA and never since. This reticence to some degree flows from embarrassment at the tactics the government has permitted and still permits in certain circumstances. In part, however, it also stems from a legitimate unwillingness to show America's interrogation palette to an enemy that has clearly trained its personnel to resist more standard techniques. Publishing a CIA field manual with the sort of detail of the army's guidance potentially risks giving Al Qaeda a road map to American interrogations, a road map the group can use both for training and for eroding America's moral high ground before the public.

It may, therefore, be necessary to maintain a certain level of ambiguity while still permitting a measure of transparency and accountability. One possibility would be publishing a document that describes the techniques in general terms while leaving the more granular details to a classified version shared only with the congressional intelligence committees. The key, however, is for Congress to force the CIA to articulate—in significant detail and in public to the maximum extent possible—what it will do and what it will not do and to put the force of law behind this list. To the extent members of Congress believe that any listed techniques violate the prohibition against "cruel, inhuman, or degrading" treatment or Common Article 3 of the Geneva Conventions, Congress would then have ample leverage to force its removal.

My guess is that such a rule would, at once, ameliorate a great deal of public and international anxiety about American interrogation policy and provide ample flexibility for all but the most exigent circumstances. The public hand-wringing about American policy, after all, does not have roots in the talismanic magic of the specific techniques approved by the Army Field Manual. There is a big gray area between what the military permits and the actual legal lines—wherever they may be. The anxiety, rather, flows from a combination of the brutality of certain specific tactics and the sense of the agency's interrogations as constituting a lawless zone in which anything goes. Clarifying that anything does not go and that what does go—while perhaps more permissive than the military's rules—falls within international humanitarian protections would go a long way toward addressing the anxiety.

Such a rule would, I suspect, probably also suffice for the preponderance of high-value detainees. Remember that even within the CIA's program, only a minority of detainees required enhanced interrogation tactics of any kind and the agency used waterboarding only thrice. Create a list of lawful interrogation tactics that approach, but do not cross, the legal lines, and officials may find that the additional flexibility this palette offers—on top of authorized military tactics—will serve to crack all but the tiniest, most committed, subset of America's enemies.

Yet Congress cannot pretend that this subset does not exist. It cannot pretend that the executive does not sometimes interrogate people in time-sensitive efforts to avert catastrophes and that these catastrophes do not constitute a surpassing ambition for suspects—an ambition they can fulfill through silence, misdirection, and lies in the face of pressure. For this group, the executive will breach the rules. That reality requires that these rules do something genuinely extraordinary: contemplate the circumstances of their own violation. Laws do this very seldomly. It's a little like taxing the sale of illicit drugs. Yet here, we must return to the fact with which we began: Almost everyone acknowledges situations in which he or she wants the interrogation lines breached. Once we reject the administration's foolish contention that the most brutal interrogations have complied with the rules, the only remaining argument should take place over the legal zone the president and his administration occupy when they do what they deem necessary in those circumstances.

This question has two distinct components: the legal status of the action by the agents in the field and the legal status of the order to take those actions. Senator McCain and B'Tselem's Montell insist on the forgivable illegality of the action in the field—that is, that the law be structured so as to render the interrogator culpable of a felony for the interrogation expected under the circumstances. This seems to me perverse. These people are not the guards at Abu Ghraib, people who sated their sadism by violating the policies designed to protect detainees from abuse. Rather, to the extent their conduct breached America's international obligations—even its domestic laws—it did so precisely *because* they were following instructions, ultimately of the president, in a situation of presumably surpassing national importance. To ask that they subject themselves to prosecution for these acts is unlike anything we ask of other officials in government service for acts we expect them to take in foreseeable situations. We don't ask police officers to face murder charges when they fire their guns and kill people in accordance with departmental policies. Congress needs to create a mechanism to recognize that in such situations, the president has the authority to immunize officers for the effectuation of his orders, for which he alone should stand accountable.

Congress, in fact, gives up little in recognizing this—because a crude such mechanism already exists as a matter of constitutional law. The president has the unreviewable and plenary power to pardon people for any infraction under federal law, and he has the implicit authority to promise to do so.[62] He can already, in other words, make clear to agents in the field that he will shield them from the consequences of any illegality associated with carrying out his will—and shoulder the burden of responsibility himself. Congress should enact a law that provides a more refined statutory device for the president to use, in lieu of the pardon power, in such situations, one that clarifies his political accountability for breaches of the normal rules and also makes sure that the legislature is kept informed and has the opportunity to object.

Congress could create this mechanism without explicitly authorizing any deviations from normal field policy, leaving ambiguous the question of whether the president himself is acting extralegally in authorizing these departures. As long as the legislature clarifies that the field personnel do not commit crimes in carrying out those deviations, it will fix accountability in the person of the president.

Congress can accomplish this relatively simply. It should forbid the president to authorize any deviations from CIA interrogation policies except by written finding to the congressional intelligence committees, identifying the need for enhanced tactics in the specific case and the individual techniques he is ordering. The law should insist that these techniques under no circumstances violate the prohibition on torture, and the finding should require the personal signature of the president. Congress should require as well that the White House annually publish the number of such findings the president issues, so that while each finding would remain classified, the public may determine whether coercive interrogation has remained an exception or is drifting towards more of a norm. The law should further immunize against all criminal and civil liability those personnel carrying out the enhanced techniques specified within such a finding.

Other commentators have suggested schemes along these lines, which loosely track the current covert action law; columnist Jonathan Rauch, for example, and scholars Philip B. Heymann and Juliette N. Kayyem have advocated allowing the president to personally authorize breaches in the normal rules by written finding to the intelligence committees and have similarly suggested requiring annual publication of the number of such authorizations.[63] The idea is to create a stopgap for the true emergency, an arrangement that recognizes what the president has the raw power to do and will face an overwhelming temptation to do, without overtly approving of it and while affixing the clearest of accountability for it.

———

A FINAL WRINKLE complicates any discussion of interrogation policy: rendition. Just as the CIA program backstops military interrogations, the Egyptians and the Jordanians potentially backstop the CIA. On this matter, human rights activists have perversely sought to bar all options. It cannot be illegal for the government to detain and interrogate dangerous people *and* illegal for it to transfer them to other governments. It cannot be that the CIA has no legitimate role to play in neutralizing bad guys whom the justice system cannot reach through traditional extraditions by facilitating their removal to countries that want them for crimes. Nor can it be the role of the CIA to police the criminal justice systems of every country that wishes to cooperate in the fight against Al Qaeda. There is simply no way to avoid making some choices about the comparative risk to human rights interests of different tactics for neutralizing terrorists. Either we're going to be holding more people ourselves for longer periods of time and letting their interrogations test our own liberalism or we're going to risk treatment by allies that falls short, sometimes far short, of the standards we would tolerate.

In this area, Congress has a limited role to play. Senator Joseph Biden has sought to require prior judicial approval for renditions; this is a recipe for failure.[64] Such a rule would either authorize judicial micromanagement of fast-moving intelligence operations overseas or create a rubber-stamp procedure that would implicate the judiciary in some of the uglier sides of the war on terror. In the end, Congress cannot successfully regulate when CIA operatives can assist foreign governments in detaining people under—or in violation of—their own laws. Nor can it usefully interpose judges to review the agency's efforts to facilitate the transfer of suspects to third countries.

It can, however, do two things. The first is to put a time limit on how long the agency can hold someone outside of both the Geneva Conventions and the administrative detention apparatus outlined in Chapter 6. It is, in my judgment, perfectly reasonable for the CIA to nab someone abroad in a secret operation—or to obtain custody of a suspect from some foreign intelligence service—and then give itself a little time to find out what he knows. This was normal fare during the Cold War; it's a part of what a clandestine service does. It is not reasonable, however, for the agency to operate a parallel Guantánamo, a detention system meant to skirt the normal rules of either warfare or counterterrorism. I don't pretend to know what the outer time limit should be; any fixed period of time is ultimately arbitrary. But Congress ought to impose one so that the United States has only a single system for long-term detentions and does not run "secret prisons" at "black sites" around the world.

The second contribution Congress can make is to define more precisely what level of certainty the government needs to obtain that countries will not torture or mistreat the suspects we transfer to them. The Convention Against Torture, to which the United States is a signatory, requires that "No State Party shall expel, return . . . or extradite a person to another State where there are substantial grounds for believing that he would be in danger of being subjected to torture."[65] And the Senate, in consenting to the treaty's ratification, interpreted the provision as applying "if it is more likely than not that he would be tortured."[66] The United States, like many countries, has thus sought to comply with the obligation not by refraining entirely from returning people to countries that torture but by seeking diplomatic assurances that the individuals will be treated properly.[67] Human rights groups have complained that these assurances sometimes amount to meaningless sheets of paper from governments with long records of mistreatment of prisoners.[68] On the other hand, executive officials argue that the assurances they obtain are real—though they do not contend that the countries that offer them always honor their assurances.[69] The fundamental problem here is that people have come to doubt the propriety of the limited guidance the legislature has offered regarding implementation of the treaty's requirements—and not just in renditions but in the far more common situations of deportations and extraditions as well.[70] Congress ought to step up to the plate and either clarify that guidance or provide new rules.

I profess a certain agnosticism as to what precise legal test Congress ought to adopt here. My own instinct is that any legislative implementation of this rule ought to permit transfers with assurances that amount to something less than real certainty—that the more people we can get rid of, in other words, the better. Many of America's detainees so far have hailed from countries with dreadful human rights records, a trend that will likely continue. There are only minimal prospects of third countries taking such people, as a general rule, so insisting on a law that forbids their repatriation effectively requires their indefinite detention by American forces. There are many reasons other than subcontracting torture why the CIA might transfer a given captive. Local intelligence services may have better language skills or expertise with certain groups, for example. What's more, the controversy over rendition largely involves cases from early in the war on terrorism, and while public law has not changed since then, policies have clearly tightened, at least in practice. As State Department legal adviser John Bellinger III put it, "Nobody has made any allegations about any renditions off the streets of Europe in years and yet they keep beating up on things that may have happened three, four or five years ago. . . . [T]here has been evolution in our laws and policies."[71] America should certainly refrain from sending people to foreign countries to be tortured. But saying that is a far cry from saying that it has to reduce the risk of abuse to zero before turning someone over.

Congress may, however, reasonably make a different judgment: that America should err on the side of caution and avoid transferring suspects to countries with known records of abuse. This would be a powerful moral statement, but it is one that Congress can only make with its eyes wide open. It cannot pretend that these suspects will simply disappear or become less dangerous. They will remain in American hands, raising controversies under American law.

The public debate often treats coercion as binary—a switch we can turn on and off, a tool we either use or do not use in dealing with our enemies. This a comforting lie we tell ourselves; even within the relatively civilized setting of the criminal justice system, custodial interrogations are inherently coercive. The right question is not whether we use coercive means but *how* coercive, when, and with whom ultimately answerable for them. And try as we might, we cannot escape the occasional conflict in interrogation policy between our needs and our values. We need to face this problem honestly, to stop lying to ourselves and to stop pretending either that brutality and torture are humane treatments or that circumstances don't sometimes push inexorably for their use. To the extent we confront the problem more candidly, we can reduce the frequency with which these conflicts arise, and we can face them when they do with accountability for our choices.

EIGHT

Surveillance Law
for a New Century

Pass through a set of double-glass doors marked "Restricted Area" on the sixth floor of the Justice Department, and walk down the hall. Stride past a row of chairs where agents of the Federal Bureau of Investigation and the National Security Agency wait to testify.

Step through a heavy door snaked with wires, then through another, and press a button on the wall. The doors will slowly swing shut, then audibly secure themselves to their frames. If you are carrying a radio, it will go dead.

You are now sealed inside a conference room with an oddly textured ceiling, no windows, and a single table running down the middle. You have entered the Foreign Intelligence Surveillance Court, the most secretive institution in the American judiciary.[1]

I WROTE THESE WORDS more than a decade ago, as a young reporter for a legal trade newspaper, when the FISA court remained unknown to most Americans—even most lawyers practicing in Washington. FISA was not then, as it became after the USA PATRIOT Act and the revelation of the National Security Agency's (NSA) warrantless wiretapping program, a common acronym in political conversation. It was, rather, among the most specialized corners of national security law, the province of a tiny group of nerdy government lawyers from the Justice Department and the security agencies and an even tinier group of civil liberties lawyers who watched the Court from the outside and tried to find avenues for litigation and challenge in an arena in which the government kept tightly under wraps virtually everything worth knowing. The Court itself was an enigma, a secret alcove in a judiciary known for openness and public proceedings, a tribunal that worked only on espionage and security cases and whose sole job was to consider government applications for secret warrants against surveillance targets. The FISA court okayed requests to snoop on foreign embassies and authorized wiretaps of suspected spies, including American citizens like Aldrich Ames—most of whom, unlike Ames, never found out they had been listened to. In its work, the Court heard from only government lawyers, never defense counsel. And at least back then, the government never lost a case before it. It was weird, spooky, and tantalizing both to me and to an enterprising editor who allowed me to spend several months trying to find out everything I could about it. It tantalized us in large part because nobody else seemed to care about it.

The description quoted above may have grown considerably out of date. The Court has grown both in the number of judges who sit on it and in its staff and is even planning to move out of the Justice Department and into a facility of its own. Yet the account remains the most contemporary physical description of the Court, for one simple reason: After the Justice Department and the FISA court's presiding judge allowed me a look at the court in 1996, they apparently never gave a second tour.[2]

In one sense, my interest during the mid-1990s in the FISA court and the 1978 law that established it was prescient. As a consequence of serial controversies that began some years later—over alleged Chinese spying on American nuclear research, over Zacarias Moussaoui's laptop, over the PATRIOT Act and the "wall" that separated intelligence from law enforcement information in the run-up to September 11, and, most ferociously, over the NSA's program—the Court has since exploded into the public's consciousness. Today, everyone seems to care about FISA: whether the Bush administration violated it, what precisely it should permit and forbid, whether it should or should not apply overseas, and if so, exactly how.

Yet the truth of the matter is that, like almost everyone who was thinking about FISA at that time, I had largely misapprehended the issue. Viewing surveillance through a post-Watergate, pre–September 11 prism, I came to the story wondering whether the Court itself was acting as a rubber stamp for government domestic snooping, a judicial gloss for a kind of modern-day COINTELPRO.[3] My investigation, sparked both by the strangeness of the institution and by the government's perfect win-loss record before it, looked at whether the Court and the law adequately protected civil liberties, whether they restrained government enough, whether they adequately separated the spies from the cops. In retrospect, these were not prescient questions. Within a few years, the country would turn considerable attention to the converse questions, which almost nobody was publicly asking at the time: whether the Court protected civil liberties *too well,* whether it restrained government *too much,* and whether it created *too rigorous* an apartheid between espionage and law enforcement. In retrospect, I should have asked whether the FISA structure was so protective as to be rigid, and therefore fragile, when a crisis would demand large volumes of expedited surveillance orders in situations of the highest stakes and lowest margin for error. The shift took place, in part, because of several high-profile instances in which the FBI could not, or failed to, obtain FISA orders in crucial cases, the most prominent being the fateful failure to examine Zacarias Moussaoui's laptop computer when authorities arrested him in the weeks before September 11. It took place also because of the administration's decision to jettison the problems the statute creates in certain circumstances by operating outside of it altogether. And it took place because of September 11 itself, because Americans in the wake of the attacks reacted quite differently to the possibility of expansive government surveillance powers than they did when Watergate abuses remained fresh in their minds. Only a few years before the attacks, I never imagined that America would come to see FISA itself as part of the problem, rather than as a perhaps inadequate piece of the solution.

The problems with FISA, and with surveillance law more generally, differ markedly from those that plague other areas of the putative law of terrorism. With respect to detention, interrogation, and trial, as we have seen, the fundamental problem lies in the law's basic underdevelopment—that is, the fact that American law evolved for other purposes and has not yet adapted itself well to a long-term global struggle against terrorism. FISA suffers from something close to the opposite problem. It is overdeveloped—or, perhaps, misdeveloped. Congress has paid careful attention to it over the years, amending it frequently, patching its holes as they have opened, trying desperately to keep it current. The statute has grown enormously complicated. Some of the complexity, to be sure, was intentional—a set of obfuscations in the law's original drafting designed to protect a then-classified NSA program. But some of it was developmental; as the world changed, Congress added more to FISA in an attempt to keep pace with changing technology and changing threats. FISA's patchwork quality is a strange fate for a law that attempts to enact a simple principle: that government should not spy on Americans without evidence of their acting as covert foreign agents.

Despite Congress's labors and an admirable and resilient flexibility in the statute itself, FISA has grown dramatically out of date. Mostly because of the development of technologies unimaginable at the time of its drafting, this venerable statute has grown overprotective of civil liberties in certain areas and inadequately protective in others. In a variety of fashions it inhibits acquisition of information the intelligence agencies probably should be getting even as it says little about one of the central privacy questions of our time: the use of giant swaths of call records—and their contents—in giant data-mining operations to identify patterns and networks of suspicious activity and communications. To put it bluntly, the communications and data infrastructure FISA sought to regulate no longer exists and the one that exists today was beyond the fathoming of legislators thirty years ago.

All of this parallels a larger obsolescence of American surveillance law in the domestic law enforcement arena, in which old high-altitude principles like the Fourth Amendment's requirement that searches and seizures be "reasonable" have crashed up against the realities of a data society, in which every step individuals take leaves digital footprints ripe for mining by industry and government alike. What is "reasonable" under such circumstances is not a question for which our legal tradition offers ready answers. The laws governing the investigative collection of transactional records like credit card data and telephone call and e-mail addressing information permit the easy acquisition of huge volumes of such data, yet offer little guidance about what government can and cannot do with it. Can it store such data forever for data-mining purposes? Can it use the companies that collect them as proxies and simply ask them to do its data mining for it? Congress has never said that it cannot do these things.[4] But if it can, then why exactly is it unthinkable for government to do in real time domestically what the NSA reportedly does with overseas communications: capturing such data in real time and analyzing them electronically for patterns of traffic and content indicative of terrorist networks? We have not as a society thought through how to regulate privacy and intelligence gathering on the network that has come into being—much less on the network into which it will some day soon evolve.

Beginning in the 1960s with the passage of the federal wiretapping law and continuing through the passage of the FISA in 1978, Congress devoted significant energy to designing surveillance regimes to authorize collection of evidence and intelligence and to restrict government from behaviors unbefitting American democracy. It was, in retrospect, an awesome legislative accomplishment, a mature and serious exploration that took account of the power of available surveillance tools, the technology that then existed, their capacity for abuse, and the relevant constitutional landscape. It crafted out of this exploration a series of rules that has served this country well for a generation—rules under which nearly all domestic wiretaps required warrants, national security investigations became subject to limited judicial oversight, and the Justice Department kept a close eye on the spooks.

Congress today needs to engage in a similar process of thinking through surveillance law for a new generation of technology, threat, and human cultural engagement with electronic communications. In part because the degree of secrecy surrounding this area makes fine policy judgments impossible at this stage and in part because of the sheer complexity of the issues, it is hard to discern with any precision what this body of law will look like. It will, however, both deeply challenge contemporary civil libertarian sensibilities and require an unprecedented level of oversight—internal and external, executive and congressional and judicial—of the intelligence and law enforcement worlds.

At the core of a new regime, I suspect, will lie two principles. The first is that government should have relatively easy access to telecommunications and other data, the mining of which has an essential role to play in combating terrorism and other transnational threats. This principle flies in the face of modern privacy orthodoxy, which analogizes all surveillance to a Fourth Amendment search and sees government acquisition of personal information as the principal threat to privacy. Civil libertarians will fiercely resist it. The second principle, the flip side of facilitated government access to information, is stricter rules of—and accountability for—the use of that material, a punishing regime of retroactive accountability for misuse of data and violation of the rules. This means creating auditable trails of information use, which costs money and significant human labor and generally consumes resources Congress will not wish to pony up. The security bureaucracy will fiercely resist it. In combination, however, these two principles offer a better approach to privacy protection in a digital age than trying to impede government access to information it often needs with rules too loose to mind the gates effectively yet which can nonetheless create significant headaches.

THE FISA AROSE as a response to the out-of-control electronic surveillance of political dissidents that came to light during the Watergate era.[5] A decade earlier, Congress had regulated wiretaps in criminal cases, requiring prior judicial approval akin to a search warrant before government could listen in on people's phone calls. It had, however, left wiretapping in national security cases without statutory guidance, and the executive branch had continued to conduct so-called black bag jobs on its own authority.[6] By the late 1970s, the courts had clarified that the Fourth Amendment and its warrant requirement applied to domestic security surveillance, so Congress sought to close the gap in the statute.[7]

The combined regime of FISA plus the criminal wiretapping law reflected a few basic understandings of electronic surveillance—all of them the product of years of debate and conceptual development, all of them deeply rooted in American constitutional values. All of them seem obvious now. None, however, was an inevitable understanding of the relationship between the individual right protected by the Fourth Amendment and the powers of the presidential preemption.

The first understanding was that wiretapping someone's phone was a kind of search that, like a raid on his house, a judge ought to approve before it happens. The second was that wiretapping in criminal investigations and intelligence gathering differ profoundly from one another and that the rules regulating them ought to differ as well. The third was that government has no place spying on its citizens; unless that person is operating on behalf of some *foreign* entity and thereby triggers the vast foreign policy and intelligence powers of the presidency, the criminal law represents the only valid source of the power to conduct surveillance against him. In other words, government can investigate someone for an alleged crime and can spy on him *to the extent that one could reasonably consider that spying as the collection of foreign intelligence.* But government possesses no legitimate power to collect information on people out of idle interest, the desire to harass political opponents, or even the understandable instinct to watch people who might be dangerous.

The mechanism the new law set up to reflect these philosophical propositions was the FISA court. Under the scheme, the intelligence agencies—through the Justice Department—would bring national security warrant requests to the super-secure tribunal, which would evaluate them under a standard different from the one applied in criminal cases. Instead of looking at whether the government had shown probable cause of a crime, the Court would decide whether the government had probable cause that the surveillance target was either a foreign power itself—like an embassy—or an "agent of a foreign power" who, on behalf of some foreign entity, "knowingly engages in clandestine intelligence gathering activities," including terrorism.[8] The Court would hear only from government lawyers and witnesses; the defense would have no opportunity to see or challenge the warrant application—

even if material from FISA surveillance later ended up in criminal cases, as it sometimes did.[9] The idea was to impose a multilayered review process on top of national security surveillance, a review process in which FBI lawyers watched over their agents, in which Justice Department lawyers watched over the FBI lawyers, and in which those Justice Department lawyers—bearing the individual signature of the attorney general or another top official—then had to present their cases to a federal judge before anyone could switch on a wiretap.

It worked shockingly well. By the mid-1990s, when I investigated the implementation of FISA, everybody connected with the process spoke of it with evident pride. Officials at all levels spoke on the record about the super-secret process—from the presiding judge of the Court to attorneys who worked on FISA cases. They released documents elucidating the system. Civil libertarians certainly harbored anxieties about this court, which had never once turned down a government warrant request. But no clear abuses of FISA had ever come to light. And given the dramatically open fashion in which the government explained its most covert judicial activity—an openness unthinkable today, incidentally—I came to take seriously the alternative explanation everyone involved posited.

"To the extent that any ongoing procedures can be without flaw, this is about as close as you can get," said James McAdams III, who then ran the Justice Department's Office of Intelligence Policy and Review, the office that both watches over the FBI and represents the government before the Court. "We have tried to think of every possible flaw and then address it—and then address it again."

The presiding judge of the Court at the time, Royce Lamberth—known generally in Washington as the bane of government lawyers for his cantankerous behavior towards them in any number of litigations—backed up McAdams. "I have been very impressed with what I have seen so far with the professionalism of both the Justice Department attorneys who are presenting the applications and the agents and officials who appear before the Court to swear to the underlying information and to answer questions posed by the Court," he told me. "I think the win-loss record is more a tribute to the superb internal review process created within the Department of Justice, now through several different administrations, than it is [a reflection] on the judges. Indeed, there might be a concern that the Justice Department has been too conservative in what they are presenting to the Court if we're approving every one."[10]

Lamberth's words foreshadowed the coming debate—and, ironically, his own role within it. In the wake of the PATRIOT Act, the FISA court issued a published opinion rejecting the new law's efforts to tear down the "wall" between intelligence and law enforcement and blasting the FBI for a series of erroneous statements in agent testimony before the Court.[11] The government had grown bolder, and the Court was no longer approving every application. In response, the Foreign Intelligence Surveillance Court of Review—the appellate body created by the FISA—convened for the first time and reversed Lamberth and his colleagues.[12] Perhaps seeing a more aggressive posture, one in which the factual rigor of presentations to the Court slipped and greater uncertainty therefore attended the Court's decisions, had made him appreciate more the value of the department's prior conservatism.

But that, in any event, was later. In the mid-1990s, Lamberth was more than content. And he was not the only one. America was not at war. It was between major adversaries and had no single overarching enemy to combat. It had no sense of acute threat from anywhere, and no foe seemed to pose a substantial challenge to its hegemony. In such a world, particularly only two decades after Watergate, FISA was an ideal statute. It allowed the surveillance the government needed. Yet it also created sufficiently layered accountability for domestic espionage that public fears of it largely withered. Domestic spying went from the stuff of national news to a kind of curio.

But to praise FISA for this accomplishment is not to romanticize it. It was a creature of its time, and it responded to the concerns of that time. And times changed—quickly. The political judgment behind the law, perfectly understandable in the wake of the intelligence abuses revealed in the 1970s, was that broad surveillance authorities pose a greater danger to the public than does any threat against which government might use those powers to protect the public. This assumption for many Americans did not survive the Septem-

ber 11 attacks, particularly when preceded by a long period in which the intelligence community behaved not as a rogue operation but within the rule of
law. As the balance of threat from our foes and our government shifted, our
attitudes towards surveillance as both protection and menace shifted with it.
Only a year before September 11, nobody was publicly arguing for a warrantless wiretapping program. As a thought experiment, ask yourself whether a
year after the next horrific attack, anyone will still be arguing against it. FISA
represented an approach that captured the zeitgeist of its moment—but it is a
moment in which many Americans no longer live.

What's more, to a degree the law's drafters never could have imagined,
FISA's vitality relied on a series of assumptions rooted in the technology of its
era. The whole structure assumes, for example, that the fundamental threat to
civil liberties posed by electronic surveillance lies in the initial interception of
a communication, rather than in the manner of its use. In the 1970s, after all,
interception of a call was virtually synonymous with *human* interception—
that is, if your phone was tapped, someone was almost certainly listening in
or, at least, your calls were being taped so that someone could listen in later.
There existed only crude mechanized means for processing intercepted materials, no sophisticated algorithms that might systematically handle them without any human ever hearing.[13] The government also lacked the ability to
cross-reference the transactional information associated with the call against
gigantic sets of similar data and examine it for patterns. Consequently, FISA is
obsessed with defining the circumstances of acquisition of information, but
beyond forbidding the retention and dissemination of data about U.S. citizens
or residents that do not constitute foreign intelligence, it says little about what
government may do with the information it acquires.[14]

Another fundamental judgment embedded within the statute is that the
intelligence agencies have already identified their target, that they already
know something about the person about whom they seek information, indeed that they know where this person is and what telecommunications facilities he or she uses. FISA quite deliberately does not contemplate the reverse
situation—in which one might identify a surveillance target by processing the
very communications traffic the statute means to shield. The law takes this

position both because the technology of its time did not support such an approach and, probably more importantly, because its drafters actively wanted to preclude domestic intelligence collection in the absence of preexisting evidence against some person. Because FISA defined "person" broadly—to include groups, entities, or governments—the law contained a measure of ambiguity about when individuals might have their communications captured in the absence of individualized warrants on the basis of broader warrants against groups to which they might be connected.[15] But clearly, FISA assumes a classic human-centered investigation, in which a suspect against whom the government can amass a known quantum of evidence uses a specific phone in the United States and the government wants to monitor that phone by way of keeping track of his activity.

The statute also assumes, for reasons of constitutional law, that the borders of the United States mean something. In the 1970s, overseas telecommunications, far from part of the daily communications culture of most Americans, was something of a rarity. Congress could, with relative safety, assume that when it required a warrant for domestic collection against a U.S. person—a citizen or permanent resident alien—it was effectively regulating the relationship between government and the polity. Yes, Americans sometimes traveled abroad and sometimes called friends and family overseas. When they did so, they potentially subjected themselves to incidental surveillance outside of FISA. But no government agency could have launched a domestic surveillance program based on overseas communications; it simply could not have relied on domestic dissidents to make enough international calls to make the collection fruitful. The compromise of making domestic calling secure and most overseas calling fair game roughly tracked the constitutional principle that the president has a free hand in foreign policy and wears the shackles of law when he operates at home.

Finally, the FISA assumed a meaningful difference between governmental collection and private-sector data collection—that a threat to civil liberties exists when government collects material about people that does not exist when private companies collect the very same material. This too made sense at the time. When commercial entities collect data about individuals, we presume they do so in order to sell things to those people—or to sell information about them. They're not trying to build criminal cases, much less violate people's civil liberties. In any event, the private sector's ability to mine large swaths of data about people was then in its infancy. And the total capacity of a private-sector database to invade a person's privacy simply could not rival the capacity of a government spy agency—much less would a spy agency pervasively *depend* upon the private sector for the collection of its data. Wiretapping, after all, traditionally involved government's breaking into private data networks—a kind of authorized theft—not a collaborative relationship between government and a group of corporate partners.

None of these assumptions has weathered the test of time. It's not just that technology has eroded them; our entire culture's interaction and engagement with technology has shifted. We use information technology pervasively in ways unimaginable a generation ago. We feel differently about privacy, and our behavior has changed in a reflection of the shifts in our feelings. Interactions that once threatened our sensibilities do so less today; others that were once innocuous have grown more menacing.

Today, for example, it is possible to intercept calls and e-mails using automated systems without subjecting them to human eyes or ears at all—a tactic with little real-world privacy impact. In fact, we eagerly allow companies to deploy such computer algorithms to "read" our e-mail and filter it for spam. We knowingly let Google filter our e-mails and target advertising to us based upon their contents. We sign up for social networking sites like Facebook, on which we create and analyze patterns of friendship and social contact in fashions strikingly similar to the pattern analyses the intelligence community uses to identify threatening groups. We let Amazon.com keep track of our book purchases to recommend future titles, and we actively help Ebay and Amazon and other sites keep track of our behavior and contentedness by rating our transactions. If our collective behavior is any indication of our fears, the idea of being constantly monitored, at least by computers, simply isn't as threatening as it used to be.

On the other hand, the capacity of data mining—by government and by the private sector alike—to invade a person's privacy has grown enormously. Companies like ChoicePoint amass enormous volumes of public-record data on people and sell them, mostly for marketing purposes. "Want the names, addresses of people taking Prozac for depression? No problem," wrote *Washington Post* reporter Robert O'Harrow, Jr., in his book on data mining. "Computer users who like to gamble online? Who like sex toys? Bible believers and Hispanic political donors? It's all available to almost anyone who wants to pay. . . . Marketers dream of perfect lists, filled with names of rich, compliant, and acquisitive people. The quest is never-ending and, now, always accelerating."[16] We leave electronic fingerprints whenever we buy something online or with a credit card or pay a toll or visit a Web site, and we call dramatically more people using many more phone numbers on many more different devices than we used to. Assemble these data and you can do all kinds of things to someone, not all as benign as targeted advertising. O'Harrow, for example, tells the harrowing story of a man whose identity thief turned out to be a multiple murderer and whose name and social security number thereby ended up on *America's Most Wanted*.[17] Surveillance law today should be at least as concerned with how information gets used as how easily government can collect it in the first place.

Technology has also significantly complicated the notion that all investigations start with a suspect and then proceed by acquiring data about that person. It is still true, of course, that investigators have to start somewhere. If you're looking for the proverbial needle in the haystack, you still have to start with a haystack—and you have to start with the right haystack. But today we have the technology to ask prospective questions about haystacks in general and to use data to identify the right stacks to search more closely. That is, we can use data to acquire suspects. We can also, having identified an investigative target, use data to expand the field around him. Telephone-addressing information offers a good example. Just as social-networking software is fun because it identifies people's overlapping circles of friends and acquaintances, patterns of communications—even without looking at the contents of those communications—can help identify networks of jihadists. I don't know how many degrees of telephone separation one needs to be from a major Al Qaeda figure in order to attract legitimate scrutiny from the NSA, but examining such data systematically only makes sense.

This is not as Orwellian as it may sound. After September 11, it would have been foolish not to ask what other Saudis and Egyptians, having spent time in Afghanistan, went on to flight schools in the United States. Having identified such people, it would also have been foolish not to see whether any of them dialed phone numbers that Mohammed Atta also called or sent e-mails to addresses with which he also corresponded.[18] Significantly, O'Harrow also tells the story of a data company that, in the wake of September 11, tried to identify high-risk potential terrorists and came up with a list of twelve hundred people, including five of the hijackers.[19] To the extent such data are available, and a lot of them are readily available, the temptation on the part of the investigators to use it will be—and should be—inexorable. Data mining represents a tool of enormous power—imperfect and potentially prone to error, to be sure, but enormous power nonetheless—far too much power for investigators and intelligence agencies to ignore.

Perhaps the most anachronistic assumption in FISA is geographical—the idea that some magic difference of principle separates overseas and domestic communications. Philosophically sound though it may be, technology has made this line impossible to hold. A substantial percentage of international communications traffic routinely passes through servers in the United States. A server in Palo Alto may store e-mail communications from Saudi Arabia to Germany, for example. And IP "packets"—that is, bits of data broken up, sent out over the network, and reassembled on arrival at their address—may take widely varying routes to reach their common destination, some through this country, some around it. On the other hand, international communications now represent a day-to-day feature of the lives of countless Americans. We e-mail, instant message, and Skype with people all over the world with no particular thought to their locations. We don't think of those communications as any more or less private than the comparable exchanges with people down the street. And pivotally, even if we exercise the discipline of reminding ourselves that the law offers our overseas communications dramatically less security than our domestic calls, we don't always even *know* which of our communicants are physically within the country. Cell phones and BlackBerries work internationally, after all, and people can access their e-mail from anywhere. Dial a local phone number and you could be calling Mexico, Canada, Qatar, or Pakistan. This problem importantly also affects government, which has to know—or, as of this writing, at least "reasonably believe"—something about where an intelligence target is physically located before deciding what law to apply.

As the reader will no doubt have picked up, the results of FISA's technological obsolescence do not all cut in the same direction. Combatants in the political wars over surveillance tend to see only the erosions technology has wrought on their values and interests in this debate. Government officials often talk about how changes in the network have brought communications FISA never intended to protect under its ambit.[20] Civil libertarians bewail the lack of data regulation in a society now driven by data. Both points are essentially correct, but essentially incomplete and in considerable tension with one another. Surveillance law has grown paradoxically overprotective and underprotective at the same time.

PRESIDENT BUSH'S POST–SEPTEMBER 11 warrantless NSA program, under which the agency nabbed suspected Al Qaeda communications in which one party was abroad, appears to have developed in response to FISA's emergent overprotectiveness with respect to international data traffic. The administration's goals here were hardly unreasonable in either policy terms or—reasonableness being the ultimate touchstone of Fourth Amendment legitimacy—constitutional terms. It aimed to filter a large stream of telecommunications data coming into the United States, identify from the addressing and perhaps content of those data patterns indicative of terrorist networks, and then switch on human surveillance of a given target once a certain quantum of evidence had been obtained.

Yet under FISA, as it existed in 2001, the legality of such a program was preposterously tricky—largely because its mind-numbing definition of "elec-

tronic surveillance" requiring approval of the special court hinged simultaneously on the technical modes of interception the government used, the
geographical location in which the spooks tapped the lines, and the location
of the target of the surveillance. If the NSA was targeting domestic people in
the course of the program, it certainly operated in grave tension with the law,
which applies whenever the spooks acquire "the contents of any wire or radio
communication sent by or intended to be received by a particular, known
United States person who is in the United States, if the contents are acquired
by intentionally targeting that United States person, under circumstances in
which a person has a reasonable expectation of privacy and a warrant would
be required for law enforcement purposes."[21]

But there's some reason to think that the bulk of the targets were abroad
and that capture of the American side of these communications was incidental to foreign surveillance. And for targets abroad, the situation changed
markedly—even if they were calling people in the United States. In that situation, the specific modality of the program would then become all important.
Had the data traffic arrived by satellite, the program would be indisputably
kosher.[22] Congress wrote radio communications out of FISA's ambit even
where the physical interception took place domestically in order to exempt
from the law's coverage the NSA's practice in the 1970s of vacuuming up
without warrants as much radio traffic as it could get. But this exemption
covered a higher percentage of traffic in the 1970s than it did by 2001. At the
time Congress passed FISA, satellite communications carried the bulk of
overseas calls (exactly how much is disputed). With the advent of fiber-optic
cables, a lot of the traffic migrated to wire.[23] And if the government sought to
acquire the communication by tapping a wire line, it mattered where physically it conducted the interception. If it tapped the line domestically, the communication was subject to FISA. On the other hand, if the agency tapped the
line *abroad,* the communication was exempt from FISA.[24] In other words, as
long as the government focused on targets overseas using operations overseas,
FISA had nothing whatsoever to say about the matter. Indeed, the original
FISA would have allowed exactly what the 2007 "fix" triggered a furor for
allowing—warrantless surveillance of communications with one end abroad

and the other end in the United States—provided either that the NSA tapped a physical wire outside the sovereign territory of the United States or captured only radio signals.

The legal problem with the NSA's warrantless program arose because the data the NSA tapped reportedly came in by fiber-optic cable, so FISA applied unless the physical tap took place *outside* the sovereign territory of the United States—a few miles offshore, for example. Since the NSA apparently got these data by securing the *onshore* cooperation of the telecommunications companies, the law and its warrant requirement appear to have covered the acquisition—notwithstanding the facts that many of the communications may have involved only foreign parties and that the distinctions between onshore and offshore collection and between cable and satellite traffic have no conceivable civil liberties significance.[25] Put simply, the intelligence community's concerns that FISA's archaic structure impaired collection of foreign traffic the law never intended to cover surely had a legitimate basis, at least until the 2007 temporary patch.

Congress has had to patch holes in FISA before, some of them highly individualized. When immigration agents detained Moussaoui the month before the September 11 attacks, FBI agents could not search his laptop computer and other belongings without a FISA warrant. They believed—rightly or wrongly—that they could not get such a warrant because they could not tie Moussaoui tightly enough to a foreign power, only to a loose group of Chechen rebels. This turned out to be a fateful failure. Moussaoui's belongings, in fact, could have tied him to Ramzi Binalshibh, one of the conspiracy's overseas masterminds. As the 9/11 Commission later wrote:

A maximum U.S. effort to investigate Moussaoui conceivably could have unearthed his connections to Binalshibh. Those connections might have brought investigators to the core of the 9/11 plot. The Binalshibh connection was recognized shortly after 9/11, though it was not an easy trail to find. Discovering it would have required quick and very substantial cooperation from the German government, which might well have been difficult to obtain.

However, publicity about Moussaoui's arrest and a possible hijacking threat might have derailed the plot. With time, the search for [9/11 hijackers Khalid al] Mihdhar and [Nawaf al] Hazmi and the investigation of Moussaoui might also have led to a breakthrough that would have disrupted the plot.[26]

Congress responded to this incident with another patch: an amendment to FISA to permit surveillance of future Moussaouis without waiting for a definitive link to a foreign terrorist group. The so-called lone wolf FISA provision considers an "agent of a foreign power" any noncitizen or resident alien in the United States who "engages in international terrorism or activities in preparation therefore."[27]

Harder to patch is FISA's exacting "probable cause" standard, which legal journalist Stuart Taylor, Jr., has called "an unduly stringent burden of proof" in some terrorism cases.[28] This standard clearly deters a lot of surveillance. Generally speaking, a high legal threshold for wiretapping is a good thing; the law's goal, after all, is to prevent government's spying on people in the absence of evidence that they are themselves spies or terrorists. Yet terrorism, particularly catastrophic terrorism, presents a different constellation of issues than does classic espionage. Leaving the bar as high for all interceptions as we set it for traditional security investigations is almost certainly not constitutionally required, and it does not serve merely to protect political dissidents from overweening government. It serves also to protect genuine operatives from discovery. As commentator K. A. Taipale has perceptively pointed out, there is no equivalent under surveillance law to what police and courts call a *Terry* stop—in which a police officer can stop an individual and conduct a limited search based on "reasonable suspicion" even before establishing "probable cause" for an arrest or a broader search.[29] If agents don't have probable cause under FISA, the law itself offers them no aid in getting it, other than the potential use of trap-and-trace or pen register devices, which offer real-time access to information about whom a target is calling and receiving calls from.

All of this tends to foster a certain risk aversion in the intelligence community. In Moussaoui's case, for example, the FISA request never even went to the FISA court. The surveillance faltered within the bureau itself. This risk aversion carries real-world consequences, largely invisible to the public and sometimes compounded by basic misunderstandings within the bureau about a horrendously complicated law. In October 2001, for example, Jessica Stern began receiving e-mails from Osama bin Laden's official "biographer" about "alleged recent sightings" of the Al Qaeda leader. Stern, a former National Security Council staffer who now teaches at Harvard, is a terrorism expert who had written a pioneering book on the possibility of terrorists using weapons of mass destruction.[30] Subsequently, she had begun spending time traveling through dangerous regions interviewing jihadists.[31] She was one of the few scholars who prior to September 11 had focused intensely on the severity of the threat of Islamist extremist terrorism. In response to the contact, she called the FBI. "I didn't know whether this was misinformation, disinformation, or truth," she later said, "whether this man was applying for a job with the CIA, hoping to confuse the CIA, or what. . . . I found the situation hair-raising—it seemed that the information might potentially be important and I wanted to make sure that it got into the right hands quickly." Stern says she invited the bureau to "come right into my house" and tap her e-mail. And given her known contacts with some dangerous jihadis, her invitation represented an intelligence source of potential value.

Yet the bureau told Stern that "they had to vet my request with someone, their lawyers, I suppose." And they later told her that they couldn't do it: "it would be illegal." The bureau was almost certainly wrong in that judgment; a consensual, positively invited search of someone's computer is always lawful. Stern says she was told subsequently that "another agency" had "taken care of the problem," but she still isn't sure.[32] It's impossible to know how much intelligence gets lost because fear and misunderstanding of the law inhibits collection it actually permits—but the volume is probably substantial and certainly was so prior to September 11.

There is a final manner in which federal surveillance laws arguably overprotect privacy: While they do little to prevent intelligence agencies from ultimately acquiring and analyzing all sorts of data, they do encumber the gathering and processing of that information *in real time*. Stewart Baker, a former general counsel of NSA and current official at the Department of Homeland Security, noted in a perceptive 2002 paper that the government has easy access "to information in a third party's hands" using a variety of legal tools. "If the government has even a casual interest in a citizen's affairs, it can fairly easily establish the predicates [to use those tools] and obtain the orders necessary to gather large amounts of data about the citizen." On the other hand, "legal restraints seem to pose a significant problem for the use of more sophisticated technologies—particularly . . . technologies that might help us identify terrorists early, as opposed to convicting them after they've killed people." These restrictions, especially the Privacy Act, don't prevent the acquisition but "are just restrictive enough to make it awkward for the government to take direct access of private databases for data-mining analysis," the perverse result being arrangements under which the government "encourage[s] or even require[s] industry to keep the databases in private hands, run pattern recognition themselves, and report suspicious results to the government."[33]

FISA itself offers a good example. No government agency could attempt domestically what the NSA does with international traffic: capturing it as it happens and analyzing it algorithmically. Instead, we pretend that such data are private, yet we also allow the agencies to obtain much of them later using a variety of inconsequential legal standards—or just by negotiating their delivery by the phone companies. This is a curious sort of civil liberties protection, especially because when the government ultimately gets the data, it gets them with no serious restrictions on or accountability for their use. Such restrictions operate in large measure to ensure inefficiency in acquisition and a measure of obfuscation of what is really happening—a kind of illusion that the law keeps such domestic data private.

This brings us to the sense in which modern surveillance law underprotects privacy in our pervasively digital era. For even as the law places roadblocks in the way of collection and acquisition of data and makes the content of communications especially difficult to acquire, it does little to regulate what government does with the material it collects. Yes, some laws and regulations make certain uses, as Baker notes, "awkward." But not so awkward that the government ultimately lacks the ability either to collect and process huge volumes of material or to contract with companies to do the job on its behalf. Intelligence and law enforcement agencies, in fact, have obtained access to gigantic volumes of material—transactional data, telecommunications addressing information from phone companies and Internet service providers, credit card records—by a variety of means, generally involving trivial standards of evidence. Government can obtain court orders for records, often by doing nothing more than declaring them "relevant" to an investigation.[34] In terrorism cases, it can also use what are called national security letters, a kind of administrative subpoena the FBI can issue without even going to court.[35] Under the unjustly infamous "library" provision of the PATRIOT Act, the government can obtain "business records" using an order from the FISA court.[36] Under both FISA and domestic criminal authorities, it can deploy pen register and trap-and-trace devices.[37] Sometimes, the government does not even bother to obtain a court order, but simply negotiates the production of large volumes of records by private companies instead.[38] As long as it doesn't try to eavesdrop—that is, to capture or listen to the words people speak or e-mail to one another—but sticks to transactional data, the government has broad access to whatever it might need, and without especially individualized suspicion. As a result, the proper parameters of governmental data processing represent one of the great domestic civil liberties questions our society has not yet squarely faced.

It is possible, even tempting, to see this question as something of a nonissue. After all, if the government obtains information lawfully, would not only a true Luddite argue that we should bar it from processing that information as efficiently as possible? And what is data mining other than the attempt to maximize the efficiency of processing large volumes of information? If a particularly resourceful FBI agent devoted himself to studying and making head or tail of this type of record manually and managed accurately to identify criminal suspects based on suspicious behaviors, calls, and purchases, we would give that agent a medal. It seems silly to forswear the attempt just because we have developed computer technologies capable of doing hundreds or thousands of years' worth of human grunt work in seconds.

Yet there comes a point at which the amalgamation, storage, retention, and processing of information becomes more than added efficiency, but a different capacity altogether. New technologies have always required legal adjustments—both legislative and judicial—to keep the privacy doctrine meaningful. As wiretapping became technologically plausible, courts struggled with whether it counted as a search for purposes of the Fourth Amendment, and the legislature struggled with the circumstances under which the law should allow it. More recently, the Court has had to decide whether looking into a home using an infrared scanning device constitutes a "search" or just represents an efficient means of gauging the heat radiating from the outside of a building.[39] We have clearly reached the point with data processing where we need to ask as a society whether we really want no meaningful rules on the subject. What kind of transactional profile renders someone suspicious? Who gets to decide? What actions can government take against someone based on a threatening-looking data picture that may contain errors or result from unfortunate coincidences?

Current surveillance law, obsessed as it is with defining the circumstances of data acquisition, makes virtually no attempt to address these questions. While it is possible that having fully considered the matter, Congress would decide to give the intelligence community a wide berth in this area, doing so by default gives government far too much. And doing so by default, while at the same time insisting that access to data be impaired by farcical legal hurdles, borders on the nonsensical.

GROSSLY COMPLICATING and distorting any serious discussion of surveillance law is that perennial—and to some degree necessary—encumbrance to democratic debate on the subject: secrecy. The public still does not know exactly what the NSA has been doing. We do not know the precise circumstances in which the agency captures data traffic, what precisely it does with it, and what precisely its data-mining algorithms look for. We do not know for sure whether the agency looks only at addressing data or also at the content of communications. We do not know exactly what triggers monitoring by humans. And we do not know how all of this interacts with more traditional

FISA surveillance. This ignorance has survived several years of investigative reporting, leaks, congressional investigations, and public statements by officials on the subject. Yet without answers to these questions, we can only speculate as to whether the NSA's program is useful and important and adequately protective of privacy, trivially useful and invasive of the privacy of innocents, or—most challenging of all—useful and important yet also invasive of the privacy of innocents.

The secrecy problem in this area is far from new. The discussions that led to FISA's original passage suffered similarly from the need to keep certain programs under wraps. The NSA, in fact, back then had a program of vacuuming up overseas microwave transmissions, a program the agency was keen to exempt from the new law. This concern profoundly influenced the statute's arcane definition of "electronic surveillance"—yet as with the current program, members of the administration and Congress could not discuss the program itself much in public. As FISA expert David S. Kris recounts the history,

> Attorney General Edward Levi . . . explained that . . . "government operations to collect foreign intelligence by intercepting international communications . . . [are] not addressed in this bill." In response to questions, Levi observed that the bill would not apply to "a radio communication of an international kind which is picked up in some kind of a sweeping operation or some other kind of operation," or to "the transatlantic kinds of sweeping overhearing." In short, as he made clear, "Congress knows that there is an important area here which is not covered by this legislation."
>
> In subsequent appearances before Congress, Levi repeated these points about the limits of FISA, and referred explicitly to NSA surveillance. For example, he explained that while "one doesn't generally discuss them in public . . . we do know that there is a kind of sweeping operation by the NSA which is dealing with international communications not covered here. And that is uncovered in this bill." Indeed, Levi summarized testimony given in a closed hearing by the Director of the NSA, General Lew Allen, about "an

awesome technology—a huge vacuum cleaner of communications—that had the potential for abuses." Levi often was quite specific in his testimony, explaining that the bill would not cover surveillance of international communications from radio waves in any location, or from wires located outside the United States, and highlighting the significance of these exemptions for NSA. . . .

In response to a Senator's question about "what is covered by this legislation," Levi replied, "it has to come under the definition of electronic surveillance. If it doesn't come under that, it goes beyond that, then we say, well, it is outside the scope." Asked whether "we really [are] talking about the thrust of the whole NSA program," Levi replied, "We are talking about that portion of the NSA program which is not covered here, and which as I say, I really don't want to discuss in any detail," but which Senators had discussed with the NSA the previous day in executive session. He went on to say that "I know you had an executive session. A great deal of that is not covered by the definition."[40]

Indeed, at no time since FISA's passage has secrecy not encumbered public discussion of surveillance law. In the 1990s, months of research could give me only a peephole view of a complicated room with elaborate furnishings. I had no idea whether I was seeing 1 percent, 3 percent, or 5 percent of the room, but I knew the vast bulk of it remained out of sight. Indeed, the peephole chiefly allowed me to see only that portion of the room that involved other people's impressions of the part that remained out of sight: Judge Lamberth's sense, subsequently eroded, of the quality of the government's presentations before the Court, McAdams's account of the precautions his office took, the occasional judicial opinion that commented upon the occasional FISA application reviewed (always under seal) by the occasional court. Public debates over FISA have always rested on layers of inference built on top of a foundation of quicksand.

The problem, however, has grown worse, and not only—or even principally—because circumstances have changed since September 11. The Bush administration has an ideological commitment to secrecy, an active desire to minimize public debate over these questions. The openness the Justice Department showed in response to my inquiries in the 1990s seems positively quaint today. The animating spirit of the current administration asks not how much it can really say in public without compromising important interests— as Levi evidently did at the time of FISA's passage and the department did as well during the Clinton administration. It asks, instead, how little it can get away with saying.[41]

AS A RESULT OF the secrecy, we have only the barest sketch of the NSA program that has provoked such a roiling controversy. The administration has described the activity in broad generalities. The Justice Department's white paper on the legal authorities supporting the program says:

> The President has acknowledged that, to counter [the Al Qaeda] threat, he has authorized the NSA to intercept international communications *into and out of the United States of persons linked to Al Qaeda or related terrorist organizations.* The same day, the Attorney General elaborated and explained that in order to intercept a communication, there must be "a reasonable basis to conclude that one party to the communication is a member of Al Qaeda, affiliated with Al Qaeda, or a member of an organization affiliated with Al Qaeda." [Emphasis added.][42]

At the press conference to which the white paper refers, then–Attorney General Alberto Gonzales and then–Principal Deputy Director of National Intelligence Michael Hayden gave a few more illuminating details. Hayden, who had headed NSA when the program commenced and later became the CIA director, described the program as more "aggressive" than traditional FISA surveillance but also emphasized that it is "less intrusive. It deals only with international calls. It is generally for far shorter periods of time. And it is not designed to collect reams of intelligence, but to detect and warn and prevent about attacks." Asked what specific inadequacies in FISA created the need for it, he said that "the whole key here is agility. . . . FISA was built for persistence.

FISA was built for long-term coverage against known agents of an enemy power." By contrast, the current program is designed "to detect and prevent. . . . It's a quicker trigger. It's a subtly softer trigger." The idea, he said, was to eliminate "any inefficiencies in our coverage of those kinds of communications" and "to be as agile as operationally required to cover these [Al Qaeda] targets." When asked whether he could guarantee that NSA had intercepted no purely domestic communications, Hayden significantly declared that "I can assure you, *by the physics of the intercept, by how we actually conduct our activities,* that one end of these communications are always outside the United States of America." [Emphasis added.][43]

Combine these comments with news stories about the data-mining dimension of the NSA's program and its tapping the switches through which pass enormous volumes of overseas and domestic traffic, and a picture begins to emerge. The agency seems to be tapping the entire bitstream at domestic switching stations in an operation akin to what General Allen described in the 1970s as "a huge vacuum cleaner of communications," subjecting that stream to some kind of data mining—probably based principally on addressing information but looking to some degree at content as well—and then "agilely" switching on human surveillance based on patterns that might not amount to probable cause under FISA for relatively brief periods of time in order to identify potential threats. The program seems like an effort to create the kind of electronic *Terry* stop that Taipale complains FISA does not authorize. Those the program identifies domestically as Al Qaeda, we can presume, the NSA refers to the FBI for investigation and perhaps longer-term surveillance under FISA. As to those who seem innocuous, the agency simply switches off the human surveillance and nobody is the wiser.

Within the general parameters of this description, one can imagine a useful and valuable program that most Americans would want continued or a menacing threat to domestic liberty that would horrify much of the public. The difference between the two programs lies in the details. How sound are the algorithms that identify suspects out of the giant mass of ones and zeros the NSA vacuums up? Is the "subtly softer" trigger still a significant evidentiary standard or does it render anyone who takes a call from a Muslim abroad liable to having her subsequent international e-mails and calls tapped? How brief a period of surveillance is Hayden talking about when he emphasizes that the duration of NSA surveillance does not generally approach longer-term monitoring under FISA? My own sense is that the program is probably relatively responsible; members of Congress of both parties, when briefed on it, have emerged impressed by the technology and been inclined to permit its use either under current authorities or by amending the law.[44] And interestingly, notwithstanding the heated political rhetoric surrounding this issue, Congress has managed a generally constructive, if so far inconclusive, policy process over the specific structural problem the NSA appears to have launched the program to address: FISA's inconsistent and sometimes burdensome application to overseas telecommunications, including those with one end in the United States and those transiting through America's domestic communications infrastructure.

This problem has been kicking around for some time, and while a lot of details remain classified, we can try to piece together a sketch of its history. The problem developed as technology increased the uncertainty as to the location of targets, brought ever more purely overseas communications within FISA's ambit, and made it more likely that surveillance involving one domestic party would require FISA court approval. Conducting the NSA's program outside of FISA was an attempt to bulldoze the statutory impediments to efficient collection. At first, the administration probably justified its authority to do so based on a broad claim of inherent presidential power, akin to the claimed power to toss aside the torture statute.[45] The program, however, was to some degree scaled back following the now-famous confrontation over then–Attorney General John Ashcroft's hospital bed in March 2004, and the legal justification probably shifted at that point too.[46] Around the same time, then-OLC-head Jack Goldsmith began a process of attempting to bring the entire program under FISA—as he put it, "working with the FISA court to give the Commander in Chief much more flexibility in tracking terrorists."[47] This process finally came to fruition, long after Goldsmith's departure, early in 2007, when Gonzales declared that a "Judge of the Foreign Intelligence Surveillance Court issued orders authorizing the Government to target for collection international communications into or out of the United States where there is probable cause to believe that one of the communicants is a member or agent of Al Qaeda or an associated terrorist organization." Gonzales called these orders "innovative" and "complex" and announced that they would preserve the "speed and agility" of the old program while providing "substantial advantages" over it and allowing it to take place under FISA.[48]

Yet shortly after this accommodation with the Court, something happened that eroded its utility. According to press accounts, the FISA court issued an order insisting that FISA does, in fact, cover some purely foreign communications if they transit through American pipes. This created a huge backlog of FISA applications and necessitated some kind of legislative response.[49]

Congress responded first with the six-month temporary fix, the so-called Protect America Act (PAA), in the summer of 2007, the soul of which reads: "Nothing in [FISA's] definition of electronic surveillance . . . shall be construed to encompass surveillance directed at a person reasonably believed to be located outside of the United States."[50]

On its face, this sentence did two things. First, it eliminated the difference between wire and radio communications. If the NSA is now trying to vacuum up the entire stream of data flowing into the United States and subjecting it to a giant data-mining operation, it ceased to matter whether the agency accomplishes this by physically tapping fiber-optic lines outside of the territorial confines of the country or at facilities on its shore. For purposes of the law, it also ceased to matter whether the signal comes in over cables or from a satellite. As long as the government reasonably believed its targets abroad, the technology it used no longer matters. Because of the way technological shifts have brought more communications under the FISA, this change likely increased greatly the volume of communications acquirable without a warrant. But it's hard to see any real civil liberties significance in letting the NSA do with wire communications what it has always been able to do with radio communications.

The second change was a relaxation of the strict geographical requirements of FISA. To avoid going to the FISA court, the government under the PAA no longer needed to *know* its target is abroad. It need merely reasonably believe as much. This change did have civil liberties consequences: It presumably increased the amount of surveillance of people who are more likely than not to be outside of the country but who may turn out to be here after all. But the change seems defensible to me. The more mobile communications become, the more paralyzing a firm geographic rule becomes. Sometimes, intelligence operatives know a terrorist's phone number or e-mail address before they can pinpoint his location with certainty. If they reasonably believe he's not in the United States, should they really have to get a court order before checking out what he's saying and to whom?

The law had important problems, most notably that because of FISA's broad definition of "person" to include groups and organizations, it could be read to allow more extensive domestic eavesdropping than Congress intended.[51] That said, it was far less outrageous than the common rhetoric imagined it. As of this writing, the PAA has expired and Congress is struggling with the design of a more permanent solution. While important differences separate the various proposals, they are in essence similar: They permit warrantless surveillance of overseas targets who might communicate with domestic figures, and they provide for limited judicial review not of the surveillance itself but of the procedures under which it takes place. Something along these lines seems likely to emerge—the latest in the growing line of patches as Congress continues its scramble to keep FISA current.

But such legislation will leave the longer-term question looming: What would the optimal surveillance regime for our modern era look like? If Congress went through in 2008 something akin to the admirable process in which it engaged in 1968 and 1978, what would it come up with today?

THIS QUESTION defies detailed answer. The degree of secrecy simply precludes the sort of granular policy prescription we can attempt for, say, detention, trial, and interrogation. Too many questions about what technology currently permits and what we can foresee it permitting within a proximate time frame remain unanswered. Too many questions regarding what exactly the NSA is doing—and what it wants to do—remain unanswered as well. The most one can do at this stage is to identify the broad principles that might guide a new generation of surveillance law and to pinpoint some of the more specific questions it will need to address.

At the core of the next generation of surveillance law will lie, I suspect, a fundamentally different approach than America took starting in the 1960s. Then the idea was to treat surveillance and data acquisitions as somehow analogous to a physical search under the Fourth Amendment—that is, to identify evidentiary thresholds government needs to meet in order to conduct different types of "searches" against a given individual "target," and to delay permission for acquisition until government reaches those thresholds. A data society strains the search analogy past the breaking point, both because the standards that government must meet to obtain these data are generally so low and because government is sometimes seeking to examine this data not to learn more about a known target but in order to identify targets in the first place. In this context, the right approach is not to pretend the data themselves are off-limits except in the face of a showing of particular need. It is, rather, to allow relatively liberal government access to data and to focus privacy regulation on the manner of its use and accountability for its use.

The first part of this marriage will deeply challenge civil libertarians, who reflexively see intrusions on privacy in enhanced government access to information. We need to accept as a society, however, that government already has relatively easy access—either by its own acquisition or because industry has access—to huge volumes of material and that current laws designed to protect these data do less to shield individual privacy than to throw ultimately evadable obstacles into the path of investigators trying to exploit information. We end up with the worst of all worlds: mythological privacy protections that yield real investigative inconveniences.

Congress ought to strip away the roadblocks to constructive, real-time government access to routine transactional data—credit card and other financial transactions and telecommunications addressing information in particular. A Markle Foundation analysis concluded that aggressive examination of available data could have identified and connected all nineteen September 11 hijackers based on two who had already been placed on a watch list and purchased airline tickets using their real names.[52] Such material is simply too powerful a tool for government to ignore, and our law should generally facilitate responsible access to it rather than perversely pretending to limit it. It would be more honest, and with honesty and clarity would come an ability on the part of policy makers to focus on ensuring that information acquired gets put to appropriate use.

To push this point from the merely controversial into the realm of what now seems radical, let me say that I don't believe that all of what the NSA is doing abroad should be off the table domestically. Specifically, Congress should explore letting the government run real-time automated evaluation of telecommunications content and addressing information. As long as the algorithms are strong, the intelligence agencies do not retain the contents of communications, and human monitoring occurs only under circumstances of heightened scrutiny, such a program should not be unthinkable.

If this sounds completely Big Brotherish, consider government DNA databases, which allow law enforcement to compare biological material collected at crime scenes with the genetic fingerprints of large samples of known criminals. Cold hits from these databases have solved a lot of crimes and freed a number of innocent people from prison. Yet the databases suffer from a similar privacy problem. Technically, the government is subjecting to a criminal investigation every person whose information resides within the database each time it queries it for a match. But except for the subject who happens to have left his DNA at the crime scene, the investigation takes place at an entirely philosophical level. The hundreds of thousands of subjects of the investigation do not know they have been investigated and the investigators don't know whom they have looked at. Such investigations pose a kind of tree falling in the forest question: If your privacy gets invaded and nobody knows, did it really happen? Our society's emerging answer in the context of DNA databases is that it didn't.[53]

With a good enough data-mining algorithm—and it can never be as good as a DNA match—electronic monitoring of telecommunications traffic amounts to something similar. Yes, the individual's electronic communications get scanned for elaborate indicators of threatening behavior—the combination, for example, of contact with terrorist figures and the use of certain keywords. But unless those patterns turn up, the computer neither notices nor cares whatever else the communication might contain. A person's love notes and business correspondence go unread. As long as no human listens to or reads them and the computers don't retain the communications but merely filter them, the process is less like traditional wiretapping than it is like spam filtering—albeit without the consent of the communication's sender or recipient and with a great deal more at stake.

The trouble is that algorithms are not perfect and false positives will arise—much more frequently than with a DNA database. The propriety of such data mining should thus hinge significantly on two factors, one technological and the other a matter of policy.

The technological question regards the integrity of the algorithms. To anyone whose credit card company has called having identified quickly an uncharacteristic pattern of financial transactions and thus aborted a fraud, the notion that one can design pattern recognition programs of enormous power to head off wrongdoing will not seem too futuristic. Modeling terrorist risk factors, however, is more difficult than modeling fraud.[54] And if the result in practice is to produce too little useful data and too many false hits, the result will burden investigators with bad tips even as it menaces the liberty of innocents. If the tool is not yet powerful enough to deploy for this purpose, in other words, the legislature should certainly spare America the prospect—at once horrifying and counterproductive—of the intelligence community's laboring to check out large numbers of innocent people fingered by "suspicious" electronic fingerprint patterns while actual terrorists hide amidst the bitstream.

The policy question involves what happens when the electronic data crunching flags someone—that is, at the point at which we leave the realm of data and at which humans come in contact with names and begin contemplating taking action against real people. This is the point, in my view, where the true invasion of privacy takes place, the first point at which the capture and processing of data about someone involves adverse consequences for that person—other than the almost metaphysical consequence of having one's data examined electronically and then ignored. Assuming a set of algorithms powerful enough to deploy responsibly, this is the policy choke point on which we ought to focus. Taipale suggests using a kind of electronic *Terry* stop, that is, allowing investigators to switch on brief warrantless surveillance to figure out whether circumstances justify the sort of longer-term monitoring that FISA contemplates and to gather material in support of an application for that monitoring.[55] This would a be structure akin to the NSA's current activity involving international communications. Another possibility would be to have heightened bureaucratic checks—even, perhaps, a judicial warrant of some sort—governing the retrieval of identities. Government would have a free hand in searching data and in winnowing them down based on terrorism risk factors. But before an agency could know whom its searches had flagged, it would have to somehow justify the integrity of its queries and the assumptions behind them. The point here is that what threatens privacy is not computerized filtering of data, but humans acting upon that filtering, whether by keeping someone off an airplane or by launching a criminal investigation of him. And it is by regulating those actions, not by regulating the access to data itself, that we can maximize privacy as data processing becomes ever more pervasive.

This idea of focusing less on the front-end acquisition of data than on the back end—what government does with the material it acquires—admittedly cuts somewhat against the current grain. After all, the entire momentum of post–September 11 intelligence has pushed for greater sharing of information between government agencies and the tearing down of the wall between intelligence and law enforcement. Restricting the use of certain information to certain bureaucratic purposes operates in some tension with this goal. It also increases inefficiency. To make data use accountable, you have to make its tapping auditable. That means more personnel, more money, and a lot more bureaucratic hassle.

But the idea here is not to re-create the wall—much less to throw needless bureaucratic roadblocks in the way of intelligence and law enforcement. It is to create accountability and a means of preventing abuse that will not encumber collection that should take place in real time. Imposing restrictions on data use aims to guard against a kind of mission creep, under which tactics we permit to prevent catastrophic terrorism become routine law enforcement behavior in areas that do not justify their use. It aims also to provide a set of rules, under which the public can rest assured that while the government uses these tools aggressively to identify America's most implacable enemies, it does not use them either recklessly with respect to the billions of innocent people whose electronic fingerprints make these datasets so powerful or maliciously with respect to political opponents.

At least for now, the first rule ought to be a Las Vegas-like principle for the most aggressive data mining: What happens in counterterrorism stays in counterterrorism. There may come a time, and it may even come soon, when we decide that this principle protects too much. Our conceptions of privacy are changing rapidly, and we may decide that mission creep isn't so bad—particularly if government is using data mining responsibly and avoiding civil liberties violations. When, for example, the public learns that a serial rapist or murderer has eluded capture and struck again because those investigating him were unable to access data available to their colleagues chasing terrorists, people might well demand broader law enforcement access. But we're not there yet. We would not contemplate radically altering the legal landscape of surveillance in order to facilitate the investigation of routine crimes and should therefore act cautiously in allowing the tools we contemplate in the law of the long war to trickle down into more routine uses. Again, if we imagine a new generation of surveillance law as part of a broader, emergent law of terrorism—a body of law distinct from the traditional law of war, the law of intelligence, and the criminal law—it follows that we might limit certain surveillance activities to terrorism alone.

The broader challenge is defining what uses of data to authorize for what purposes. The details of this of this task are probably better suited to executive rule making than to congressional legislation. But the project of both forcing executive consideration of data policies and defining the broad principles of such an undertaking is a legislative function Congress has shirked far too long. The government needs clear rules, and the public needs to debate those rules. At the extremes, the question of what uses we permit for what sort of data is easy. Should local parking enforcement officers query people's health records when they write them a ticket to figure out if they are really handicapped and therefore entitled to park in designated spaces? Of course not. Should airline security officers know when a former Guantánamo detainee buys a ticket to New York? Of course. Obviously, both the immediacy of the threat and the sensitivity of the data bear on the propriety of using those data for particular purposes.

The problem gets devilishly tricky, however, in the large middle space of a very wide spectrum. So far, American policy deals with it piecemeal, with excessive secrecy from government, shrill criticism from privacy activists, and abdication from Congress. The legislature could begin by pushing the executive branch to articulate and define its authorized data uses—in public where possible—in the counterterrorism arena.[56]

Intricately connected to the notion of defining rules for data use is accountability for those uses. And Congress could easily create a regime of accountability. Inspector general audits, internal checks, and reporting requirements to the courts, to Congress itself, and to the public may sound like meaningless bureaucratic drudgery. But this sort of multilayered accountability, of which FISA itself provides an excellent example, creates redundant mechanisms for the exposure of abuses. It can also create at every stratum of the bureaucracy the fear of that exposure, which can have a powerful disciplining effect on behavior. And it can create a body of material—public and classified—that enables ongoing debate as to whether the counterterrorism bang of a given surveillance tactic or policy is worth its civil liberties buck. A limited version of this exists today—the occasional requirement of a "privacy impact statement," an audit by the Government Accountability Office, or an inspector general review. Making these accountability mechanisms more pervasive, vibrant, regular, rigorous, and—to the extent possible—public offers a better avenue for restraining executive abuse than pretending to subject acquisition of data to judicial review that isn't real.

Critically, these oversight mechanisms must somehow incorporate oversight of the algorithms themselves, since so much depends on their integrity, and they will need to guarantee as well better mechanisms for correcting errors in the data. Data-mining schemes that seem like voodoo will ultimately acquire the disregard many people now harbor for the "science" of polygraph testing. And any data-mining effort that relies on bad data will produce bad results. Data errors have already wreaked havoc in data-mining efforts used in airline security.[57] And while strong human analysis of data-mining "hits" can mitigate this problem, it cannot compensate for it entirely. Where the underlying technology isn't strong, any system will spend scarce investigative energy on wild goose chases—otherwise known as innocent people. If the public is going to have any comfort with this sort of investigative tactic, it needs ongoing reassurance of both the science behind it and the fuel driving it. There is actually precedent for such accountability. In the early 1990s, when the NSA was trying to get companies to use an encryption system it had developed with a back-door access mechanism for law enforcement use, many people doubted the strength and integrity of the algorithm. In response, the NSA invited in a panel of outside experts to publicly review what was then still a classified system.[58] The goal, in short, is a series of systemic checks on the integrity and reasonable deployment of the information systems on which our security aparatus grows daily more dependent. Done properly, this will both enhance privacy protection and maximize the investigative utility of data-mining. Done badly—or not at all—it will continue to maximize controversy over surveillance while dampening both the value of data and public confidence in their responsible use.

Organizing such an effort will require a different orientation both from the legislature and from the executive branch. Congress will need to think bigger, not merely about the patchable deficiencies in FISA but about the broader landscape of surveillance law—how it has changed, how it will change in the future as patches pile up upon patches, and what the principles might look like that could obviate the need for those patches by at once restraining and enabling government as shifts in law and technology continue. It will have to organize itself for sustained legislative fact gathering and oversight. This effort will not result in a single piece of legislation but a redirection over time. Congress will have to begin a process of rethinking some of the first principles of surveillance law, and it will have to keep working on it and not imagine that its work is done the first time a bill becomes law.

On the executive side, the next president is going to have to enable this debate by sharing significantly more information with Congress and the public. Yes, such openness involves risks of disclosing secrets to the enemy. But America is not a society of secret law, and ultimately, Congress must justify its public laws in public terms. It cannot do so when its members do not know what they do not know and when the public does not know even a fraction of what members of Congress do know. At a minimum, the executive branch will need to display a far greater openness with the congressional intelligence committees, which the current administration has too often kept needlessly in the dark about matters solidly within their purview.

If this all sounds hopelessly ambitious, some cause for optimism lies in the process that led to modern wiretapping law in the first place. For more than a decade, Congress struggled with new technology, intelligence programs and abuses, the relevance of America's constitutional tradition, and the practicalities of applying that tradition. The result of this labor was a surveillance architecture that served America well for a generation. But FISA was not, as matters turned out, a statute for all time, and the architecture now needs a substantial renovation. Surely the institution that managed its imagination and creation can now handle its reimagination and retrofitting. Surely Congress can provide a surveillance law for a new century, rules under which the intelligence agencies can learn what they need to know about America's enemies while respecting an appropriate measure of data privacy for the rest of us.

Conclusion

ON DECEMBER 5, 2007, just as I was completing a draft of this manuscript, the Supreme Court heard oral arguments in the case of *Boumediene v. Bush*, the latest round of litigation over the jurisdiction of the courts at Guantánamo Bay. For connoisseurs of oral arguments, the day was a treat, pitting two of the great advocates of our time against one another before an engaged group of justices in a high-stakes case freighted with liberty and national security.

Seth P. Waxman, who served as solicitor general in the Clinton administration, argued for the detainees and engaged in a lengthy colloquy with Justice Antonin Scalia over whether centuries of habeas corpus cases required federal court jurisdiction over the Guantánamo cases or precluded it. Current Solicitor General Paul D. Clement, arguing for the government, contended that compared with the scope of habeas at the time the Constitution was adopted, current law represents a "remarkable liberalization of the writ, not some retrenchment or suspension" of it. They argued over ancient British cases and over cases in India. The argument even touched on whether the Isle of Jersey was considered part of the British crown's sovereign territory for habeas purposes. It was, in its own way, a dazzling display.

Unless, that is, you're trying to design a legal architecture for a long confrontation with international jihadist terrorism—in which case it all seems somehow empty. Indeed, all of it, or nearly all of it, banks on the same premise on which both the administration and its foes have leaned incessantly since September 11: the notion that our constitutional tradition, if sifted through enough, can answer our current questions, that we can debate history and centuries-old legal principles long enough to figure out how to handle Khalid Sheikh Mohammed and the very scary future that he represents.

It's an illusion. We can't.

In a few months—possibly before this book sees publication, possibly days or weeks afterward—the Court will rule in this case. The day it does, the country's legal, political, and journalistic elites will convulse in discussion of the future of habeas at the base and beyond, whether Guantánamo must now be closed, and who it all will help and hurt in a presidential election some months down the road. We will dissect whether the Bush administration has suffered another "stinging defeat" or has snatched victory from its jaws. We will proclaim the decision a great victory for the rule of law or a dangerous shackling of the military. We will debate whether the Court is right or wrong. We will psychoanalyze Justice Anthony Kennedy—who, as the Court's swing vote, will almost surely control the case's disposition. We will have no doubt of the moment's momentousness.

Yet the following day, America will still hold nearly three hundred people at Guantánamo Bay under rules it has failed to define in law. It will still have failed to agree on standards for its highest-stakes interrogations, and it will still have no idea how to manage surveillance in a pervasively data-driven society. We will still, as a political culture, busy ourselves contesting every component of the powers of presidential preemption—the result being that if American forces catch Ayman al Zawahiri or Osama bin Laden the day after the decision, we will still have nothing remotely approaching a consensus regarding what to do with them, where to do it, or what rights they should have. The answers to our questions don't lie in the Constitution or in the historical reach of habeas corpus. As Richard Posner once quipped to me, "The Constitution is old—old and short." It cannot answer our contemporary problems in this area, because the Founders not only did not address them, they did not address anything close enough to them for lawmaking by useful analogy.

A close parallel to the problem of overreliance on the founders as a source for our law has developed in America's intellectual and policy discussions of legal approaches to terrorism: the assumption that the answers are obvious. How obvious it is that we should close Guantánamo, abstain from interrogations that trouble our collective conscience, and either try our enemies in court or define them as not our enemies. How equally obvious that the president has the power to do whatever is necessary to win the war, that what is necessary is a matter for his unreviewable judgment, that anxieties about civil liberties constitute—as John Ashcroft once put it—nothing more than "the phantoms of lost liberty," and that we don't make errors in identifying the enemy.

It is so much easier this way. Everybody gets to define the good guys and the bad guys in our domestic disputes in a fashion that oh so neatly tracks preexisting political predilections. Liberals get to dismiss conservatives as insufficiently attentive to liberty; conservatives can dismiss liberals as weak and insufficiently serious about the threats to our way of life. Ironically, by virtue of both sides' willingness to engage the battle on these terms, both caricatures become more true, not less.

Yet the answers here are no more obvious than they are written in the Constitution. They are terrifyingly, dangerously, paralyzingly nonobvious. The more one studies them, in fact, the less obvious they get, until their nonobviousness becomes the only obvious thing about them. These are questions that require designing systems to balance risk in situations in which at every stage we know a lot less than we need to know to make wise decisions. And one way or another, when we get those systems wrong, terrible things will happen. In this project, we are the Founders. We should stop pretending otherwise. The place to look for the answers to these foundational design questions is in our own minds and intellects, in our own hearts and values, and in our own willingness to take risks for liberty and to take risks with liberty.

It is too late for the Bush administration. It has no trust on Capitol Hill, and it has no time. And even at this late date, it has too much ambivalence about the project—too much residual insistence that it has all the power it needs. It has lost the personnel who most strongly believed in engaging Congress. And not until seven years into Bush's tenure did the president hire an attorney general with the public stature and apparent inclination to make the attempt. Bush also has too much baggage. Locked in a death grip with its critics, his administration can at most speak credibly to a fraction of the country. For presidential leadership in this arena, America will have to await Bush's successor.

The great question in that regard is what attitude that successor will adopt. Will he or she ask, when faced with the possibility of working with Congress, "Why are you trying to give away the president's power?"—as vice presidential counselor David Addington did? Or will he or she see it as former Deputy Attorney General Jamie Gorelick did in the 1990s as a means of building executive power by involving the other branches in its exercise? I suspect that the next administration will see Gorelick's attitude as more attractive than the Bush administration did—that is, will see in it the opportunity to stem the endless tide of litigation and build a long-term foundation and legal safe harbor for actions that will inevitably garner controversy but for which accountability might be diffused.

My guess is that this will be true whether the next president is Democratic or Republican, whether it is John McCain, Barack Obama, or Hillary Clinton. A Democratic president, even one who has run for office talking of closing Guantánamo and restoring habeas, will face a new reality on taking office: He or she will suddenly be responsible for preventing the next attack and will need to wield powers about which liberal anxiety runs high and upon whose legitimacy Democrats have spent several years casting aspersions. Even if the new president magically arranges the repatriation resettlement or prosecution of all Guantánamo detainees, he or she will inevitably have to take actions that look at times surprisingly similar to those of the Bush administration. Going to Congress will create political cover. It will create a sharp break with the past in tone, legitimacy, and procedure, even while allowing much substantive action to reflect continuity with prior practice. McCain's incentives would be slightly different. The author of the McCain amendment has never seen eye to eye with the Bush administration on this constellation of issues and may well wish not to adopt as his own its controversies and battles. Going to Congress would allow him to transcend Bush's narrow ideological skirmishes with domestic foes and build consensus for fighting the foreign ones. It will allow him to define an approach of his own, one that does not carry the taint of a particularly unpopular predecessor.

The other critical variable is the posture that Congress itself adopts. This is already changing. The past year has seen considerably more legislative exploration of the rules of the road, particularly concerning interrogation, detention, and surveillance. Much of this activity has been constructive, some less so. Much, however, has been oppositional—attempts to throw roadblocks in the way of administration policy. This is probably a healthy development given Congress's previous posture of lapdoglike obedience to the executive. It is, however, an interim stage, a kind of adolescence beyond which the legislature will have to mature before a fully adult conversation with the presidency can proceed. Congress has to begin seeing itself not principally as a counterweight or an opposition stronghold or even as a center for oversight but as a coequal branch, a partner in policy making responsible for the design of systems and for monitoring their use. It badly needs, in short, to take ownership of these issues.

We need to cultivate a different intellectual climate about these questions as well—one less conditioned by personality, political party, and the current war in Iraq. We need a climate more sensitive to the awesome task at hand: designing a law for a long war, a war that isn't quite a war, but isn't quite anything else either, a war we have still not compellingly defined and may never fully define and yet will need to regulate and prosecute anyway. More than six years after September 11 and who knows how long before the next catastrophic strike, we have come to this project late, far too late to tarry longer.

ACKNOWLEDGMENTS

THIS BOOK HAS BEEN by far the most difficult project of my career, involving at once a greater breadth of subject matter than either of my two previous books and a volume of data unlike anything I have worked with before. As such, it simply would not have come into being without the support and help of people and institutions for whom the following acknowledgments are but meager repayment.

As I did with both of my previous books, I wrote this one quickly following some years of intellectual germination. The germination took place at the *Washington Post* editorial page. My attempt to imagine the law of the long war began around the page's conference table in the company of a diverse group of powerful minds meeting daily to chew over the issues of the moment. I am forever grateful to Fred Hiatt and my former colleagues for their support, friendship, engagement, and disagreement over nine uncommonly excellent years. Those conversations affect every page of this work.

The task of translating the many, often conflicting thoughts of those several years into a coherent argument would have been impossible had I not ended up at the Brookings Institution, which has given me a wonderful new intellectual and professional home since my departure from the *Post*. I am particularly grateful to Pietro Nivola, who encouraged me to join the Governance Studies program at Brookings, and to Strobe Talbott and Bill Antholis for their unstinting support of my work in particular and of building a vibrant space for the study of legal affairs at Brookings more generally. A special word for thanks as well to the people—Bethany Hase, Erin Carter, and Gladys Arrisueño—who make the trains run on time, run at all in fact, at Governance Studies, without whom I would never have had time to set pen to paper. I could not be more delighted to find myself at Brookings and look forward to haunting its halls for many years to come.

The book itself began as a lengthy essay in *Policy Review,* whose editor, Tod Lindberg, gave me space to ruminate on the role of judges in the war on terrorism. More generally, the Hoover Institution, which publishes *Policy Review,* has provided through its Task Force on National Security and Law both generous support and a particularly stimulating intellectual climate for the nonideological discussion of the legal framework that governs counterterrorism. The astute reader may also notice that several of the ideas and themes fleshed out in these pages had their origins in columns I wrote in the *New Republic Online* and the *Atlantic,* which have provided a terrific platform for my essays in recent years. My chapter on detention and trial had its origins in a paper I wrote for Brookings with Mark Gitenstein, "A Legal Framework for Detaining Terrorists: Enact a Law to End the Clash over Rights."

Two people gave me particular assistance in navigating the world of New York publishing. My agent, Gail Ross, pushed me to think ambitiously about telling legal stories to general audiences. And my editor, Vanessa Mobley, stepped into this project midstream and midcrisis, and provided excellent guidance in framing difficult ideas both rigorously and accessibly. Her wise counsel and challenging suggestions improved the manuscript in countless ways, large and small.

The manuscript also benefited enormously from helpful suggestions from a number of people. In particular, Matt Waxman and Jonathan Rauch read each chapter within days of its drafting and offered perceptive comments that were invaluable as I revised. Many components of the book's thesis emerged in conversations over the years with Jack Goldsmith, whose deep thought on these subjects has greatly influenced my own thinking on them and who read and commented on each chapter. Richard Posner, Bill Galston, Hannah Neprash, and Peter Berkowitz each read, critiqued, and provoked changes in the manuscript. And incisive comments from David Kris, Jim Baker, and Shane Harris greatly improved my chapter on surveillance law.

I had first-rate research assistance throughout the writing of this book, particularly in connection with the processing of the large volume of declassified government records about Guantánamo detainees. Griha Singla, as an intern at Brookings, began the process of constructing a database of information about the detainees, a task in which Erin Miller and Rakim Brooks participated as well. When Griha went back to college, she passed the torch to my research assistant, Zaahira Wyne, who has slaved ever since at completing and polishing the database, assisted at times by Julia Pilcer and Dayana Medevsky. The data in Chapter 3 are the fruits of the combined efforts of this team, under Zaahira's and Griha's leadership. Dominique Melissinos gave me extensive help with footnotes. And Becca Rosen, assisted by Christine Lai, checked every fact in the book; if you have found no mistakes in the text, it is only because she found them first. I also owe a debt of gratitude to Emily Messner, who spent a grueling day helping reality check data.

This is the second book I have written in substantial part at the Modern Times Café at Politics and Prose. So once again, a word of thanks goes to the staff there for their cheer, black coffee, and warmth, and for the homey office they provide away from home and office.

Finally, I could not have made a dent in writing this, or any, book without the support and encouragement of my family. My wife and—now that I have joined her at Brookings—colleague, Tamara Cofman Wittes, made sure I had time to write, though she was polishing off a book herself, and was an endless source of support and encouragement at a time of transition and professional instability. She was, as always, a critical sounding board for ideas, both good ones and those that, well, seemed good at the time. My daughter Miriam, who as a two-year-old almost derailed my first book project by, as she put it, "bumping down the stairs" to interrupt my early-morning work sessions, now sometimes joins them with reading of her own or brings her homework to the café with me for a work date. My son Gabriel has kept me smiling with his affectionate creativity and his ever-warm solicitude for "Daddy's book."

He suggests that since I dedicated my first book to his sister and his mother before he existed, it's now his turn and I should dedicate this book to him—which seems like a good idea to me. It is, after all, ultimately about the law under which he will grow up, a law that needs to protect him without itself menacing him.

Notes

Introduction

1. *Hamdan v. Rumsfeld*, 126 S. Ct. 2749 (2006).

2. Public Law 109-366.

3. Bush announced the transfer of the detainees from the CIA's secret program to Guantánamo on September 6, 2006. The transcript is available at http://www.whitehouse.gov/news/releases/2006/09/20060906-3.html.

4. The circumstances of Hoess's capture are described in Laurence Rees, *Auschwitz: A New History* (New York: PublicAffairs, 2005), 288–89. I am indebted to Charles Lane for bringing this incident to my attention.

5. Under Supreme Court doctrine, an investigative tactic that "shocks the conscience" is considered to violate the substantive due process requirements of the Fifth Amendment. See *Rochin v. California*, 342 U.S. 165 (1952).

6. Combatant Status Review Tribunal for Ghassan Abdallah Ghazi Al Shirbi, ISN #682, CSRT Set 30, 2073–77, available at http://www.dod.mil/pubs/foi/detainees/csrt_arb/. All subsequent citations of CSRT testimony and ARB records are available at the same site under the heading "Combatant Status Review Tribunal (CSRT) and Administrative Review Board (ARB) Documents."

7. The charge sheet in *United States v. Ghassan Al Sharbi* is available at http://www.defenselink.mil/news/Nov2005/d20051104sharbi.pdf. The military's spelling of the detainee's name in his military commission case differs from that in his CSRT record.

8. The transcript of the military commission case of *United States v. Ghassan Abdullah Al Sharbi*, April 27, 2006, session, is available at http://www.defenselink.mil/news/Apr2006/Vol%203

%20-%20al%20Sharbi%20-%20(R.%201-58)%20(27%20Apr%2006%20session)%20(R).pdf. See especially ibid., 14–15, 20.

9. Combatant Status Review Tribunal Record for Faruq Ali Ahmed, ISN #032, Publicly Filed CSRT Records, 165–90. The allegation that Faruq Ali Ahmed went to high school with some of the mujahedeen with whom he allegedly traveled appears in "Unclassified Summary of Evidence for Administrative Review Board in the Case of Ahmed, Faruq Ali," ISN #032, ARB Round 1 Factors, 35–37.

10. Administrative Review Board Round I hearing for Faruq Ali Ahmed, ISN #032, ARB Round 1 Set 5, 20035–51.

11. See Amnesty International press release, "USA: Guantánamo Must Be Closed Immediately," June 22, 2007, available at http://www.amnesty.org/en/alfresco_asset/687402ff-a2d1-11dc -8d74-6f45f39984e5/amr511102007en.html.

12. Jean-Paul Akayesu was convicted of genocide by the International Criminal Tribunal for Rwanda (ICTR), in part based on allegations of sexual violence. See *Prosecutor v. Akayesu*, No. ICTR-96-4-T, September 2, 1998. The International Criminal Tribunal for the former Yugoslavia (ICTY) held as well that rape could, under certain circumstances, constitute torture. See *Prosecutor v. Delalic*, No. IT-96-21-T, November 16, 1998.

13. Public Law 107-40.

14. *Rasul v. Bush*, 542 U.S. 466 (2004).

15. *Hamdi v. Rumsfeld*, 542 U.S. 507 (2004).

16. The Detainee Treatment Act passed as part of Public Law 109-148 on December 30, 2005. See Title X of the Department of Defense, Emergency Supplemental Appropriations to Address Hurricanes in the Gulf of Mexico, and Pandemic Influenza Act, 2006.

17. *Hamdan v. Rumsfeld*, 126 S. Ct. 2749 (2006).

18. Early efforts to make sense of the data have been shrill and polemical. See, for example, Andy Worthington, *The Guantánamo Files: The Stories of the 774 Detainees in America's Illegal Prison* (London: Pluto Press, 2007).

Chapter 1: The Law of September 10

1. The National Commission on Terrorist Attacks Upon the United States, also known as the 9/11 Commission, released its report (*9/11 Commission Report*) on July 22, 2004. The quoted text appears on 132.

2. Steve Coll, *Ghost Wars: The Secret History of the CIA, Afghanistan, and Bin Laden, from the Soviet Invasion to September 10, 2001* (New York: Penguin Press, 2004), 428.

3. John Yoo, *War by Other Means: An Insider's Account of the War on Terror* (New York: Atlantic Monthly Press, 2006), 2–4.

4. Joseph Margulies, *Guantánamo and the Abuse of Presidential Power* (New York: Simon & Schuster, 2006), 4–5.

5. Ibid., 13–14.

6. See *United States v. Salameh*, 152 F.3d 88 (2d Cir. 1998).

7. See *United States v. Abdel Rahman,* 189 F.3d 88 (2d Cir., 1999).

8. See *United States v. Ressam,* 474 F.3d 597 (9th Cir., 2007).

9. See indictment in *United States of America v. Usama Bin Laden,* 98-CR-1023 (S.D.N.Y., unsealed November 4, 1998).

10. Coll, *Ghost Wars,* 425–26.

11. Ibid., 139–44.

12. Ibid., 492–94.

13. While I served on the *Washington Post* editorial board, the *Post* editorialized repeatedly against the use of secret evidence in these cases. See, for example, "The Constitution and Terrorism," *Washington Post,* March 27, 1998, A24; "Not-So-Secret Evidence," *Washington Post,* July 22, 1998, A16; "A Blow for Secret Evidence," *Washington Post,* August 6, 1999, A20; and "Secret Evidence," *Washington Post,* November 3, 1999, A34.

14. See, for example, *Detroit Free Press v. Ashcroft,* 303 F.3d 681 (6th Cir., 2002). Circuit Judge Damon J. Keith, writing for the majority, held that the government could not close immigration proceedings on a blanket basis but had to close hearings on a case-by-case basis.

15. Testimony of Michael Scheuer before Joint Hearing of the Subcommittee on International Organizations, Human Rights, and Oversight, and the Subcommittee on Europe of the House Committee on Foreign Affairs on "Extraordinary Rendition in U.S. Counterterrorism Policy: The Impact on Transatlantic Relations," April 17, 2007.

16. See Daniel Benjamin, "5 Myths About Rendition (and That New Movie)," *Washington Post,* October 21, 2007, B3.

17. Richard A. Clarke, *Against All Enemies: Inside America's War on Terror* (New York: Free Press, 2004), 143–45.

18. See Jane Mayer, "Outsourcing Torture: The Secret History of America's 'Extraordinary Rendition' Program," *New Yorker,* February 14, 2005, 106. For a more detailed account of the Albania operation, see Andrew Higgins and Christopher Cooper, "Cloak and Dagger: A CIA-Backed Team Used Brutal Means To Crack Terror Cell," *Wall Street Journal,* November 20, 2001, A1.

19. Tenet disclosed this fact during his keynote address at the Distinguished Service Award Banquet in Washington, DC, on December 11, 2002. The transcript of Tenet's remarks is available at https://www.cia.gov/news-information/speeches-testimony/2002/dci_speech_12112002.html.

20. Noted cases of erroneous transfers include those of Canadian-Syrian dual national Maher Arar, a case that did not technically involve a rendition, and Khaled El-Masri, a German citizen of Lebanese extraction. The Canadian Commission of Inquiry into the Actions of Canadian Officials in Relation to Maher Arar, headed by Justice Dennis O'Connor, released its report, entitled "Report of the Events Relating to Maher Arar," on September 18, 2006. See also *El-Masri v. United States,* 479 F3d. 296 (4th Cir., 2007).

21. See Scheuer testimony.

22. See Article 3 of all four Geneva Conventions.

23. The most famous of these is *Miranda v. Arizona,* 384 U.S. 436 (1966).

24. See Article 16 of the "United Nations Convention against Torture and Other Cruel, Inhuman

or Degrading Treatment or Punishment," adopted on December 10, 1984. The Convention against Torture came into force on June 26, 1987.

25. Ibid., Article 2.

26. See 18 U.S.C. §§2340–2340A.

27. The War Crimes Act was codified at 18 U.S.C. §2441 (1996).

28. The so-called Torture memo, formally titled "Standards of Conduct for Interrogation under 18 U.S.C. §§2340-2340A," has been published in *The Torture Papers: The Road to Abu Ghraib*, Karen J. Greenberg and Joshua L. Dratel, eds. (Cambridge: Cambridge University Press, 2005), 172–217.

29. William R. Levi, "Identifying and Explaining Change: Development of U.S. Interrogation Policy 1949–2006." Levi's paper, an undergraduate thesis, remains sadly unpublished.

30. Brandt Goldstein, *Storming the Court* (New York: Scribner, 2005), 20.

31. Ibid., 77–78.

32. See *Haitian Centers Council v. Sale*, 823 F. Supp. 1028 (E.D.N.Y. 1993).

33. The decision by the Second Circuit, *Haitian Centers Council v. McNary*, 969 F.2d 1326 (2d Cir., 1992), was vacated as moot by the Supreme Court, see 509 U.S. 918 (1993). For a discussion of the decision to vacate the court order that forced the closure of the Guantánamo camp, see *Storming the Court*, 298–300.

34. Ibid., 298.

35. *Cuban American Bar Association Inc. v. Christopher*, 43 F.3d 1412 (11th Cir., 1995). The court first articulated this principle in *Haitian Refugee Center, Inc. v. Baker*, 953 F.2d 1498 (11th Cir., 1992).

36. Judicial tolerance of civil commitment of the mentally ill is by no means a recent development. See, for example, *Minnesota ex rel. Pearson v. Probate Court of Ramsey*, 309 U.S. 270 (1940).

37. See, for example, *Addington v. Texas*, 441 U.S. 418 (1979); *Foucha v. Louisiana*, 504 U.S. 71 (1992).

38. See *Kansas v. Hendricks*, 521 U.S. 346 (1997).

39. See, for example, Thomas S. Szasz, *The Myth of Mental Illness: Foundations of a Theory of Personal Conduct* (New York: Harper and Row, 1974). See, in particular, the preface to the second edition, vii–xii.

40. See *Shaughnessy v. United States ex rel. Mezei*, 345 U.S. 206 (1953).

41. See Brief for the Petitioners in *Crawford v. Martinez* (No. 03-878), 7–9.

42. See *Zadvydas v. Davis*, 533 U.S. 678 (2001).

43. See *Clark v. Martinez*, 543 U.S. 371 (2005).

44. Justice Sandra Day O'Connor provided the pivotal fifth vote for the majority in *Zadvytas*. Whether Chief Justice John Roberts or Justice Samuel Alito would vote to follow through on the Court's suggestion that such a statute, interpreted literally, would face due process difficulties seems very much open to question.

45. Writing for the majority in *Zadvydas*, Breyer specifically noted that "the provision authorizing detention does not apply narrowly to 'a small segment of particularly dangerous individuals,' . . . say suspected terrorists, but broadly to aliens ordered removed for many and various

reasons." Breyer went on to emphasize that the Court here was not "consider[ing] terrorism or other special circumstances where special arguments might be made for forms of preventive detention and for heightened deference to the judgments of the political branches with respect to matters of national security." O'Connor reiterated these sentiments in *Clark,* noting that "the Government has other statutory means for detaining aliens whose removal is not foreseeable and whose presence poses security risks. Upon certifying that he has 'reasonable grounds to believe' an alien has engaged in certain terrorist or other dangerous activity specified by statute . . . the Secretary of Homeland Security may detain that alien for successive six-month periods."

46. See 8 U.S.C. §1226a.

47. Breyer wrote in *Zadvydas* that "the alien's release may and should be conditioned on any of the various forms of supervised release that are appropriate in these circumstances, and the alien may no doubt be returned to custody upon a violation of those conditions." Justice O'Connor reiterated this point in her concurrence in *Clark,* in which she stated, "[A]ny alien released as a result of today's holding remains subject to the conditions of supervised release. . . . And, if he fails to comply with the conditions of release, he will be subject to criminal penalties— including further detention."

48. The legitimacy of distinguishing between honorable soldiers and other combatants was well ingrained in state practice by the time Francis Lieber first set out to codify the laws of war during the Civil War era. See, for example, Francis Lieber, "Guerrilla Parties Considered with Reference to the Laws and Usages of War," published in Richard Shelly Hartigan, *Lieber's Code and the Law of War* (Chicago: Precedent, 1983), 31–44.

49. See *Ex Parte Quirin,* 317 U.S. 1 (1942).

50. Formally known as the "Protocol Additional to the Geneva Conventions of 12 August 1949, and relating to the Protection of Victims of International Armed Conflicts," Protocol I significantly weakened the requirement that prisoners of war observe the laws of war in exchange for their privileged status. It also required that those denied the status of POW nonetheless "be given protections equivalent in all respects to those accorded to prisoners of war by the Third Convention and by this Protocol." See generally Article 44.

51. Marco Sassòli, "The Status of Persons Held in Guantánamo under International Humanitarian Law," *Journal of International Criminal Justice,* Vol. 2 (2004): 96–106.

52. Margulies, *Guantánamo and the Abuse of Presidential Power,* 79.

53. See U.S. Army Regulation 190–8, Chapter 1, Section 6e(10).

54. See President Reagan's "Message to the Senate Transmitting a Protocol to the 1949 Geneva Conventions," January 29, 1987.

55. See Third Geneva Convention: Relative to the Treatment of Prisoners of War, Article 5.

56. Bush made this declaration in a memorandum on February 7, 2002, entitled "Humane Treatment of al Qaeda and Taliban Detainees." A copy is published in *The Tortune Papers,* 134–35.

57. See Third Geneva Convention, Article 4. The Taliban's status under Article 4 is a bit hazy. Depending on one's approach, its fighters could be seen either as "Members of the armed forces

of a Party to the conflict" or as "Members of other militias and members of other volunteer corps . . . belonging to a Party to the conflict." If the Taliban is viewed as a militia, its obligation to follow the four criteria as a condition for POW treatment is explicit in the convention. If it is seen as the armed forces of Afghanistan—and only a few countries had ever recognized it as such—the case for treating its soldiers as privileged belligerents becomes a great deal stronger.

58. For a general history of the use of military tribunals in the United States see Louis Fisher, *Military Tribunals and Presidential Power: American Revolution to the War on Terrorism* (Lawrence: University Press of Kansas, 2005).

59. In writing for the majority in *Ex Parte Quirin,* Chief Justice Harlan Fiske Stone wrote: "By the Articles of War . . . Congress has provided rules for the government of the Army. It has provided for the trial and punishment, by courts . . . martial, of violations of the Articles by members of the armed forces and by specified classes of persons. . . . But the Articles also recognize the 'military commission' appointed by military command as an appropriate tribunal for the trial and punishment of offenses against the law of war not ordinarily tried by court martial. . . . Article 15 declares that 'the provisions of these articles conferring jurisdiction upon courts martial shall not be construed as depriving military commissions . . . or other military tribunals of concurrent jurisdiction in respect of offenders or offenses that by statute or by law of war may be triable by such military commissions . . . or other military tribunals.'" The Court majority in *Hamdan* acknowledged that Article 21 of the Uniform Code of Military Justice contains language "which is substantially identical to the old Article 15 and was preserved by Congress after World War II." See 126 S. Ct. 2749, 2774 (2006).

60. See 18 U.S.C. §2511(2)(f).

Chapter 2: The Administration's Response

1. Representative Barbara Lee (D-CA) voted against the Authorization for Use of Military Force in the House of Representatives. Ten representatives and two senators did not vote. All other members of both bodies, 420 representatives and 98 senators, supported the bill. For the House vote, see *Congressional Record,* 107th Cong., 1st sess., 2001, H5683. For the Senate vote, see *Congressional Record,* 107th Cong., 1st sess., 2001, S9421.

2. Public Law 107-40.

3. President Bush used these phrases during a telephone conversation with Mayor Rudolph Giuliani and Governor George Pataki on September 13, 2001. The transcript is available at http://www.whitehouse.gov/news/releases/2001/09/20010913-4.html.

4. Donald H. Rumsfeld, "A New Kind of War," *New York Times,* September 27, 2001, A21.

5. The transcript of Bush's news conference, given with British Prime Minister Gordon Brown on July 30, 2007, at Camp David can be found at http://www.whitehouse.gov/news/releases/2007/07/20070730.html.

6. President Bush called the detainees "bad people" at a press conference with British Prime Minister Tony Blair on July 17, 2003. White House spokesman Ari Fleischer called the detainees among the "worst of the worst" in a press briefing on January 23, 2002. On January 27, 2002,

Defense Secretary Donald H. Rumsfeld called them "among the most dangerous, best trained, vicious killers on the face of the earth" during a press briefing en route from Andrews AFB, Maryland, to Guantánamo Bay. The transcripts are available, respectively, at http://www .whitehouse.gov/news/releases/2003/07/20030717-9.html, http://www.whitehouse.gov/news/ releases/2002/01/20020123-18.html, and http://www.defenselink.mil/transcripts/transcript.aspx ?transcriptid=2320.

7. Bush news conference, July 30, 2007.

8. John Yoo, *War by Other Means: An Insider's Account of the War on Terror* (New York: Atlantic Monthly Press, 2006), 148.

9. See, for example, John Yoo, "The Continuation of Politics by Other Means: The Original Understanding of War Powers," *California Law Review* 84 (1996): 167–305; "Kosovo, War Powers, and the Multilateral Future," *University of Pennsylvania Law Review* 148 (2000): 1673–731; "Politics as Law?: The Anti-Ballistic Missile Treaty, the Separation of Powers, and Treaty Interpretation" (book review), *California Law Review* 89 (2001): 851–915.

10. See Jack L. Goldsmith, *The Terror Presidency: Law and Judgment Inside the Bush Administration* (New York: W. W. Norton and Company, 2007), 85. For an account of their efforts, see Jane Mayer, "The Hidden Power," *New Yorker,* July 3, 2006, 44.

11. See *Walker v. Cheney,* 230 F. Supp. 2d 51 (D.D.C. 2002).

12. Goldsmith, *The Terror Presidency,* 126.

13. Ibid., 124.

14. See Brief for Respondents in *Hamdan v. Rumsfeld* (No. 05-184).

15. See Brief Amicus Curiae of the American Civil Liberties Union in Support of Petitioner in *Hamdan v. Rumsfeld* (No. 05-184).

16. See Brief of Amici Curiae Human Rights First, Physicians for Human Rights, Center for Victims of Torture, Advocates for Survivors of Torture and Trauma, Boston Center for Refugee Health and Human Right, Center for Justice & Accountability, Doctors of the World-USA, Global Lawyers and Physicians, Heartland Alliance for Human Needs & Human Rights, Program for Survivors of Torture and Severe Trauma, Rocky Mountain Survivors Center, Torture Abolition and Survivors Support Coalition International in *Hamdan v. Rumsfeld* (05-184).

17. Senator Jay Rockefeller, chairman of the Senate Select Committee on Intelligence, released a statement on August 1, 2007, regarding the need for an interim legislative fix to FISA. The press release stated that the "Administration has offered a proposal that would . . . permanently grant the Attorney General excessive surveillance powers by giving him sole authority to direct surveillance while completely removing the FISA Court from the process. That is simply unacceptable." Yet the Democratic alternative, H.R. 3356, failed passage in the House of Representatives and its Senate counterpart, S. 2011, failed to pass as well. After this failure, Democrats did not block passage of S. 1927 as an interim measure, which President Bush signed as the Protect America Act of 2007 on August 5, 2007. It became Public Law 110-55.

18. Neal K. Katyal and Laurence H. Tribe, "Waging War, Deciding Guilt: Trying the Military Tribunals," *Yale Law Journal,* Vol. 111 (2002): 1259–1310. See especially 1259–60, 1265–68.

19. Goldsmith, *The Terror Presidency*, 123–24.

20. The conference "Institutionalizing the War on Terror through Congressional Legislation" was held on April 10, 2006, and was sponsored by the American University Washington College of Law and the Hoover Institution. Other panel members included Bradford Berenson, Amanda Frost, Jamin Raskin, and David Rivkin; the discussion was moderated by Daniel Marcus. The webcast of the panel's discussion is available at http://147.9.135.143/mediasite/viewer/?peid =bbc4bdf6-0903-49af-8a30-a6fc7da0253a.

21. Benjamin Wittes, "Aldrich Ames' Legal Legacy: Surveillance Court Gets New Powers," *Legal Times,* November 7, 1994.

22. Ibid.

23. Editorial, "Black Bag Jobs," *Washington Post,* July 20, 1994, A18.

24. Wittes, "Aldrich Ames' Legal Legacy."

25. See, for example, Robert H. Bork, *Coercing Virtue: The Worldwide Rule of Judges* (Washington, D.C.: The AEI Press, 2003).

26. Memorandum from Patrick F. Philbin and John C. Yoo to William J. Haynes II, "Possible Habeas Jurisdiction over Aliens Held in Guantánamo Bay, Cuba," December 28, 2001, published in *The Torture Papers, 29–37: The Road to Abu Ghraib,* Karen J. Greenberg and Joshua L. Dratel, eds. (Cambridge: Cambridge University Press, 2005).

27. Goldsmith, *The Terror Presidency*, 134.

28. This quotation is taken from memory of a conversation several years old. It may not be exact. Goldsmith does not recall the conversation but does not dispute my recollection of it either.

29. *Johnson v. Eisentrager,* 339 U.S. 763 (1950).

30. Oral argument for *Rumsfeld v. Padilla* (No. 03-1027) took place on April 28, 2004. The transcript is available at http://www.supremecourtus.gov/oral_arguments/argument_transcripts/03-1027.pdf.

31. The Combatant Status Review Tribunal process is outlined in a memorandum from the Deputy Secretary of Defense to the Secretaries of the Military Departments, Chairman of the Joint Chiefs of Staff, and Under Secretary of Defense for Policy. The memo is entitled "Implementation of Combatant Status Review Tribunal Procedures for Enemy Combatants Detained at U.S. Naval Base Guantánamo Bay, Cuba" and can be found at http://www.defenselink.mil/news/Aug2006/d20060809CSRTProcedures.pdf. For the results of the CSRT hearings, see then–Secretary of the Navy Gordon England's remarks on March 29, 2005, at a Defense Department Special Briefing on Combatant Status Review Tribunals. A transcript is available at http://www.defenselink.mil/transcripts/transcript.aspx?transcriptid=2504. During this briefing, England explained, "It should be emphasized that a CSRT determination that a detainee no longer meets the criteria for classification as an enemy combatant does not necessarily mean that the prior classification as [an enemy combatant] was wrong."

32. The Administrative Review Board process is outlined in a memorandum from the Deputy Secretary of Defense to the Secretaries of the Military Departments, Chairman of the Joint Chiefs of Staff, and Under Secretary of Defense for Policy. The memo, entitled "Revised Imple-

mentation of Administrative Review Procedures for Enemy Combatants Detained at U.S. Naval Base Guantánamo Bay, Cuba," is available at http://www.defenselink.mil/news/Aug2006/ d20060809ARBProceduresMemo.pdf.

33. Senior Defense officials discussed the completion of the second round of the ARBs during a press conference on March 6, 2007. The transcript of the press conference is available at http:// www.defenselink.mil/transcripts/transcript.aspx?transcriptid=3902.

34. See Article 5 of the Third Geneva Convention Relative to the Treatment of Prisoners of War.

35. According to the Sourcebook of Criminal Justice Statistics of the Bureau of Justice Statistics, the federal acquittal rate in 2005 was 0.6 percent. However, when considering both acquittals and cases dismissed, the rate increases to 10 percent.

36. See President Bush's signing statement on December 30, 2005, of the Department of Defense, Emergency Supplemental Appropriations to Address Hurricanes in the Gulf of Mexico, and Pandemic Influenza Act, 2006 (H.R. 2863). Bush indicated that the executive branch would interpret the treatment provisions of Title X "in a manner consistent with the constitutional authority of the President to supervise the unitary executive branch and as Commander in Chief and consistent with the constitutional limitations on the judicial power, which will assist in achieving the shared objective of the Congress and the President, evidenced in Title X, of protecting the American people from further terrorist attacks." Although the actual internal interpretation of the treatment provisions by the Office of Legal Counsel remains unavailable, the New York Times reported that "the Justice Department issued [a] secret opinion, one most lawmakers did not know existed." This "document declared that none of the C.I.A. interrogation methods violated that standard." The article contends that the opinion "delivered what the White House wanted: a statement that the standard imposed by Mr. McCain's Detainee Treatment Act would not force any change in the C.I.A.'s practices, according to officials familiar with the memo. Relying on a Supreme Court finding that only conduct that 'shocks the conscience' was unconstitutional, the opinion found that in some circumstances not even waterboarding was necessarily cruel, inhuman or degrading, if, for example, a suspect was believed to possess crucial intelligence about a planned terrorist attack, the officials familiar with the legal finding said." See Scott Shane, David Johnston, and James Risen, "Secret U.S. Endorsement of Severe Interrogations" New York Times, October 4, 2007, A1. The administration later confirmed publicly that it regarded waterboarding's legality as, in some circumstances, an open question under the McCain amendment.

37. See Part II of the majority opinion in Hamdan.

38. See Public Law 109-366, §7.

Chapter 3: The Real Guantánamo

1. The information in these paragraphs was either given in briefings by uniformed service members or observed first hand on a site visit to Guantánamo in April 2007.

2. The transcript of Fleischer's press briefing, given on January 23, 2002, is available at http://www .whitehouse.gov/news/releases/2002/01/20020123-18.html.

3. The transcript of Rumsfeld's press briefing, given January 27, 2002, en route from Andrews AFB, Maryland to Naval Station Guantánamo Bay, Cuba, is available at http://www.defenselink.mil/transcripts/transcript.aspx?transcriptid=2320.

4. Mark Denbeaux and Joshua Denbeaux, "Report on Guantánamo Detainees: A Profile of 517 Detainees Through Analysis of Department of Defense Data," February 8, 2006, is available at http://law.shu.edu/news/guantanamo_report_final_2_08_06.pdf.

5. Corine Hegland, "Empty Evidence," *National Journal,* February 3, 2006.

6. Editorial, "They Came for the Chicken Farmer," *New York Times,* March 8, 2006, A22.

7. Editorial, "The Real Agenda," *New York Times,* July 16, 2006, section 4, 11.

8. Mark Denbeaux and Joshua Denbeaux, "No-Hearing Hearings: An Analysis of the Government's Combatant Status Review Tribunals at Guantánamo," November 17, 2006, is available at http://law.shu.edu/news/final_no_hearing_hearings_report.pdf.

9. See, for example, Neil A. Lewis, "Freedom for Chinese Detainees Hinges on Finding a New Homeland," *New York Times,* November 8, 2004, A17. See also Carol D. Leonnig, "Panel Ignored Evidence on Detainee," *Washington Post,* March 27, 2005, A1; Carlotta Gall and Andy Worthington, "Time Runs Out for an Afghan Held by U.S.," *New York Times,* February 5, 2008, A1.

10. See, for example, Worthington, *The Guantánamo Files.*

11. Joseph Felter and Jarret Brachman, "CTC Report: An Assessment of 516 Combatant Status Review Tribunal (CSRT) Unclassified Summaries," July 25, 2007, is available at http://www.ctc.usma.edu/csrt/CTC-CSRT-Report-072407.pdf.

12. Denbeaux and Denbeaux, "No-Hearing Hearings."

13. For information on this program, see Josh White and Robin Wright, "After Guantánamo, 'Reintegration' for Saudis," *Washington Post,* December 10, 2007, A1.

14. The data reported in this chapter are fleshed out in greater detail in a more technical paper, Benjamin Wittes and Zaahira Wyne, "The Detainee Population of Guantánamo: An Empirical Examination," forthcoming 2008.

15. The allegations summaries list 345 detainees as associates of Al Qaeda, the Taliban, or other hostile groups. By contrast, they list 156 members and only 41 fighters.

16. It is unclear how many detainees were sold to U.S. forces for bounty. A number of detainees claim to have been "sold," and the military did offer bounties in some instances. See Nancy Gibbs with Viveca Novak, "Inside 'The Wire'," *Time,* November 30, 2003, 40; Michelle Faul, "Guantánamo Detainees Say Arabs, Muslims Sold for U.S. Bounties," Associated Press, May 31, 2005; Carol J. Williams, "Detainee Lawyers See Stacked Deck," *Los Angeles Times,* November 13, 2007, A14.

17. Compare, for example, CSRT hearing for Yusef Abbas, ISN #275, Set 20, 1623–30, to CSRT hearing for Akhdar Qasem Basit, ISN #276, Set 16, 1363–68. Both acknowledge traveling from China and receiving training at the Uighur training camp at Tora Bora on the AK-47 rifle with the intention of fighting the Chinese government. Both acknowledge fleeing when the United States began bombing the region. The CSRTs deemed the former an enemy combatant and the latter no longer an enemy combatant.

18. CSRT hearing for Salih Uyar, ISN #298, CSRT Set 29, 2015–21.

19. CSRT Summary of Evidence for Sadik Ahmad Turkistani, ISN #491, 414.

20. CSRT hearing for Karam Khamis Sayd Khamsan, ISN #586, CSRT Set 26, 1859–65.

21. CSRT hearing for Zakirjan Asam, ISN #672, CSRT Set 29, 2001–14.

22. CSRT hearing for Mustaq Ali Patel, ISN #649, CSRT Set 18, 1470–76.

23. CSRT hearing for Shed Abdur Rahman, ISN #581, CSRT Set 3, 272–94, Sets 22–23, 1722–54.

24. CSRT hearing for Mohammed Nasim, ISN #958, CSRT Set 51, 3572–81.

25. CSRT hearing for Janat Gul, ISN #953, CSRT Set 29, 2030–47.

26. CSRT hearing for Nasibullah Darwaish, ISN #1019, CSRT Set 43, 2837–43.

27. The military has not identified the list of detainees cleared for release or transfer under pre-CSRT procedures. I have attempted to reconstruct it, though my effort may be either somewhat incomplete or somewhat over inclusive.

28. CSRT hearing for Mohammed Hashim, ISN #850, CSRT Set 34, 2442–44.

29. CSRT hearing for Walid Muhammad Salih Bin 'Attash, ISN #10014. The CSRT hearings for the high-value detainees were released separately from those of the other detainees. Bin 'Attash's transcript is available at http://www.defenselink.mil/news/transcript_ISN10014.pdf.

30. CSRT hearing for Khalid Sheikh Muhammed, ISN #10024, available at http://www.defenselink.mil/news/transcript_ISN10024.pdf.

31. ARB Round II hearing for Abd Al Rahman Al Zahri, ISN #441, ARB II Transcripts, 2285–93.

32. See, for example, CSRT hearing for Muhsin Muhammad Musheen Moqbill, ISN #193, CSRT Set 47, 3210–17; CSRT hearing for Yasim Muhammed Basardah, ISN #252, CSRT Set 44, 2930–38; CSRT hearing for Khalil Rahman Hafez, ISN #301, CSRT Set 11, 1153–54.

33. CSRT hearing for Adnan Mohammed Ali, ISN #105, CSRT Set 10, 1126–32.

34. CSRT hearing for Salim Ahmed Salim Hamdan, ISN #149, CSRT Set 51, 3538–46.

35. CSRT hearing for Abdul Haq Wasiq, ISN #4, CSRT Set 16, 1375–86.

36. CSRT hearing for Mullah Norullah Noori, ISN #6, CSRT Set 42, 2730–33.

37. CSRT hearing for Abdul Rauf Aliza, ISN #108, CSRT Set 50, 3478–80; ARB I hearing, ARB I Set 3, 874–80.

38. CSRT hearing for Dawd Gul, ISN #530, CSRT Set 44, 3014–20.

39. CSRT hearing for Mohammed Sharif, ISN #532, CSRT Set 33, 2312–21; ARB I hearing, ARB I Set 7, 2055–68.

40. CSRT hearing for Fahed Nasser Mohamed, ISN #13, CSRT Set 50, 3462–66; ARB I hearing, ARB I Set 2, 624–29.

41. ARB I hearing for Mohammed Ali Abdullah Bwazir, ISN #440, ARB I Set 6, 20430–44.

42. CSRT hearing for Hafez Qari Mohamed Saad Iqbal Madni, ISN #743, CSRT Set 1, 46–58.

43. CSRT hearing for Zia Ul Shah, ISN #15, CSRT Set 42, 2752–68.

44. CSRT hearing for Mahrar Rafat Al Quwari, ISN #519, CSRT Set 31, 2145–52.

45. CSRT hearing for Mohammed Ahmad Said Al Edah, ISN #33, CSRT Set 28, 1970–78.

46. See, for example, CSRT hearing for Samir Naji Al Hasan Moqbel, ISN #43, CSRT Set 47, 3192–98.

47. See, for example, CSRT hearing for Ab Aljallil Allal, ISN #156, CSRT Set 8, 971–79.

48. See, for example, ARB I hearing for Muhammad Ben Moujan, ISN #160, ARB I Set 1, 483–89.

49. See, for example, CSRT hearing for Ridouane Khalid, ISN #173, CSRT Set 7, 792–804.

50. See, for example, CSRT hearing for Salih Uyar, ISN #298, CSRT Set 29, 2015–21.

51. CSRT hearing for Riduan Bin Isomuddin, ISN #10019, available at http://www.defenselink
.mil/news/transcript_ISN10019.pdf; CSRT hearing for Majid Khan, ISN #10020, available at
http://www.defenselink.mil/news/transcript_ISN10020.pdf.

52. CSRT hearing for Bessam Muhammed Saleh Al Dubaikey, ISN #340, CSRT Set 29, 2022–29A.

53. CSRT hearing for Omar Hamzayavich Abdulayev, ISN #257, CSRT Set 20, 1606–13.

54. See *In Re Guantánamo Detainee Cases,* 355 F. Supp. 2d 443 (D.D.C. 2005).

55. CSRT hearing for Murat Kurnaz, ISN #61, CSRT Set 9, 1055–64.

56. Carol D. Leonnig, "Panel Ignored Evidence on Detainee." See also Carol D. Leonnig, "Evidence of Innocence Rejected at Guantánamo," *Washington Post,* December 5, 2007, A1.

57. See "Administrative Review Board Assessment and Recommendation ICO ISN 061 (Turkey/
Germany)," ARB II Decision Memos, 39–46. See also Mark Landler, "Guantánamo Prisoner
Goes Home," *New York Times,* August 26, 2006, A2.

58. CSRT Summary of Evidence for Abdul Razzak, ISN #942, 670.

59. CSRT hearing for Abdul Razzak, ISN #942, CSRT Set 18, 1517–21. See also ARB Round I hearing for Abdul Razzak, ARB I Transcripts, Set 9, 21288–301.

60. See, for example, CSRT haring for Nasrullah, ISN #886, CSRT Set 33, 2336–57; CSRT hearing
for Ismat Ullah, ISN #888, CSRT Set 31, 2234–50.

61. Carlotta Gall and Andy Worthington, "Time Runs Out for an Afghan Held by U.S.," *New York
Times,* February 5, 2008, A1.

62. See CSRT records for Bensayah Belkacem, ISN #10001, Publicly Filed CSRT Records, 4851–90;
Sabir Mahfouz Lahmar, ISN #10002, Publicly Filed CSRT Records, 4891–946; Mohammad
Nechle, ISN #10003, Publicly Filed CSRT Records, 4947–5000; Mustafa Ait Idr, ISN #10004,
Publicly filed CSRT Records, 5001–53; Lakhdar Boumediene, ISN #10005, Publicly Filed
CSRT Records, 5054–68; and Boudella Al Hajj, ISN #10006, Publicly Filed CSRT Records,
5069–134.

63. "Unclassified Summary of Evidence for Administrative Review Board in the Case of Adel Hussein, Hassan," ISN #940, ARB Round I Factors, 749–51.

64. ARB I hearing for Hassan Adel Hussein, ISN #940, ARB I Set 9, 21260–76.

65. CSRT record for Hassan Adel Hussein, ISN #940, Publicly Filed CSRT Records, 4287–315. See
also "Administrative Review Board Assessment and Recommendation ICO ISN 940 (Sudan),"
ARB I Decision Memos, 625–31.

66. See CSRT record for Hassan Anvar, ISN #250, Publicly Filed CSRT Records, 1734–67. Anvar is
a Uighur, which probably explains the CSRT's difficulty with his case. See also CSRT record for
Abdullah Mohammad Khan, ISN #556, Publicly Filed CSRT Records, 2835–68. Khan's case is
particularly interesting. It was sent back twice after two successive CSRTs determined him to be
no longer an enemy combatant. A third determined him to be an enemy combatant. The cir-

cumstances of capture in Khan's case, at least as described in his subsequent ARB proceeding, seem to back this designation: He was allegedly captured with explosives residue on his hands. See "Unclassified Summary of Evidence for Administrative Review Board in the Case of Khan, Abdullah Mohammad," ARB I Factors, 929–31. See also CSRT record for Abdullah Hamid Abdalsalam Alghazawy, ISN #654, Publicly Filed CSRT Records, 3244–90. The record states: "On 24 November 2004, a Tribunal unanimously determined that the detainee was not properly designated as an enemy combatant. Following that Tribunal, CSRT intelligence personnel conducted another search of the Government Information for evidence relevant to ISN #654's status. They collected additional evidence which eventually became exhibits R-17 through R-20. . . . [T]he additional evidence, along with the original evidence and original Tribunal Decision Report, was presented to Tribunal panel #32 to reconsider the detainee's status. Following their consideration of the new information, along with the original information, the second Tribunal unanimously determined that the detainee was properly classified as an enemy combatant."

67. See, for example, "Unclassified Summary of Evidence for Administrative Review Board in the Case of Al Mudhaffan, Abdel Qadir Hussein," ISN #40, ARB I Factors, 48–50.

68. See, for example, "Unclassified Summary of Evidence for Administrative Review Board in the Case of Al Shamyri, Mustafa Abdul/Qawi Abdul Aziz," ISN #434, ARB I Factors, 1075–77.

69. See, for example, "Unclassified Summary of Evidence for Administrative Review Board in the Case of Azani, Saad Masir Mukbl Al," ISN #575, ARB I Factors, 1048–49.

70. See Neil A. Lewis, "Freed From Guantánamo but Stranded Far From Home," *New York Times,* August 15, 2006, A15.

71. Compare, for example, Faruq Ali Ahmed, ISN #32, the young Yemeni man discussed in the Introduction with British national Feroz Ali Abbasi, ISN #24. The former denied all suggestions of belligerency, of which evidence seemed relatively weak and associational, yet both rounds of ARB review have insisted on the necessity of continuing to hold him. By contrast, Abbasi acknowledged having gone to Afghanistan committed to jihad and participating in meetings with top Al Qaeda figures; he was even slated for trial by military commission, yet he was sent home as part of a blanket release of British detainees early in 2005. I describe this case in more detail in Chapter 6.

72. See Denbeaux and Denbeaux, "No-Hearing Hearings."

73. The memorandum "Implementation of Combatant Status Review Tribunal Procedures for Enemy Combatants detained at Guantánamo Bay Naval Base, Cuba," issued on July 29, 2004, is available at http://www.defenselink.mil/news/Jul2004/d20040730comb.pdf.

74. Even some of those who participated in the CSRT process had anxieties on this front. Lieutenant Colonel Stephen Abraham, who served on CSRT panels, complained in an affidavit filed in the Supreme Court's Guantánamo litigation both of serious inadequacies in tribunal access to intelligence information and of interference by the chain of command in CSRT findings. See "Declaration of Stephen Abraham," June 15, 2007, filed in *Khaled A.F. Al Odah et al. vs. United States,* No. 06–1196.

75. Stimson's estimate was given in a conversation on January 25, 2007.

76. For a startling example, see the letter from a coalition of human rights and civil liberties groups to Senator Carl Levin (D-MI.), sent April 23, 2007. Levin had been contemplating legislation to beef up the CSRTs and give detainees more procedural protections within the CSRT process. The groups objected, arguing that "if Congress tinkers with the CSRT process in a way that gives it a greater veneer of due process respectability, it will be seen by some as an adequate substitute for habeas corpus, and the critical effort to restore habeas rights to detainees will flounder." The letter can be found at http://www.constitutionproject.org/pdf/Letter_to_Senator_Levin_4-23-07.pdf.

Chapter 4: The Necessity and Impossibility of Judicial Review

1. Editorial, "Reaffirming Rule of Law," *New York Times,* June 29, 2004, A26.

2. Editorial, "A Victory for the Rule of Law," *New York Times,* June 30, 2006, A22.

3. David B. Rivkin, Jr., and Lee A. Casey, "Bush's Good Day in Court," *Washington Post,* August 4, 2004, A19.

4. Ronald Dworkin, "What the Court Really Said," *New York Review of Books,* August 12, 2004.

5. On behalf of the plurality in *Hamdi,* Justice Sandra Day O'Connor wrote: "We conclude that detention of individuals falling into the limited category we are considering, for the duration of the particular conflict in which they were captured, is so fundamental and accepted an incident to war as to be an exercise of the 'necessary and appropriate force' Congress has authorized the President to use."

6. See Public Law 109-366.

7. Article I, Sec. 9 of the Constitution contains the following language: "The Privilege of the Writ of Habeas Corpus shall not be suspended, unless when in Cases of Rebellion or Invasion the public Safety may require it."

8. The transcript of the oral argument in *Boumediene v. Bush,* No. 06-1195, can be found at http://www.supremecourtus.gov/oral_arguments/argument_transcripts/06-1195.pdf.

9. For efforts by detainee lawyers to get the Court to consider the substantive questions now, see Brief for the Boumediene Petitioners, *Boumediene v. Bush,* No. 06-1195, August 2007. The brief spends a great deal of energy arguing not only that "the [Constitution's] Suspension Clause prevents Congress from abrogating Petitioners' access to the Great Writ," as it did in the MCA, but also that the Court should adopt a narrow *substantive* definition of a detainable enemy combatant. "[T]he government has failed to show any lawful basis for Petitioners' imprisonment," the lawyers write, and after nearly six years of detention, "Petitioners are therefore entitled to immediate habeas relief."

10. *Ex Parte Merryman,* 17 F. Cas. 144 (Cir. Ct. Dist. Md., 1861).

11. See *Journal of the House of Representatives,* 37th Cong., 1st sess., July 5, 1861, 23–35.

12. *Dred Scott v. Sandford,* 60 U.S. 393 (1856).

13. *Korematsu v. United States,* 323 U.S. 214 (1944).

14. For a good general discussion of the subject of judicial tolerance and intolerance of executive

claims of necessity during wartime, see William H. Rehnquist, *All the Laws but One: Civil Liberties in Wartime* (New York: Alfred A. Knopf, 1998).

15. See Brief of Amici Curiae Specialists in Israeli Military Law and Constitutional Law in Support of Petitioners, *Boumediene v. Bush,* 06-1195, August 2007.

16. As the U.S. Court of Appeals for the Fourth Circuit summarized the government's position in an early appeal in the *Hamdi* litigation, for example, "In its brief before this court, the government asserts that 'given the constitutionally limited role of the courts in reviewing military decisions, courts may not second-guess the military's determination that an individual is an enemy combatant and should be detained as such.' The government thus submits that we may not review at all its designation of an American citizen as an enemy combatant—that its determinations on this score are the first and final word." See *Hamdi v. Rumsfeld,* 296 F.3d 278 (4th Cir., 2002).

17. See Title X of Public Law 109-148, Section 1005(e).

18. That the D.C. Circuit judges aimed at conducting a serious review became clear quickly once the first DTA review cases, *Bismullah v. Gates,* Nos. 06-1197 and 06-1397, got under way. The panel, after hearing oral arguments on the preliminary question of how much evidence concerning each detainee the government should have to disclose, rejected government suggestions that it limit its review to the record of the CSRT itself. See 2007 U.S. App. LEXIS 17255 (D.C. Cir., July 20, 2007). Rather, the panel ordered the government to produce evidence far beyond the actual record to "all the information a [CSRT] *is authorized to obtain and consider* [emphasis added], . . . defined by the Secretary of the Navy as 'such reasonably available information in the possession of the U.S. Government bearing on the issue of whether the detainee meets the criteria to be designated as an enemy combatant.'" The court required that it receive all evidence concerning each case and adopted a presumption that detainee counsel receive access to classified material, too. It permitted the government to withhold from counsel, though not from the court, access to certain highly sensitive information. After the panel declined to reconsider its decision in October 2007, the full court split five to five over whether to rehear the matter, thereby upholding the panel's ruling. See *Bismullah v. Gates,* 2008 U.S. App. LEXIS 2278 (D.C. Cir., 2008). The government, in response, petitioned the Supreme Court for review on February 14, 2008.

19. *Boumediene v. Bush* oral argument transcript.

20. In its decision in *Boumediene v. Bush,* 476 F.3d 981 (D.C. Cir., 2007), for example, the court panel wrote that "Precedent in this court and the Supreme Court holds that the Constitution does not confer rights on aliens without property or presence within the United States"—a ruling that could conceivably survive the decision's reversal by the Supreme Court on its main jurisdictional point. A more extensive discussion appears in *Al Odah v. United States,* 321 F.3d 1134 (D.C. Cir., 2003), an earlier jurisdictional decision that the Supreme Court reversed in *Rasul;* again, the reversal did not disturb the lower court's discussion of extraterritorial application of constitutional rights.

Chapter 5: The Case for Congress

1. Congressional and presidential approval ratings reflect the Real Clear Politics average of polls as of March 24, 2008.

2. I was one of the first of this group. During my tenure on the *Washington Post* editorial page, the *Post* argued repeatedly for more extensive congressional involvement in designing the law of counterterrorism. For an early example, see Editorial, "The Stakes for Liberty," *Washington Post*, December 31, 2002, A16: "With Congress so far unwilling to get involved in defining reasoned boundaries, the courts have been the only realistic check on the Bush administration's unilateral assertions of power. This is a far-too-passive means of making law in such a fateful area. In the American system, the national legislature is primarily responsible for determining what the law should be. If, through inaction, it effectively cedes that power to the president, the new rules will reflect the presidency's interests at the expense of all others. That's a dangerous prospect for civil liberties and, in the long run, for effective counterterrorism as well." Other advocates of a more extensive congressional role included American University law professor Kenneth Anderson, who organized a conference on the subject in 2006 and wrote an essay in the *New York Times Magazine* advocating an enhanced legislative role. See Kenneth Anderson, "It's Congress's War, Too," *New York Times Magazine*, September 3, 2006, 20.

3. Lord Byron, *Don Juan*, Canto I, stanza I.

4. John Yoo, *War by Other Means: An Insider's Account of the War on Terror* (New York: Atlantic Monthly Press, 2006), 233.

5. Ibid., 239.

6. John Hart Ely, *War and Responsibility: Constitutional Lessons of Vietnam and Its Aftermath* (Princeton: Princeton University Press, 1995), ix.

7. Congress set up the 9/11 Commission in Title VI of Public Law No. 107-306. Its own investigation, the "Joint Inquiry into Intelligence Community Activities Before and After the Terrorist Attacks of September 11, 2001," was published as S. Rept. No. 107-351 and H. Rept. No. 107-792, 107th Cong., 2d sess., December 2002.

8. Public Law 107-56.

9. Ibid., Section 412.

10. See Section 202 of administration's original proposal, advanced in the wake of the attacks and dubbed the Anti-Terrorism Act of 2001. A copy of the draft is available at http://www.epic.org/privacy/terrorism/ata2001_text.pdf.

11. Public Law 107-56, Section 203. See generally Title II.

12. Ibid., Section 206.

13. Ibid., Section 218.

14. Ibid., Section 213.

15. Ibid., Section 215.

16. Ibid., Section 216.

17. *9/11 Commission Report,* 181–82, 266–72.

18. Public Law 108-458, Section 6001.

19. The Department of Homeland Security was created by the Homeland Security Act (HSA) of 2002, Public Law 107-296. The director of national intelligence was the creation of the Intelligence Reform and Terrorism Prevention Act of 2004, Public Law 108-458.

20. Criticism of the Department of Homeland Security has been widespread, more the norm than the exception, particularly since Hurricane Katrina. The intelligence reform legislation, by contrast, has generally won wide acclaim. Prominent commentators, however, have vociferously dissented. Richard Posner, for example, wrote a trenchant book criticizing the 9/11 Commission report and the implementation of its recommendations in the Intelligence Reform Act. "In responding, prematurely and hastily, to the commission's proposal," he writes, "Congress did not plug the gaps in the commission's analysis or rectify the deficiencies in the commission's organizational recommendations. The Intelligence Reform Act is a backward step in the reform of the U.S. intelligence system." See Richard Posner, *Preventing Surprise Attacks: Intelligence Reform in the Wake of 9/11* (Lanham: Rowman & Littlefield, 2005), 200.

21. Public Law 109-148, Section 1002(a).

22. Ibid., Section 1003(a).

23. Ibid., Section 1003(d).

24. See Army Field Manual 2-22.3, "Human Intelligence Collector Operations," September 6, 2006.

25. Vice President Cheney outlined this standard explicitly in an interview with ABC News on December 18, 2005. "There's a definition that's based on prior Supreme Court decisions and prior arguments. And it has to do with . . . three specific amendments to the Constitution. And the rule is whether or not it shocks the conscience. If it's something that shocks the conscience, the court has decreed that crosses over the line.

"Now, you can get into a debate about what shocks the conscience and what is cruel and inhuman. And to some extent, I suppose that's in the eye of the beholder. But I believe and we think it's important to remember that we are in a war against a group of individuals, a terrorist organization, that did, in fact, slaughter 3,000 innocent Americans on 9/11, that it's important for us to be able to have effective interrogation of these people when we capture them. And the debate is over the extent to which we're going to have legislation that restricts or limits that capability.

"Now, I say we've reached a compromise. The President signed on with the McCain amendment. We never had any problems with the McCain amendment. We had problems with trying to extend it as far as he did, but ultimately, as I say, a compromise was arrived at. And I support the compromise." A transcript can be found at http://www.whitehouse.gov/news/releases/2005/12/20051218-4.html.

26. Mukasey confirmed in testimony before the Senate Judiciary Committee on January 30, 2008 "that waterboarding is not among the techniques currently authorized for use in the CIA program." Given that, he went on, "I don't think it would be appropriate for me to pass definitive judgment on the technique's legality"—a matter he described as "not an easy question. There are some circumstances where current law would appear clearly to prohibit waterboarding's use. But other circumstances would present a far closer question."

27. A transcript of the president's remarks, delivered September 6, 2006, can be found at http://www.whitehouse.gov/news/releases/2006/09/20060906-3.html.

28. Public Law 109-148, Section 1005.

29. Ibid.

30. Public Law 109-366, Section 5.

31. Ibid., Section 6.

32. Ibid., Section 8.

33. Ibid., Section 7.

34. Neal K. Katyal and Laurence H. Tribe, "Waging War, Deciding Guilt: Trying the Constitutionality of the Military Tribunals," *Yale Law Journal*, Vol. 111 (2002): 1259–1310.

35. Editorial, "The Fear of Fear Itself," *New York Times*, August 7, 2007, A18.

36. Editorial, "Warrantless Surrender: Congress Is Stampeded into Another Compromise of Americans' Rights," *Washington Post*, August 6, 2007, A16.

37. Public Law 110-55, Section 2.

38. As of late February 2008, Congress and President Bush were at something of a standoff over renewal of the Protect America Act—albeit a standoff whose resolution seemed very probable. The Senate and the House of Representatives had passed competing versions of H.R. 3773, and the House had allowed the temporary law to sunset. The major sticking point between Bush and congressional Democrats, however, was not the substance of the new authority but whether to grant telecommunications carriers retroactive immunity for their earlier cooperation with the National Security Agency's warrantless wiretapping program. It seems likely that Congress will ultimately bless some version of the new authority.

39. Posner made this remark at a meeting of the Hoover Institution Task Force on National Security and the Law in September 2007.

40. The quoted language appears as Article 3 in all four of the 1949 Geneva Conventions.

41. Public Law 109-366, Section 6.

42. See, for example, Chapter 11 of the *9/11 Commission Report*, which accuses the government in the years prior to the attacks of "four kinds of failures: in imagination, policy, capabilities, and management."

Chapter 6: The Twin Problems of Detention and Trial

1. Human Rights Watch expressed these concerns in a letter to then National Security Advisor Condoleezza Rice on January 28, 2002, a copy of which can be found at http://hrw.org/press/2002/01/us012802-ltr.htm. See also Jamie Fellner, "U.S. Must Take the High Road with Prisoners of War," *Newsday*, January 16, 2002, A30.

2. A copy of the letter, date June 22, 2007, can be found at http://hrw.org/english/docs/2007/06/22/usdom16239.htm.

3. See Constitution Project letter to Senator Carl Levin, April 23, 2007.

4. Jerry Markon, "Lindh Asks Bush to Reduce Sentence; Attorneys for U.S. Taliban Fighter Say Fellow Soldier Wasn't Charged," *Washington Post*, September 29, 2004, A2.

5. For an account of the case of the Lackawanna Six, see Dina Temple-Raston, *The Jihad Next Door: The Lackawanna Six and Rough Justice in the Age of Terror* (New York: Public Affairs, 2007).

6. The full record of the first military commission completed post-September 11, *United States of America v. David Hicks*, is available at http://www.defenselink.mil/news/Mar2007/US%20v%20David%20Hicks%20ROT%20(Redacted).pdf.

7. Al-Qahtani is ISN #63. His case and interrogation are discussed in greater detail in Chapter 7. The charges filed against him and his five codefendants can be found at http://www.defenselink.mil/news/Feb2008/d20080211chargesheet.pdf.

8. See *United States v. Moussaoui*, 01-455-A (E.D. Va.).

9. The government, in a biographical sketch of Binalshibh at the time of his transfer to Guantánamo, alleged that he "was slated to be one of the 11 September hijacker pilots" but was "unable to obtain a US visa, despite four attempts." In 2000, he "tried to convince a US citizen in San Diego via e-mail to marry him to gain entry into the United States, but [Mohamed] Atta convinced him to abandon the idea." The biographical sketch of Binalshibh, along with those of the other high-value detainees, is available at http://www.odni.gov/announcements/content/DetaineeBiographies.pdf.

10. For information on Padilla's confinement in military custody, see *Padilla v. Hanft*, 423 F.3d 386 (4th Cir., 2005). See also *Padilla v. Hanft*, 432 F.3d 582 (4th Cir., 2005). For information on his criminal prosecution see *United States v. Hassoun*, 04-60001-CR (S.D. Fla.).

11. The former chief prosecutor for the military commissions, in a law review article defending Guantánamo Bay, says seventy-five detainees will eventually be charged. See Morris D. Davis, "In Defense of Guantánamo Bay," *Yale Law Journal Pocket Part*, Vol. 117 (2007): 21. See also William Glaberson, "Witness Names to Be Withheld from Detainees," *New York Times*, December 1, 2007, A1; Josh White, "Evidence from Waterboarding Could Be Used in Military Trials," *Washington Post*, December 12, 2007, A4.

12. CSRT hearing for Bashir Nasir Ali Al Marwalah, ISN #837, CSRT Set 4, 384–89.

13. This sort of criminal case could be the wave of the future. In a fascinating essay, law professors Robert Chesney and Jack Goldsmith argue that since September 11, the systems of criminal trial and military detention have actually converged a great deal. The military's detention apparatus has evolved towards greater procedural protectiveness and the criminal justice system has "quietly established the capacity for convicting terrorists based on something very close to associational status." See Robert Chesney and Jack Goldsmith, "Terrorism and the Convergence of Criminal and Military Detention Models" *Stanford Law Review*, Vol. 60 (forthcoming 2008).

14. Al Shirbi CSRT transcript.

15. CSRT Written Submission of Feroz Ali Abbasi, ISN #24, CSRT Set 5, 465–672.

16. Solomon Moore, "U.S. Troops Kill 11 Militiamen Linked to Iraqi Cleric," *New York Times*, December 28, 2007, A8.

17. CSRT Summary of Evidence for Ali Hamza Ahmed Suleiman Al Bahlul, ISN #39, CSRT Summaries, 44–45. Al Bahlul also faces charges before a military commission.

18. See CSRT Procedures Memorandum.

19. The idea of a national security court has been advanced by a politically diverse array of legal scholars and commentators. See, for example, Jack L. Goldsmith and Neal Katyal, "The Terrorists' Court," *New York Times,* July 11, 2007, A19. Katyal, a former Justice Department official in the Clinton administration, represented Salim Hamdan in his case before the Supreme Court. See also Andrew McCarthy and Alykhan Velshi, "We Need a National Security Court," July 15, 2007, available at http://www.defenddemocracy.org/research_topics/research_topics_show.htm ?doc_id=510024.

20. See Section 1023 of S. 1547, The National Defense Authorization Act for Fiscal Year 2008.

21. Estimates of the number of released detainees who have returned to the battle vary. Authorities have named seven but suggested that the actual number may be around thirty or even more. One former detainee, Abdullah Mehsud, became a major Taliban leader in Pakistan after his release. He was killed in 2007. See Griff Witte, "Taliban Leader Once Held by U.S. Dies in Pakistan Raid," *Washington Post,* July 25, 2007, A1.

22. In his opinion in *Hamdan,* Justice John Paul Stevens wrote that the Uniform Code of Military Justice (UCMJ) "conditions the President's use of military commissions on compliance not only with the American common law of war, but also with the rest of the UCMJ itself, insofar as applicable, and with the 'rules and precepts of the law of nations,' . . . including . . . the four Geneva Conventions signed in 1949. . . . The procedures that the Government has decreed will govern Hamdan's trial by commission violate these laws." The clear implication here is that a commission could be constituted lawfully. Justice Breyer's concurrence, joined by three other justices, makes this point even more clearly. The Court's striking down of the commissions, he wrote, "ultimately rests upon a single ground: Congress has not issued the Executive a 'blank check.' . . . Indeed, Congress has denied the President the legislative authority to create military commissions of the kind at issue here. *Nothing prevents the President from returning to Congress to seek the authority he believes necessary.*" [Emphasis added.]

23. For a brief overview of the differences, see David B. Rivkin, Jr., and Lee A. Casey, "Family Feud: The Law in War and Peace," *National Interest,* May 1, 2007.

24. McCarthy and Velshi, "We Need a National Security Court," 48.

25. *United States v. Abdel Rahman et al.,* 189 F.3d 88 (2d Cir., 1999).

26. Michael B. Mukasey, "Jose Padilla Makes Bad Law: Terror trials hurt the nation even when they lead to convictions," *Wall Street Journal,* August 22, 2007, A15.

27. U.S. District Judge Leonie Brinkema strongly defended the federal judiciary as the proper forum for terrorism trials in a keynote speech at a conference entitled "Terrorists and Detainees: Do We Need a New National Security Court?" The conference was sponsored by American University Washington College of Law and the Brookings Institution on February 1, 2008. An audio recording of Judge Brinkema's remarks are available at http://www.wcl.american.edu/podcast/audio/20080201_WCL_TAD.mp3.

28. The full docket in the Moussaoui case is available at http://notablecases.vaed.uscourts.gov/1:01 -cr-00455/DocketSheet.html.

29. For a procedural history of the case, see *Ali Saleh Kahlah Al-Marri v. Wright*, 487 F.3d 160 (4th Cir., 2007).

30. See, for example, the American Bar Association's Model Rules of Professional Conduct, specifically Rule 4.2 on "Communication with Person Represented by Counsel": "In representing a client, a lawyer shall not communicate about the subject of the representation with a person the lawyer knows to be represented by another lawyer in the matter, unless the lawyer has the consent of the other lawyer or is authorized to do so by law or a court order."

31. Section 3 of the MCA lays out rules and standards for the commissions in the form of a series of additions to the UCMJ. Added as Chapter 47A of Title 10 of the United States Code, these included Sections 948, 949, and 950. Section 949a(b)(1)(A) gives the accused the right "to present evidence in his defense, to cross-examine the witnesses who testify against him, *and to examine and respond to evidence admitted against him on the issue of guilt or innocence and for sentencing*, as provided for by this chapter." [Emphasis added.] That right is somewhat qualified by the Byzantine procedures for protecting classified information outlined in 10 U.S.C. §949d(f), but these rules do not permit the admission of evidence to which the defendant cannot respond.

32. The general admissibility of evidence probative to a reasonable person appears in 10 U.S.C. §949a(b)(2)(A). The specific admissibility of hearsay appears in 10 U.S.C., §949a(b)(2)(E).

33. See Federal Rule of Evidence 802, which creates a baseline, with exceptions, under which hearsay is generally *not* admissible. This rule has a direct parallel in the Military Rules of Evidence.

34. Section 948r(b) of Title 10 of the United States Code requires that "a statement obtained by use of torture shall not be admissible in a military commission under this chapter, except against a person accused of torture as evidence that the statement was made." This stricture, however, is qualified by 10 U.S.C. §948r(c), which treats statements obtained by lesser forms of coercion in a more nuanced fashion. "A statement obtained before December 30, 2005 (the date of the enactment of the Defense Treatment Act of 2005) in which the degree of coercion is disputed may be admitted only if the military judge finds that . . . the totality of the circumstances renders the statement reliable and possessing sufficient probative value; [and] . . . the interests of justice would best be served by admission of the statement into evidence." By contrast, "a statement obtained on or after December 30, 2005 (the date of the enactment of the Defense Treatment Act of 2005) in which the degree of coercion is disputed may be admitted only if the military judge finds that . . . the totality of the circumstances renders the statement reliable and possessing sufficient probative value; . . . the interests of justice would best be served by admission of the statement into evidence; and . . . the interrogation methods used to obtain the statement do not amount to cruel, inhuman, or degrading treatment prohibited by section 1003 of the Detainee Treatment Act of 2005."

35. McCarthy and Velshi, "We Need a National Security Court," 41.

36. 10 U.S.C. §948a(1)(i).

37. *Ex parte Quirin*, 317 U.S. 1 (1942).

38. As of this writing, the Supreme Court has two such cases before it, both appeals from decisions

of the D.C. Circuit Court of Appeals. See *Munaf v. Geren,* 482 F.3d 582 (D.C. Cir., 2007). See also *Omar v. Harvey,* 479 F.3d 1 (D.C. Cir., 2007).

39. The *New York Times,* for example, editorializing during Padilla's belated trial on his treatment while in custody as an enemy combatant, concluded that his abuse had been so extreme that "We will probably never know if Mr. Padilla was a would-be terrorist" or not. See Editorial, "The Jose Padilla Trial," *New York Times,* March 1, 2007, A18. Nonetheless, on his conviction a few months later, it editorialized that "It is hard to disagree with the jury's guilty verdict against Jose Padilla, the accused, but never formally charged, dirty bomber." Padilla, the paper argued, "should have been charged as a criminal and put on trial in a civilian court" at the outset. See Editorial, "The Padilla Conviction," *New York Times,* August 17, 2007, A22. Legal journalist Dahlia Lithwick declared the "abuse" of Padilla "futile" and "*aimed at the wrong man* [emphasis added] and carried out for years"—as though Padilla were some kind of innocent. See Dahlia Lithwick, "Abuseless," *Slate,* February 27, 2007.

40. For an account both of how the government officials responsible for Padilla experienced the case at the time and of whom they believed Padilla to be, see James Comey's press conference on the case, which took place on June 1, 2004. Comey was deputy attorney general at the time of the press conference, but was serving as U.S. attorney in New York at the time Padilla's case began. A transcript is available at http://www.cnn.com/2004/LAW/06/01/comey.padilla.transcript/index.html.

41. Ibid.

42. See, for example, Editorial, "When, and Whom, to Commit; In Virginia Tech's Bloody Wake, a Rethinking of Standards," *Washington Post,* September 16, 2007, B6. The editorial praises Virginia Republican legislators for "delving into a range of tough questions, many of which seek to strike the right balance between public safety and the protections of privacy and individual liberty." It goes on to criticize current law in the state for "requir[ing] that authorities determine that an individual poses an 'imminent danger' to self or others, or be unable to care for himself, before they can order involuntary detention. That high hurdle, once embraced by a majority of states, has kept many unstable and dangerous people from receiving the care they need. In the case of Seung Hui Cho, the Virginia Tech gunman, officials who examined him in late 2005 after he had made a suicide threat could not agree whether he met the standard. Ultimately, a special justice decided that outpatient treatment was adequate for Mr. Cho—who then never received it."

Chapter 7: An Honest Interrogation Law

1. This exchange occurred at New York University School of Law on September 23, 2004. A transcript appears in *The Torture Debate in America,* Karen J. Greenberg, ed. (Cambridge: Cambridge University Press, 2006). The quoted remarks appear on pages 17–21.

2. Evan Thomas and Michael Hirsh, "The Debate Over Torture," *Newsweek,* November 21, 2005, 26.

3. John McCain, "Torture's Terrible Toll," *Newsweek,* November 21, 2005, 34.

4. Mark Bowden, "The Dark Art of Interrogation," *Atlantic*, October 2003, 51.

5. See David Luban's essay, "Liberalism, Torture, and the Ticking Bomb" in *The Torture Debate in America*, 35–83, especially 44. The article is reprinted from the *Virginia Law Review*.

6. Roth made these remarks on CNN on March 2, 2003.

7. Henry Shue, "Responses to the Debate on Torture," *Dissent*, Summer 2003.

8. See Richard A. Posner, "The Best Offense," *New Republic*, September 2, 2002, 28.

9. See 18 U.S.C. §2340.

10. An example of such a case shows up in the decision by Israel's High Court of Justice to ban coercive interrogation tactics involving a "moderate degree of physical pressure." According to the court, one of the applicants "was arrested . . . and interrogated by" the General Security Services (GSS). "He appealed to this Court . . . [and] claimed to have been tortured by his investigators. . . . His interrogation revealed that he was involved in numerous terrorist activities in the course of which many Israeli citizens were killed. He was instrumental in the kidnapping and murder of [an] IDF soldier. . . . Additionally, he was involved in the bombing of the Cafe 'Appropo' in Tel Aviv, in which three women were murdered and thirty people were injured. He was charged with all these crimes and convicted at trial. He was sentenced to five consecutive life sentences plus an additional twenty years of prison.

"A powerful explosive device, identical to the one detonated at Cafe 'Appropo' in Tel Aviv, was found in the applicant's village (Tzurif) subsequent to the dismantling and interrogation of the terrorist cell to which he belonged. Uncovering this explosive device thwarted an attack similar to the one at Cafe 'Appropo.' According to GSS investigators, the applicant possessed additional crucial information which he only revealed as a result of their interrogation. Revealing this information immediately was essential to safeguarding state and regional security and preventing danger to human life." See *Public Committee Against Torture in Israel v. State of Israel*, 38 I.L.M. 1471 (Isr. H.C.J. 1999).

11. Cesare Beccaria, *An Essay on Crimes and Punishments*, Edward D. Ingraham, trans. (Philadelphia: Philip H. Nicklin, 1819), 63–64.

12. Darius Rejali, *Torture and Democracy* (Princeton: Princeton University Press, 2007), 478.

13. Chris Mackey and Greg Miller, *The Interrogators: Task Force 500 and America's Secret War against Al Qaeda* (New York: Back Bay Books, 2005), xxix–xxx.

14. Ibid., xxx.

15. Ibid., 468.

16. Ibid., 354–64.

17. Ibid., 285–89.

18. Ibid., 476.

19. Ibid., 477.

20. The Schlesinger Report, officially titled "Final Report of the Independent Panel to Review DoD Detention Operations," was published in August 2004 and can be found in *The Torture Papers*, 908–75. The quoted language appears ibid., 924.

21. See "Army Regulation 15–6: Final Report: Investigation into FBI Allegations of Detainee Abuse

at Guantánamo Bay, Cuba Detention Facility" (The Schmidt Report), April 1, 2005, as amended June 9, 2005, 20.

22. *Public Committee Against Torture in Israel v. State of Israel.*

23. President Bush made these comments in announcing the transfer of the high-value detainees to Guantánamo on September 6, 2006. The transcript is available at http://www.whitehouse.gov/news/releases/2006/09/20060906-3.html.

24. Ron Suskind, *The One Percent Doctrine: Deep Inside America's Pursuit of Its Enemies Since 9/11* (New York: Simon & Schuster, 2006), 99–101, 111, 115–18. To a considerable degree, the debate over the effectiveness of the CIA's program was an institutional debate; the CIA stands by its program, while FBI officials doubt its effectiveness and doubt specifically how much Abu Zubaydah really knew and how much of an insider he really was. For a summary of the controversy, see Dan Eggen and Walter Pincus, "FBI, CIA Debate Significance of Terror Suspect," *Washington Post,* December 18, 2007, A1.

25. Suskind, *The One Percent Doctrine,* 228–30.

26. Ibid., 114–15. See also Eggen and Pincus, "FBI, CIA Debate Significance of Terror Suspect."

27. The Kiriakou interview was broadcast on ABC's *World News with Charles Gibson* and *Nightline* on December 10, 2007. A video of the full interview is available at http://abcnews.go.com/video/playerindex?id=3979409.

28. Lawrence Wright, "The Spymaster: Can Mike McConnell Fix America's Intelligence Community?" *New Yorker,* January 21, 2008, 42.

29. Mackey and Miller, *The Interrogators,* 477.

30. Robert Coulam, "Approaches to Interrogation in the Struggle Against Terrorism: Considerations of Cost and Benefit," in *Educing Information: Interrogation: Science and Art* (Washington: Center for Strategic Intelligence Research, 2006), 7–16. The quoted language appears on 8.

31. Randy Borum, "Approaching Truth: Behavioral Science Lessons on Educing Information from Human Sources," in *Educing Information,* 17–43. The quoted language appears on 35.

32. Paul Lehner, "Options for Scientific Research on Eduction Practices," in *Educing Information,* 303–10. The quoted language appears on 305.

33. Mackey and Miller, *The Interrogators,* 11.

34. Ibid., 181.

35. Army Field Manual 34–52, "Intelligence Interrogation," September 28, 1992, Chapter 3.

36. See *9/11 Commission Report,* 248.

37. Adam Zagorin and Michael Duffy, "Inside the Interrogation of Detainee 063," *Time* magazine, June 20, 2005, 26. The detention logs themselves are available at http://www.time.com/time/2006/log/log.pdf.

38. The Schmidt Report, 20.

39. See Memorandum from General James T. Hill for the Chairman of the Joint Chiefs of Staff, "Counter-Resistance Techniques," October 25, 2002, in *The Torture Papers,* 223. The memo forwards a request from Major General Michael E. Dunlavey, commanding general of the Joint Task Force 170 at Guantánamo, also ibid., 225–35.

40. Ibid.

41. Memorandum from William J. Haynes II to Secretary of Defense, "Counter-Resistance Techniques," November 27, 2002, in ibid., 236–37.

42. "Working Group Report on Detainee Interrogations in the Global War on Terrorism; Assessment of Legal, Historical, Policy, and Operational Considerations," April 4, 2003, ibid., 286–359. See, particularly, 340–47.

43. Memorandum from Donald Rumsfeld for the commander, US Southern Command, "Counter-Resistance Techniques in the War on Terrorism," April 16, 2003, ibid., 360–63.

44. See the Schlesinger Report in *The Torture Papers,* 911.

45. See, for example, Tim Golden, "In. U.S. Report, Brutal Details of 2 Afghan Inmates' Deaths," *New York Times,* May 20, 2005, A1. See also Josh White, "Documents Tell of Brutal Improvisation by GIs," *Washington Post,* August 3, 2005, A1.

46. "Investigation of Intelligence Activities at Abu Ghraib" (The Fay-Jones Report), August 2004, in *The Torture Papers,* 987–1131. The quoted language appears on 989.

47. The Schmidt Report, 14–20.

48. Qahtani interrogation logs.

49. Adam Zagorin, "'20th Hijacker' Claims That Torture Made Him Lie," *Time* magazine, March 3, 2006.

50. See generally, the Schmidt Report.

51. Army Field Manual 2-22.3, "Human Intelligence Collector Operations," September 6, 2006.

52. 18 U.S.C. §2340.

53. Ibid.

54. Evan Wallach, "Drop by Drop: Forgetting the History of Water Torture in U.S. Courts," *Columbia Journal of Transnational Law,* Vol. 45 (2007): 468.

55. See Dan Eggen, "Cheney Defends 'Dunk in the Water' Remark," *Washington Post,* October 28, 2006, A2.

56. The CIA, in conjunction with Italian intelligence officials, arranged the 2003 abduction and transfer to Egypt of a radical Egyptian cleric living in Milan. The cleric, named Hassan Mustafa Osama Nasr and generally known as Abu Omar, alleged torture by Egyptian authorities. The affair led to criminal charges in Italy against more than thirty American and Italian operatives.

57. For the nearly immediate news coverage of the capture of Abu Zubaydah, see Michael R. Gordon, "A Top Qaeda Commander Believed Seized in Pakistan," *New York Times,* March 31, 2002, A12. For the comparably quick announcement of Binalshibh's capture, see James Risen, "U.S. Says Suspect Tied to 9/11 and Qaeda is Captured in Raid," *New York Times,* September 14, 2002, A1. In the case of Khalid Sheikh Mohammed, White House spokesman Ari Fleischer confirmed the capture in a press conference two days after it had taken place: the "President expresses his deep appreciation and gratitude to President Musharraf and to the government of Pakistan for their efforts this past weekend that led to the capture of Khalid Sheik Mohammed, the mastermind of the September 11th attack," he said. "This is a very serious development and a blow to al Qaeda. The President is appreciative to Pakistan for their fine efforts that they have

been carrying out in the war against terror and their fine work in this most recent success." A transcript is available at http://www.whitehouse.gov/news/releases/2003/03/20030303-3.html#2.

58. See, for example, *United States v. Moussaoui*, 365 F.3d 292 (4th Cir. 2004), which replaced the detainees' names with asterisks. The *Washington Post*, in covering the decision, included the following: "the witness access issue escalated when [the district judge in the case] ordered depositions of two more detainees, identified by sources as Khalid Sheik Mohammed, the former al Qaeda operations chief, and Mustafa Ahmed Hawsawi, alleged paymaster to the hijackers." See Jerry Markon, "Terror Case Is Cleared for Trial; Moussaoui Can't Talk to Detainees, Appeals Court Says," *Washington Post*, April 23, 2004, A1.

59. Hayden gave this estimate in testimony before the Senate Intelligence Committee on February 5, 2008. Specifically, he testified that "in the life of the CIA detention program, we have held fewer than a hundred people. And . . . fewer than a third of those people have had any techniques used against them—enhanced techniques—in the CIA program."

60. Such legislation actually passed the Congress as Section 327 of the Intelligence Authorization Act for Fiscal Year 2008, H.R. 2082. President Bush vetoed the bill.

61. For information about the military's contemplation of a classified appendix, see Eric Schmitt, "New Army Rules May Snarl Talks with McCain on Detainee Issue," *New York Times*, December 14, 2005, A1. No such appendix was ultimately included.

62. Article II, Section 2 of the Constitution says: "The President shall . . . have Power to Grant Reprieves and Pardons for Offences against the United States. . . ."

63. See Jonathan Rauch, "The Right Approach to Rough Treatment," *National Journal*, September 23, 2006. See also Philip B. Heymann and Juliette N. Kayyem, *Protecting Liberty in an Age of Terror* (Cambridge: The MIT Press, 2005), Chapter 1, which deals with coercive interrogation.

64. See the National Security with Justice Act of 2007, S. 1876, 110th Cong., 1st sess., introduced July 25, 2007.

65. Convention Against Torture and Other Cruel, Inhuman or Degrading Treatment or Punishment, Article 3.

66. Reservations, Understandings, and Declarations, Convention Against Torture and Other Cruel, Inhuman or Degrading Treatment or Punishment, Amendment No. 3200–3203, *Congressional Record*, 101st Cong., 2nd sess., 1990, S17486–92.

67. See 8 C.F.R. §208.18(c)

68. See, for example, "Still at Risk: Diplomatic Assurances No Safeguard Against Torture," Human Rights Watch, April 2005, available at http://hrw.org/reports/2005/eca0405/eca0405.pdf.

69. See "Second Periodic Report of the United States of America to the Committee Against Torture," submitted May 6, 2005.

70. The State Department argues as a purely legal matter, that the torture convention does not apply to renditions overseas, only to people detained on U.S. territory. This view, however, has no practical significance since the government applies the same "more likely than not" legal standard, as a matter of policy, to renditions overseas.

71. See Phillipe Sands, "'A decision was made not to talk about these things': Transcript: A State

Department Lawyer Is Questioned on the Bush Administration's Position on Torture," *Guardian,* November 5, 2007.

Chapter 8: Surveillance Law for a New Century

1. Benjamin Wittes, "Inside America's Most Secretive Court," *Legal Times,* February 19, 1996, 1.
2. After *Legal Times* published my profile of the FISA court, the Justice Department received a series of requests from other news organizations to see the court as well. In response, according to a Justice Department public affairs officer at the time, department officials decided to disallow such tours in the future. James Baker, who ran the department's Office of Intelligence Policy and Review for several years, says he is unaware of any subsequent journalists' being shown the court's chamber. I cannot, however, exclude the possibility that an exception was made at some point.
3. In one story I wrote, I even framed the issue that way directly. See Benjamin Wittes, "Unmasking the Court of No Appeal: A Secret Federal Surveillance Tribunal Takes Exception to the Bill of Rights," *Harper's Magazine,* November 1997, 78.
4. For a useful summary of relevant laws, their restrictions, and their holes, see Stewart A. Baker, "The Regulation of Disclosure of Information Held by Private Parties," in *Protecting America's Freedom in the Information Age: A Report of the Markle Foundation Task Force,* The Markle Foundation, October 2002, 161–73.
5. An early Senate Judiciary Committee report on the incipient FISA described it as "a recognition by both the executive branch and the Congress that the statutory rule of law must prevail in the area of foreign intelligence surveillance." The need for such legislation, the committee wrote, "has become all too apparent in recent years. This legislation is in large measure a response to the revelations that warrantless electronic surveillance in the name of national security has been seriously abused. These abuses were initially illuminated in 1973 during the investigation of the Watergate break-in. Since that time, however, the Senate Select Committee to Study Governmental Operations with Respect to Intelligence Activities, chaired by Senator Church . . . has concluded that every President since Franklin D. Roosevelt asserted the authority to authorize warrantless electronic surveillance and exercised that authority. While the number of illegal or improper national security taps and bugs conducted during the Nixon administration may have exceeded those in previous administrations, the surveillances were regrettably by no means atypical." See Senate Judiciary Committee Report No. 94–1035, 94th Cong., 2d sess., July 15, 1976, 9–10.
6. See Title III of the Omnibus Crime Control and Safe Streets Act of 1968, Public Law 90-351. In Section 2511(3), this law explicitly disclaimed any regulation of national security surveillance and took a broad view of that surveillance it carved out: "Nothing contained in this chapter . . . shall limit the constitutional power of the President to take such measures as he deems necessary to protect the Nation against actual or potential attack or other hostile acts of a foreign power, to obtain foreign intelligence information deemed essential to the security of the United States, or to protect national security information against foreign intelligence activities. Nor

shall anything contained in this chapter be deemed to limit the constitutional power of the President to take such measures as he deems necessary to protect the United States against the overthrow of the Government by force or other unlawful means, or against any other clear and present danger to the structure or existence of the Government. The contents of any wire or oral communication intercepted by authority of the President in the exercise of the foregoing powers may be received in evidence in any trial hearing, or other proceeding only where such interception was reasonable, and shall not be otherwise used or disclosed except as is necessary to implement that power."

7. See, most important, *United States v. United States District Court,* 407 U.S. 297 (1972). In deciding this case, the Court specifically emphasized that it was not considering surveillance involving "activities of foreign powers or their agents," thereby leaving open a question that it has never subsequently resolved: whether the president may conduct foreign intelligence surveillance without a warrant without violating the Fourth Amendment.

8. See Public Law 95-511, Section 101(b).

9. Ibid., Sections 103–06. For an interesting early example of FISA material making its way into a criminal case against an alleged terrorist, see *United States v. Isa,* 923 F.2d 1300 (8th Cir., 1991).

10. The McAdams quotation appears in Benjamin Wittes, "Inside America's Most Secretive Court." The quotations from Lamberth appear in Benjamin Wittes, "The FISA Court Speaks," *Legal Times,* February 19, 1996.

11. *In Re All Matters Submitted to the Foreign Intelligence Surveillance Court* (FISC 2002).

12. *In re: Sealed Case,* 310 F.3d 717 (2002).

13. The intelligence community clearly had some capability at the time to do automated processing. In a FISA hearing in 1977, a telecommunications engineer who had worked for both the CIA and the Western Electric arm of AT&T, testified: "[O]ne must observe that a broadband intercept surveillance operation injected into a single microwave link, for instance, *permits the scanning of hundreds of thousands of messages in a single day with sophisticated computer-like equipment operated unattended, or by one or two persons.* . . .

    "It must be understood that when a warrant would be issued for a certain targeted objective to be sought through the broadband system, this does not ordinarily mean that special equipment is installed for that objective alone. The equipment is already in place in our microwave long lines network. What it really means is that *a new set of punched cards are inserted into the system to operate as a new addition to the watch list of called telephone and telegraph numbers or to the trigger word lexicon.*" [Emphasis added.] See *Foreign Intelligence Surveillance Act of 1977,* Hearings before the Subcommittee on Criminal Laws and Procedures of the Committee on the Judiciary, United States Senate, 95th Cong., 1st sess., June 14, 1977, 119.

14. FISA at various points requires the use of so-called minimization procedures, which are defined in 50 U.S.C. §1801(h) as "specific procedures . . . that are reasonably designed in light of the purpose and technique of the particular surveillance, to minimize the acquisition and retention, and prohibit the dissemination, of nonpublicly available information concerning uncon-

senting United States persons consistent with the need of the United States to obtain, produce, and disseminate foreign intelligence information." Minimization procedures are supposed to "require that nonpublicly available information, which is not foreign intelligence information . . . shall not be disseminated in a manner that identifies any United States person, without such person's consent, unless such person's identity is necessary to understand foreign intelligence information or assess its importance." More generally, the intelligence community is barred from retaining information on Americans that does not constitute legitimate foreign intelligence. See, for example, Executive Order 12333, December 4, 1981.

15. FISA defines a "person" in 50 U.S.C. §1801(m) as "any individual, including any officer or employee of the Federal Government, or any group, entity, association, corporation, or foreign power." For a discussion of the significance of this provision, see David S. Kris, "Modernizing the Foreign Intelligence Surveillance Act," November 15, 2007, 32–35. Kris's paper, published as a working paper of the Series on Counterterrorism and American Statutory Law, a joint project of the Brookings Institution, the Georgetown University Law Center, and the Hoover Institution, is available at http://www.brookings.edu/~/media/Files/rc/papers/2007/1115_nationalsecurity_kris/1115_nationalsecurity_kris.pdf. I am the general editor of this series.

16. Robert O'Harrow Jr., *No Place to Hide* (New York: Free Press, 2005), 47.

17. Ibid., Chapter 3.

18. For an example of this kind of analysis in the 9/11 investigation, see K. A. Taipale, "The Ear of Dionysus: Rethinking Foreign Intelligence Surveillance," *Yale Journal of Law and Technology,* Vol. 9 (2006–7): 152–53.

19. Robert O'Harrow, *No Place to Hide,* 98–102.

20. For example, the NSA's director, Keith Alexander, wrote to Congress in 2006 that when "FISA was enacted into law in 1978, almost all transoceanic communications into and out of the United States were carried by satellite" and therefore "intentionally omitted from the scope of FISA." But change in technology, he wrote, "rather than a considered judgment by Congress, has resulted in the considerable expansion" of FISA's scope. Alexander's letter to the Senate Judiciary Committee, dated December 19, 2006, is available at http://www.fas.org/irp/congress/2006_hr/alexander-qfr.pdf.

21. For FISA's inclusion of communications targeting domestic communications acquired by any technical means, see 50 U.S.C. §1801(f)(1).

22. See 50 U.S.C. §1801(f)(3).

23. For an excellent discussion of this history, see David Kris, "Modernizing the Foreign Intelligence Surveillance Act," 9–27.

24. For the law's exclusion of wire-line surveillance of overseas targets, see 50 U.S.C. §1801(f)(2).

25. The most direct evidence that the NSA acquired this data for its warrantless program domestically is the testimony of Mark Klein, a former AT&T employee who has stated that the NSA had a special room in a company data-routing facility in San Francisco used to divert data traffic. See "Declaration of Mark Klein in Support of Plaintiffs' Motion for Preliminary Injunction," filed in *Hepting v. AT&T Corp.,* C-06-0672-VRW (N.D. CA). See also Eric Lichtblau and James

Risen, "Spy Agency Mined Vast Data Trove, Officials Report," *New York Times,* December 24, 2005, A1.

26. *9/11 Commission Report,* 276. The commission's broader discussion of this episode begins on p. 273.

27. 50 U.S.C. §1801(b)(1)(C)

28. Stuart Taylor Jr., "Rights, Liberties, and Security," in *Agenda for the Nation,* Henry J. Aaron, James M. Lindsay and Pietro S. Nivola, eds. (Washington: Brookings Institution Press, 2003), 446.

29. K. A. Taipale, "The Ear of Dionysus: Rethinking Foreign Intelligence Surveillance," 157. The phrase "*Terry* stop" is a reference to *Terry v. Ohio,* 392 U.S. 1 (1968).

30. Jessica Stern, *The Ultimate Terrorists* (Cambridge: Harvard University Press, 2000).

31. Jessica Stern, *Terror in the Name of God: Why Religious Militants Kill* (New York: Ecco/Harper-Collins, 2003).

32. Stern made these remarks in an e-mail exchange in December 2007.

33. Stewart Baker, "The Regulation of Disclosure of Information Held by Private Parties."

34. Ibid. Baker's paper contains a useful overview of the relevant legal standards for acquisition of different categories of records.

35. 18 U.S.C. §2709 allows the FBI to obtain telephone billing information in terrorism cases on request from phone companies by certifying that the records are "relevant" to a counterterrorism investigation.

36. See 50 U.S.C. §1861.

37. 18 U.S.C. §3123 authorizes pen register and trap and trace orders in criminal investigations, while 50 U.S.C. §1842 allows the FISA court to issue them in national security investigations.

38. See Leslie Cauley, "NSA has massive database of Americans' phone calls," *USA Today,* May 11, 2006, A1. This story, which reported that the NSA had amassed a huge database of the addressing data of domestic American calls, appears to have overstated the degree of participation by telecommunications carriers. The newspaper ran a substantial correction some weeks later. See "A Note to Our Readers," *USA Today,* June 30, 2006, A2. Yet the core of the story withstood the paper's subsequent investigation. See Susan Page, "Lawmakers: NSA Database Incomplete; Some Who Were Briefed About the Database Identify Who Participated and Who Didn't," *USA Today,* June 30, 2006, A2.

39. *Kyllo v. United States,* 533 U.S. 27 (2001).

40. David S. Kris, "Modernizing the Foreign Intelligence Surveillance Act," 14–16. The excerpt is reprinted with permission from the Brookings Institution.

41. See, for example, Memorandum for Heads of all Federal Departments and Agencies from John Ashcroft, Attorney General, October 12, 2001, "The Freedom of Information Act," available at http://www.usdoj.gov/oip/foiapost/2001foiapost19.htm.

42. U.S. Department of Justice White Paper, "Legal Authority Supporting the Activities of the National Security Agency Described by the President," January 19, 2006, 5.

43. A transcript of the press conference, which took place on December 19, 2005, can be found at http://www.whitehouse.gov/news/releases/2005/12/20051219-1.html.

44. See, for example, Walter Pincus, "Spying Necessary, Democrats Say; But Harman, Daschle Question President's Legal Reach," *Washington Post,* February 13, 2006, A3.

45. This is admittedly speculation on my part. It is based in large measure on the "torture" memo's exceptionally broad view of the presidential power to ignore statutes that in his judgment encumbered his ability to fight the enemy. The logic of this memo, if accepted, would amply justify departures from FISA as well as in situations in which the president felt shackled by the surveillance law in confronting the enemy.

46. This point is also speculative, but there is considerable circumstantial evidence to support it. By the time the program became public late in 2005, the administration was not relying on a pure presidential power argument to support it. It relied, rather, principally on the theory that the Authorization of the Use of Military Force (AUMF) that Congress passed in the wake of the attacks implicitly authorized surveillance of the enemy as a power incident to the war powers Congress had invoked. See Department of Justice White Paper on NSA Activities. On leaving government, OLC head Jack Goldsmith—who played a key role in the hospital room confrontation—wrote a lengthy article on the scope of the powers the AUMF had conveyed to the president. See Curtis A. Bradley and Jack Goldsmith, "Congressional Authorization and the War on Terrorism," *Harvard Law Review,* Vol. 118 (May 2005): 2047–133. The article's reasoning in some respects anticipates that of the White Paper, which followed several months later. Particularly in light of Goldsmith's subsequent criticisms of the executive branch's "go it alone approach" in his book, it seems preponderantly likely that, while at OLC, he reformulated many broad assertions of inherent executive power as more modest statutory arguments that track those in the White Paper, where the executive relies first on Congress's backing in the AUMF and only secondarily on its inherent power to act even without legislative blessing.

47. Goldsmith, *The Terror Presidency,* 182.

48. Gonzales made this announcement in a letter to the Senate Judiciary Committee on January 17, 2007.

49. See, for example, Carol D. Leonnig and Ellen Nakashima, "Ruling Limited Spying Efforts; Move to Amend FISA Sparked by Judge's Decision," *Washington Post,* August 3, 2007, A1.

50. Public Law 110-55, Section 2.

51. See Kris, "Modernizing the Foreign Intelligence Surveillance Act," 32–35.

52. See *Protecting America's Freedom in the Information Age,* 28.

53. The state of Virginia pioneered the aggressive use of this sort of DNA database. In recent years, more states and the federal government have gotten in on the act. See, for example, John Wagner, "O'Malley Wants DNA Database Expanded; Samples Would Be Taken from Those Arrested for, Not Just Convicted of, Crimes," *Washington Post,* January 11, 2008, B6; Patrick McGeehan, "Spitzer Wants DNA Sampling in Most Crimes," *New York Times,* May 14, 2007, A1. For a general discussion of the controversy surrounding these databases nationwide, see

Rick Weiss, "Vast DNA Bank Pits Policing Vs. Privacy; Data Stored on 3 Million Americans," *Washington Post,* June 3, 2006, A1.

54. For a discussion of the challenges in this area, see Shane Harris, "More Than Meets the Ear," *National Journal,* March 18, 2006; Shane Harris, "Terrorist Profiling, Version 2.0," *National Journal,* October 21, 2006.

55. Taipale, "The Ear of Dionysus," 157–61.

56. For a good discussion of the concept of authorized use, see *Mobilizing Information to Prevent Terrorism: Accelerating Development of a Trusted Information Sharing Environment,* Third Report of the Markle Foundation Task Force, July 2006, 32–40.

57. Problems with the so-called No Fly List have prompted numerous news stories concerning people unable to get on airplanes without extensive additional security because of some circumstance beyond their control, like having a name similar to the name or alias of a suspected terrorist. An amusing example in 2004 was Senator Edward Kennedy. For a not so amusing example, see Ralph Blumenthal, "Pilot on Watch List Finds Career Stalled," *New York Times,* March 28, 2005, A10.

58. See Ernest F. Brickell et al., "SKIPJACK Review Interim Report: The SKIPJACK Algorithm," July 28, 1993.

INDEX

Abbasi, Feroz Ali, 159–60
ABC News, 196
Abdulayev, Omar Hamzayavich, 94
Abu Ghraib, 65, 74, 122, 191, 192, 199, 202–3, 213
Abu Hafs (Mohammed Atef), 159–60
Addington, David, 51–52, 58, 61, 63, 134, 259
administrative detention rules
  admission of evidence in, 164–65
  counsel and, 164–65
  fact finding and, 164, 166
  national security court model for, 165–66
  nature of detainees and, 160–62
  public accounting in, 169–70
  risk of injustice in, 166–68
Administrative Review Boards (ARB), 66–67, 76–78, 79, 82–99, 158
  of Al Zahri, 88
  Detainee Treatment Act and, 140
  government allegations summarized from, 81–82
  of Kurnaz, 95
Afghanistan, 6, 13, 15, 23, 41, 44, 47–48, 49, 75, 82, 88, 89, 93, 95, 98, 124, 140, 156, 192, 201, 232
African embassy bombings of 1998, 23, 87–88

Albania, 27–28
Al-Farouq training camp, 158
Ali Ahmed, Faruq, 5–6, 7
Aliza, Abdul Rauf, 90
Allen, Lew, 241–42, 244
Al Qaeda, 3, 4–5, 6, 11, 12, 13, 14, 16, 20, 21, 23, 25, 26, 27–28, 48, 51, 53, 57, 106, 113, 115, 116, 125, 135, 139, 153, 157, 163, 177, 180, 184, 187, 190, 198, 199, 212, 215, 233, 246
  anthrax program of, 195
  detention policy and, 33–35, 38, 41, 42, 56
  diffused network of, 49–50
  among Guantánamo detainees, 79–81, 86–88, 90–95, 98–100
  POW status and, 41
  war model for fight against, 44–46
Al Shirbi Ghassan Abdallah Ghazi, 4–7, 159
Al Zahri, Abdul Rahman, 36, 88
Al Zawahiri, Ayman, 27, 50, 257
Amazon.com, 230
American Civil Liberties Union, 53, 60–61
American University, 58
America's Most Wanted (television show), 231
Ames, Aldrich, 59–60, 220
Amnesty International, 6–7, 170
anthrax, 195
Argentina, 183

Army, U.S., 40, 203
Article 5 tribunals, 41, 164
Ashcroft, John, 181, 245, 258
Atef, Mohammed (Abu Hafs), 159–60
Atta, Mohammed, 200, 232
Auschwitz, 3
Authorization for the Use of Military Force
    (AUMF), 12, 25

Baker, Stewart, 237–38
Beccaria, Cesare, 191
Bellinger, John, III, 217
Benjamin, Daniel, 26
Berenson, Bradford, 58
Berger, Sandy, 26
Biden, Joseph, 215
Bilgin, Selcuk, 95, 126
Bill of Rights, 108, 168, 175
Binalshibh, Ramzi, 97–98, 156, 169, 194, 195,
    208, 235
Bin 'Attash, Walid, 87
bin Laden, Osama, 5, 6, 23, 24, 25, 49–50, 82,
    84, 89, 91, 92, 159, 194, 237, 257
    in CIA's kidnap scheme, 19–21
Bosnia, 96
Boumediene v. Bush, 111, 126, 256–57
Breyer, Stephen, 37, 112
B'Tselem (human rights group), 184, 190,
    213
Bush, George W. 12, 14, 37, 45, 47, 48, 50, 131,
    133, 140, 151, 154, 187, 196, 198, 233
    CIA secret interrogations and, 204–7
    successors to, 259–60
    on torture policy, 194–95
    unlawful combatant debate and, 40–41
Bush (GHW) administration, 31, 32
Bush (GW) administration, 3, 6, 8, 9, 15, 19,
    20, 25, 26, 27, 39, 43, 61, 70, 112, 127,
    134, 141, 169, 170, 174, 257, 258–59
    combatant decision of, 16–17
    detainment policy of, 30–33
    executive-legislative relations and, 69–71
    executive power debate and, 50–54
    Guantánamo jurisdiction debate and, 104–6
    interrogation policy and, 28–30, 187, 205–7
    9/11 response of, 24–25
    public announcement of arrests by, 208–9
    rendition program and, 207–8
    secrecy and, 242–43
    "torture" as defined by, 206
    war model of, 12–14, 44, 48
    war powers debate and, 54–55

Bwazir, Mohammed Ali Abdullah, 91
Byron, George Gordon, Lord, 132

Casey, Lee A., 106
Central Intelligence Agency (CIA), 2, 23–24,
    27, 28, 55, 68, 93, 122, 141, 188, 214, 215
    Ames case and, 59–60
    bin Laden kidnap scheme of, 19–21
    bin Laden unit of, 26
    Counterterrorism Center of, 24
    Detainee Treatment Act model and, 139–40,
        210, 212
    interrogation policy of, 29–30, 186, 194,
        195–96, 204–7, 209–12
    9/11 warning and, 137
    rendition program of, 25–26, 30, 186–87,
        215–16
    torture issue and, 29–30, 147–48
    waterboarding and, 147–48
Chechnya, 158
Cheney, Dick, 51–52
Cho, Seung-Hui, 182
ChoicePoint, 231
civil liberties, 9, 22, 53, 168
    FISA and, 221–23, 226–33, 235, 238, 239,
        246–47, 248, 252
    presidential powers and, 50–51
Civil War, U.S., 11, 63, 120
Clarke, Richard, 26
    on rendition program, 26–27
Clement, Paul D., 256
Clinton, Bill, 19, 32
    bin Laden kidnap scheme and, 19–21
    counterterrorism strikes and, 23–24
    Lewinsky scandal and, 24
    rendition program and, 26–27
Clinton, Hillary, 259
Clinton administration, 21, 24, 26, 59, 134,
    207, 243, 256
Coast Guard, U.S., 31, 72
COINTELPRO, 221
Cold War, 216
Cole, USS, 87–88
Coll, Steve, 21, 24
Combatant Status Review Tribunal (CSRT),
    69, 74–78, 79, 125–27, 154, 155, 158, 160,
    164, 166
    of Ali Ahmed, 5–6
    of Al Saigh, 89
    of Al Shirbi, 4–5
    of Bin 'Attash, 87–88
    of Bwazir, 91

Detainee Treatment Act and, 140
errors in, 82–83
government allegations summarized from,
81–82
of Hamdan, 89
of Hashim, 87
judicial review and, 125–27
of Kurnaz, 94–95
of Madni, 91
of Mohamed, 91, 97
of Nasim, 82–83
of Noori, 90
of Rahman, 82
of Shah, 91–92
of Uighurs, 82, 98–99
of Wasiq, 89–90
Congress, U.S., 2, 8, 12, 25, 35, 37, 38, 43, 102,
107, 111, 112, 113, 123, 124, 125, 129,
131–50, 152, 160, 171, 178, 182, 224, 229,
240, 245, 249
approval rating of, 131
Detainee Treatment Act passed by, 138–40,
142
detainee trials and, 174–77
executive branch's relations with, 56–58,
133–34, 260
FISA modernization and, 143–44, 145, 222,
223, 234, 235–36, 246–47
interrogation policy and, 187–88, 209–18
legal framework for war on terror and,
10–11, 15, 55–58
MCA and, 140–43
military force authorization and, 44–45
presidential power debate and, 50–54
rendition program and, 216–17
surveillance policy and, 252–55
war on terror legislation of, 135–44
war on terror role of, 131–33
see also Senate, U.S.
Constitution, U.S., 9, 14, 17, 53, 61, 107, 110,
119, 126, 153, 174, 178, 179, 189, 256
contemporary problems in terrorism and,
257–58
Eighth Amendment of, 68, 139
Fifth Amendment of, 68, 139
Fourteenth Amendment of, 68, 139
Fourth Amendment of, 222, 224–25, 233,
240, 248
overseas detainees and, 127
presidential preemption in war on terror
and, 144–45
and rights of aliens, 114–16

Convention Against Torture, 216
counterterrorism policy, 104, 124, 138, 142,
157
congressional role in, 131–33
executive-judiciary conflict on, 13–16
military's role in, 23–24
Counterterrorism Security Group, 27
Croatia, 27
Cuba, 31
Mariel boat lift and, 36–37
Cutler, Lloyd, 27

Darwaish, Nasibullah, 83
data mining, 239–40
accountability and, 252–54
of DNA databases, 249–50
mission creep and, 251–52
new technology and, 223–24
public vs. private searches and, 229–31
D.C. Circuit Court of Appeals, 125–28, 140,
166
Defense Department, U.S., 27, 29, 58, 68, 74,
79, 97, 101, 140, 158, 161, 203
Democratic Party, U.S., 21, 56, 57, 141, 143,
210, 259
Denbeaux, Mark, 74
Dershowitz, Alan, 185
Detainee Treatment Act (DTA), 10, 56–57,
68–69, 107–8, 110, 138, 142, 144, 176,
184, 188, 203–4
CIA and, 139–40, 210, 212
interrogations and, 138–40
judicial review and, 125–26
limited impact of, 138–39
McCain Amendment to, 68, 203, 206
detention, detention policy, 2, 13, 15–16, 22,
28, 33–38, 56, 65, 103, 123–24, 222
of aliens, 36
CSRT and, 66–67
due process and, 37
framework needed for, 157–61
Geneva Conventions and, 154–55
habeas corpus review and, 152–55
of high-value detainees, 212–13
human rights groups and, 153–55
immigration law and, 36
indefinite, 33–34, 168
individual menace criteria for, 161–62, 163
in laws preceding 9/11, 22–23
of local and global fighters, 161
long-term, 151–52, 170
of mentally ill, 34–35, 163–64, 181

detention, detention policy (*cont.*)
  outside U.S., 31–33
  of POWs, 34
  preventative, 162–64
  of sex offenders, 34
  trials and, *see* terrorism trials
  war model and, 48–49
  see also Guantánamo detainees
DNA databases, 249–50
Dred Scott decision, 120
Dubaikey, Bessam Muhammed Saleh Al, 94
due process, 16, 37, 76, 98, 118, 145, 155
Dworkin, Ronald, 106

*Educing Information: Interrogation: Science and
  Art,* 197–98
Egypt, 26, 28, 187, 215
Eighth Amendment, 68, 139
Eleventh Court of Appeals, U.S., 33
Ellis Island, 36
Ely, John Hart, 133
enemy combatants, 5, 6–7, 16, 30, 66, 70, 105,
    146, 151, 154, 163
  detention program and, 33–35
  distinguishing among, 41–42
  Geneva Conventions and, 38–41
  human rights and, 6–7
  judicial review and, 105–8
  POWs and, 38
Espionage and Sedition Acts, 22
executive branch, 9, 10, 14, 116, 131, 147, 149,
    224
  enhanced presidential powers and, 12–13
  FISA and, 42–43
  judicial branch and, 14–16
  legislative branch's power debate with,
    50–54, 56–58, 132–34, 260
  and response to 9/11, 22

Facebook, 230
Federal Bureau of Investigation (FBI), 21, 27,
    55, 170, 195, 203, 219, 221, 226, 227, 235,
    237, 239, 244
  Ames case and, 59–60
  9/11 warnings and, 137
Fifth Amendment, 68, 139
Fleischer, Ari, 74
Foreign Intelligence Surveillance Act (FISA),
    42–43, 57, 59–61
  civil liberties concerns and, 221–23, 226–33,
    235, 238, 239, 246–47, 248, 252

congressional modernization of, 143–44,
    145, 222, 223, 234, 235–36, 246–47
  criminal investigations and, 225–26
  data mining and, *see* data mining
  Fourth Amendment and, 233, 240
  government vs. private data collection and,
    229–31
  international communications and, 229,
    232–33, 243–47
  lone wolf provision of, 236
  Moussaoui case and, 235–37
  9/11 and, 227–28, 232
  obsolescence of, 222–23
  origins of, 224–25
  Protect America Act and, 246–47
  "person" as defined in, 229, 247
  physical searches amendment to, 60–61
  privacy and, 230–31, 237–40, 250–53
  review process and, 225–26
  secrecy problem and, 240–43, 247–48, 253
  technology and, 223–24, 228–31
  Terry stop tactic and, 236, 244, 251
  USA PATRIOT Act and, 136–38, 227
  wiretaps and, 136, 143, 233–35
  see also surveillance, surveillance policy
Foreign Intelligence Surveillance Court,
    219–21, 225–27, 236–37, 239, 245, 246
Founders, 17, 257–58
Fourteenth Amendment, 68, 139
Fourth Amendment, 222, 224–25, 233, 240,
    248

Geneva Conventions, 23, 28, 29–30, 66–67,
    107, 112, 113, 142, 193, 198, 204, 208,
    215
  Common Article 3 of, 141, 147–48, 176,
    212
  enemy combatants and, 38–41
  Fourth, 39, 160
  POWs in, 39–40
  Protocol I and, 39, 40
  Third, 39, 40–41, 154–55, 160, 164
  war on terror and, 160–61
Germany, 95
Goldsmith, Jack, 51–52, 58, 63, 64, 245
Goldstein, Brandt, 31–32
Gonzales, Alberto, 243, 245–46
Google, 230
Gore, Al, 27, 207–8
Gorelick, Jamie, 60, 61, 62, 64, 134, 259
Government Accountability Office, 51, 253

Green, Joyce Hens, 94
Guantánamo Bay, 2, 5, 12, 14, 22–23, 38, 42,
    49, 56, 63, 68, 104, 112, 115, 116–17,
    123–24, 140, 142, 155, 187, 257, 258
  administration policy and, 77–78
  camps of, 73
  Denbeaux report on, 74
  detainees of, *see* Guantánamo detainees
  detention facilities of, 73–74
  Haitian refugee crisis and, 30–32
  jurisdiction debate and, *see* Supreme Court,
    U.S.
  New York Times editorial on, 75
  oddities of, 72–73
  operation of, 73–74
  public perception of, 73
  size of, 72
  as symbol, 153
Guantánamo detainees:
  allegations against, 81, 83–84, 99–100
  ARB process and, 76–78, 79, 81–99
  CSRT hearings and, 74–78, 79, 81–99
  declining population of, 167
  held by mistake, 82
  interrogation abuses and, 200–204
  military commissions debate and, 112–13
  national origins of, 78–79
  overview of, 78–86
  releases of, 100
  review mechanism for, 100–102
  trial system and, 175–76
  Uighurs among, 82, 98–99
  who admit nothing, 93–94
  who admit Taliban or al Qaeda member-
    ship, 86–90, 93, 159–60
  who are forced into Taliban service, 90
  who deny terrorist affiliations, 90–92,
    94–96, 99
  who "don't know" if they are terrorists,
    158–59
  who give no statements, 97–98
Gul, Dawd, 90
Gul, Janut (Hammdidullah), 83

habeas corpus, writ of, 1–2, 3, 14, 22, 63, 65,
    68, 107, 125, 126, 127, 128, 131, 152–54,
    179
  jurisdiction debate and, *see* Supreme Court,
    U.S.
  Lincoln and, 9, 118–20
  MCA and, 141–42

  proper place of, 129
  Taney on, 118–19
Haiti, 30–31
Hamas, 25
Hambali (detainee), 93–94, 194
Hamdan, Salim, 89
Hamdan v. Rumsfeld, 2, 14, 15, 57, 68, 89, 104,
    105–7, 109–10, 112, 114, 138, 140, 148,
    168, 177
Hamdi, Yaser Esam, 156, 179
Hamdi v. Rumsfeld, 14, 64, 105, 106–7, 155, 177
Hammdidullah (Janut Gul), 83
Hashim, Mohammed, 87
Hayden, Michael, 209, 243–44, 245
Haynes, William J., II, 201
Hazmi, Nawaf Al, 236
Hekmati, Abdul Razzaq, 96
Heymann, Philip B., 214
Hicks, David, 125, 156
High Court of Justice, Israeli, 193
Hoess, Rudolf, 3–4, 7, 9, 121–22, 208
Homeland Security Department, U.S., 138,
    238
human rights, 1–3, 8, 22, 53, 104, 122, 127,
    148, 168, 175
  of criminals, 9–10
  detainee trials and, 170–71
  enemy combatants and, 6–7
  Guantánamo detainees and, 153–55
  interrogation policy and, 215–16
  of released detainees, 167
  see also civil liberties
Human Rights Watch, 154–55, 185
Hundred Years War, 34
Hussein, Hassan Adel, 96–97

immigration, 47, 55, 136, 163
  Mariel boat lift episode and, 36–37
Immigration and Customs Enforcement, U.S.,
    138
Immigration and Naturalization Service, 138
Indonesia, 91
Intelligence Science Board, 197
interrogation, interrogation policy, 2, 22,
    28–30, 56, 103, 146, 147–48, 157, 159,
    173, 183–218, 222
  Abu Ghraib abuses and, 199, 202
  Army Field Manual and, 139, 210–12
  Bush administration and, 28–30
  CIA and, 29–30, 186–87, 194, 195–96,
    204–7, 209–12, 214

interrogation, interrogation policy (*cont.*)
  coercive, 194–97, 210–11
  congressional framework for, 209–18
  Congress's role in, 187–88, 209–18
  in conventional conflicts, 198–99
  criminal liability of field personnel and,
    213–14
  Detainee Treatment Act model and, 138–40,
    142, 144, 210, 212
  Educing Information report on, 197–98
  Guantánamo Bay abuses and, 200–202
  of high-value detainees, 212–13
  human rights interests and, 215–16
  Israeli experience of, 193–94
  judicial jurisdiction and, 15–16
  McCain Amendment and, 68, 203, 206
  of POWs, 198–99
  president's role in, 213–14
  proposed categories of, 200–201
  public announcement of arrests and, 208–9
  of Qahtani, 193, 200, 202–3
  rendition program and, 207–8, 215–18
  Schlesinger Report and, 193, 199, 201
  ticking time bomb scenario and, 184–86,
    189–90
  see also torture
Iran, 82
Iraq, 13, 49, 74, 112, 140, 192, 201, 202, 260
Isle of Jersey, 256
Israel, 25, 123, 183, 189
  interrogation experience of, 193–94
Italy, 208

Jackson, Robert H., 65, 114, 115–16
Jammat al Tabliq, 94–95
Japanese Americans, internment of, 22, 33,
    121
Jemaah Islamiyah, 84, 93–94, 194
Jews, 159–60
J-I operatives, 194
Johnson v. Eisentrager, 114–15
Jordan, 215
judicial branch, 10, 13, 142
  executive branch and, 14–16
  executive power debate and, 62–64
  see also judicial review; Supreme Court, U.S.
judicial review, 103–30, 140, 141
  administration policy and, 104–5
  Boumediene case and, 111, 126
  CSRT and, 125–27
  Detainee Treatment Act and, 125–26
  enemy combatant issue and, 105–8

  habeas corpus debate and, 110–12
  international conflicts and, 117–18,
    120–21
  jurisdiction issue and, 109–12
  and Lincoln's suspension of habeas corpus,
    118–20
  and rights of overseas aliens, 114–16
  surveillance issue and, 108–9
  war on terror and, 103–4, 105, 122–24, 125,
    128–30
  of wartime detainees, 113–14
  see also Supreme Court, U.S.
Justice Department, U.S., 19, 20, 21, 27, 31, 32,
    138, 168, 173, 179, 219–20, 223, 225,
    226–27, 243
  Ames case and, 59–60
  Office of Intelligence Policy and Review of,
    226
  Office of Legal Counsel (OLC) of, 19, 24,
    51, 58
  "torture memo" of, 29, 50

Karzai, Hamid, 83, 95–96
Katyal, Neal K., 142
Kayyem, Juliette N., 214
Kennedy, Anthony, 257
Kiriakou, John, 196
Korean War, 39
Kris, David S., 241
Krongard, A. B., 195
Kurnaz, Murat, 94–95, 97, 126

Lackawanna Six, 156, 179
Lake, Anthony, 26
Lamberth, Royce, 226–27, 242
legislative branch, 104
  executive branch's power debate with,
    50–54, 56–58, 133–34, 260
  see also Congress, U.S.; Senate, U.S
Leonnig, Carol D., 95
Levi, Edward, 241–42, 243
Levi, William, 29–30
Levin, Carl, 155
Lewinsky, Monica, 24
Lewis, Anthony, 183–84, 185
Libya, 23
Libyan Islamic Fighting Group, 84
Lincoln, Abraham, 9, 118
  on habeas corpus, 119–20
Lindh, John Walker, 155–56, 179
Los Angeles International Airport, 23
Luban, David, 185

McAdams, James, III, 226, 242
McCain, John, 184–85, 187, 206, 213, 259–60
McCain Amendment, 68, 203, 206
McCarthy, Andrew, 171, 176
McConnell, Mike, 196
Mackey, Chris, 192–93, 196, 199, 201
Madni, Hafez Qari Mohamed Saad Iqbal, 91
Mansfield, Lord, 110
Margulies, Joseph, 22
Mariel boat lift, 36–37
Markle Foundation, 248
Marri, Ali Saleh Kahlah al, 172
Marwalah, Bashir Nasir Al-, 158–59
Masri, Sheikh Abu Hafs Al, 88
Massoud, General, 89
Mayer, Jane, 28
Mengele, Josef, 3
Merryman, John, 118
Mihdhar, Khalid al, 236
military commissions, 42, 51–52, 58, 104, 108,
        112, 125, 140–41, 146, 151, 158, 170,
        174–75, 176, 177, 178
    detainee trials and, 168–69
    failure of, 156
Military Commissions Act (MCA), 2, 10, 14,
        57, 69, 147–48
    authorization of, 140–43
    habeas corpus and, 141–42
    trial process and, 174–76
Mohamed, Fahed Nasser, 91
Mohammed, Khalid Sheikh, 47, 84, 88, 97,
        121, 169, 178, 187, 189–90, 194–96, 208,
        209, 257
Montell, Jessica, 184, 190, 213
Moss, Randy, 19–20, 22
Moussaoui, Zacarias, 137, 172–73, 209
    FISA surveillance failure and, 235–37
    laptop issue and, 220–21
    trial of, 171–72
Mukasey, Michael, 139, 171–72

Nasim, Mohammed, 82–83
National Journal, 74–75
National Security Agency (NSA), 2, 222, 223,
        232, 246, 247, 249, 251, 254
    warrantless wiretap program of, 219–20,
        233–35, 238, 240–41, 243–45
National Security Council (NSC), 20–21, 24,
        26, 58
National Security Court, 171
New Yorker, 28
New York Times, 75, 96, 105, 183

9/11 Commission, 19, 188
Noori, Mullah Norullah, 90
Northern Alliance, 74, 80, 81, 83, 88–89, 91,
        158
Nuremberg war crimes trial, 3, 9, 118

Obama, Barack, 259
Office of Intelligence Policy and Review, 226
Office of Legal Counsel (OLC), 19, 24, 51, 58
O'Harrow, Robert, Jr., 231, 232
Omar, Mullah, 88

Padilla, Jose, 156, 171, 173, 178–81
Pakistan, 5, 74, 75, 80, 84, 91, 93
Palestinians, 25
Patriot Act, *see* USA PATRIOT Act
Philbin, Patrick, 63
Posner, Richard A., 144–45, 185, 190, 257
presidential powers, 2, 4, 12–13, 14, 21, 24, 45,
        55
    civil liberties and, 50–51
    Clinton administration and, 20
    Congress and debate on, 50–54
    response to 9/11 and, 22
    scope of, 53–54
prisoners of war, 30, 34, 38, 66–67, 154, 164,
        198–99, 210
Privacy Act, 238
Protect America Act (PAA), 246–47

Qahtani, Mohammad Al-, 156, 193, 200, 202
Qassem, Talaat Fouad, 27
Quwari, Mahrar Rafat Al, 92–93

Rahman, Omar Abdel, 23, 170, 171
Rahman, Shed Abdur, 82
Rasul v. Bush, 14, 15, 22, 56, 64–65, 69, 104,
        106–7, 109–10, 112, 114, 125, 138
Rauch, Jonathan, 214
Razzak, Abdul, 95–96, 97
Reagan, Ronald, 23, 40
Reagan administration, 24, 26
Reid, Richard, 155, 173
Rejali, Darius, 191–92, 198
rendition program:
    Bush administration and, 207–8
    CIA and, 25–26, 30, 186–87, 215–16
    Clarke on, 26–27
    of Clinton administration, 20–21, 207
    interrogation policy and, 207–8, 215–18
    precedents for, 25–28
    prior to 9/11, 22–23

Reno, Janet, 20, 59–60
Republican Party, U.S., 55, 57, 210
Ressam, Ahmed, 23
Rivkin, David B., Jr., 106
Roth, Kenneth, 185
"roving wiretaps," 136
Rumsfeld, Donald, 46–47, 74, 201
Rwanda, 9

Sadat, Anwar, 27
Saigh, Adnan Muhammad Ali Al, 89
Sassòli, Marco, 39–40
Saudi Arabia, 5, 78, 79
Scalia, Antonin, 256
Scheuer, Michael, 26, 28
Schlesinger Report, 193, 199, 201
Second Circuit Court of Appeals, U.S., 32, 171
Senate, U.S., 40, 56, 133
    Armed Services Committee of, 155
    Convention Against Torture ratified by, 216
September 11, 2001 terrorist attacks, 2, 10, 20,
    25, 45, 88, 94, 104, 115, 122, 137, 163,
    171, 172, 180, 194, 198, 200, 221, 235–36
    FISA and, 227–28, 232
    legal response to, 21–22
    roundup of aliens after, 25, 151
    surveillance of hijackers and, 248–49
    warning failure of, 137
    Yoo on response to, 21
Shah, Zia Ul, 91–92
Sharif, Mohammed, 90
Shibh, Ramzi Bin al-, 47
Shue, Henry, 185, 198
sleep deprivation, 196, 210–11
State Department, U.S., 26, 217
Stern, Jessica, 237
Stevens, John Paul, 110, 112
Stimson, Charles, 101–2
Sudan, 23–24
Supreme Court, U.S., 5, 8, 14–15, 28–29, 32,
    34, 36–37, 42, 60, 89, 104, 126, 140, 141,
    144, 148, 168, 175, 177, 178, 209
    Boumediene case of, 111, 126, 256–57
    Dred Scott decision of, 120
    Eisentrager decision of, 114–15
    executive power debate and, 62–64
    Haitian refugee crisis and, 32
    Hamdan decision of, 2, 14, 15, 57, 68, 89,
        104, 105–7, 109–10, 112, 114, 138, 140,
        148, 168, 177
    Hamdi decision of, 14, 64, 105, 106–7, 155,
        177

habeas jurisdiction debates and, 15–16,
    63–66, 68–70, 111–12, 114, 115, 138,
    256
POW-unlawful combatant issue and, 38–39
Rasul decision of, 14, 15, 22, 56, 64–65, 69,
    104, 106–7, 109–10, 112, 114, 125, 138
Terry stop tactic and, 236
war on terror role of, 121–22
surveillance, surveillance policy, 2, 17, 50, 55,
    103, 143, 219–55
    Congress and, 252–55
    DNA databases and, 249–50
    domestic, 12, 42–43
    Fourth Amendment and, 222, 224–25
    judicial review and, 108–9
    new technology and, 223–24
    of 9/11 hijackers, 248–49
    Terry stop tactic and, 236, 244, 251
    USA PATRIOT Act and, 136–37
    see also data-mining; Foreign Intelligence
        Surveillance Act (FISA)
Suskind, Ron, 195
Syria, 187

Taipale, K. A., 236, 244, 251
Tajikistan, 82
Taliban, 6, 33, 35, 38, 41–42, 45, 177
    among Guantánamo detainees, 79–81, 84,
        86–92, 95, 100
Taney, Roger, 9, 120, 121
    on habeas corpus, 118–19
Taylor, Stuart, Jr., 236
Tenet, George, 28
terrorism, terrorists, 4, 10, 21
    Constitution and, 257–58
    legal system and, 11–12
    see also war on terror; *specific individuals
        and events*
terrorism trials:
    of citizens, 178–81
    civilian detention problem for military trials
        and, 168
    court-martial process and, 173–74
    detention standards and, 156–57
    discovery rules in, 175
    in federal courts, 171–73, 177
    Guantánamo status and, 175–76
    human rights concerns in, 170–71
    illegal combatant status and, 177–78
    MCA standards in, 174–76
    military commissions and, 168–69
    of Moussaoui, 171–72

offshore, 175–76
successful, 170–72
Terry stop, 236, 244, 251
Thirty Years War, 34
Timerman, Jacobo, 183–84, 185
Tomahawk missiles, 23
torture, 2, 4, 53, 122, 139, 148, 164, 175, 186,
    187–88, 192, 205, 216, 217
  Bush administration's definition of, 206
  Bush's speech on, 194–95
  CIA and, 29–30, 147–48
  culture of, 189
  KSM's experience of, 189–90
  ticking time bomb scenario and, 184–86,
    189–90
  Timerman's view of, 183–84
  U.N. Convention against, 29
  value of information from, 191–98
  see also interrogation, interrogation policy
Torture and Democracy (Rejali), 191–92
"torture memo," 29, 50
Tribe, Laurence H., 142

Uighurs, 82, 98–99
U.N. Convention Against Torture, 29
Uniform Code of Military Justice (UCMI),
  107, 112, 173–74
United States Army Field Manual on Intelligence Interrogation, 139, 188, 203–4,
  210–12
USA PATRIOT Act, 10, 37, 55, 56
  FISA and, 136–38, 219, 227
  incohesiveness of, 135–36
  "library" provision of, 239

Viet Cong, 39–40
Vietnam War, 39–40
Virginia Tech shootings, 181–82

Wag the Dog (film), 24
War Crimes Act (1996), 29
war on terror, 8, 16, 19, 103, 140
  allied governments and, 147
  Congress and legal framework for, 10–11,
    55–64, 67–68

Congress's role in, 131–35, 144–45
  domestic law and, 147
  executive authority debate and, 50–51
  flexibility in, 148–49
  Geneva Conventions and, 160–61
  as ideological struggle, 50
  judicial review and, 103–4, 105, 109,
    122–24, 125, 128–30
  lack of ending to, 48–49
  law model for, 45, 47, 54–55
  military's role in, 47–48
  as new kind of war, 46–47
  principles of constitution needed for,
    144–46
  purpose of, 146–47
  role of judiciary in, 103–4, 109, 117, 121–22
  Rumsfeld on, 46
  Supreme Court's role in, 121–22
  ultimate goal of, 149–50
  victory in, 50
  war model of, 12–14, 44–50, 54–5
  see also interrogation, interrogation policy;
    surveillance, surveillance policy
Washington Post, 60–61, 95, 106, 143, 231
Wasiq, Abdul Haq, 89–90
waterboarding, 139, 147–48, 186, 187, 196,
  211, 212
  prohibition of, 205–6
Watergate scandal, 22, 62, 137, 221, 224, 227
Waxman, Seth, 256
World Trade Center, 23, 170, 173
World War I, 22, 121
World War II, 11, 12, 34, 39, 42, 63
  internment of Japanese Americans in, 22,
    33, 121

Yazid (terrorist), 195
Yemen, 78
Yoo, John, 19, 50, 51, 62–63, 133
  on 9/11 response, 21
Yousef, Ramzi, 173
Yugoslavia, 9

Zubair (detainee), 194
Zubaydah, Abu, 5, 96, 181, 194, 195, 196, 208

About the Author

Benjamin Wittes is a Fellow and Research Director in Public Law at the Brookings Institution. He is a columnist for the *New Republic Online,* a contributing editor for the *Atlantic Monthly,* and a member of the Hoover Institution's Task Force on National Security and Law. Between 1997 and 2006, he served as an editorial writer for the *Washington Post,* specializing in legal affairs. He is the author of two prior books, and his essays have appeared in a wide range of journals and magazines.